Questions o
Cultural Iden ity

Questions of Cultural Identity

Edited by
STUART HALL
and
PAUL DU GAY

SAGE Publications
London · Thousand Oaks · New Delhi

Editorial selection and matter © Stuart Hall and Paul du Gay, 1996
Chapter 1 © Stuart Hall, 1996
Chapter 2 © Zygmunt Bauman, 1996
Chapter 3 © Marilyn Strathern, 1996
Chapter 4 © Homi K. Bhabha, 1996
Chapter 5 © Kevin Robins, 1996
Chapter 6 © Lawrence Grossberg, 1996
Chapter 7 © Simon Frith, 1996
Chapter 8 © Nikolas Rose, 1996
Chapter 9 © Paul du Gay, 1996
Chapter 10 © James Donald, 1996

First published 1996. Reprinted 1996, 1997

SAGE Publications Ltd
6 Bonhill Street
London EC2A 4PU

SAGE Publications Inc
2455 Teller Road
Thousand Oaks, California 91320

SAGE Publications India Pvt Ltd
32, M-Block Market
Greater Kailash - I
New Delhi 110 048

British Library Cataloguing in Publication data

A catalogue record for this book is
available from the British Library

ISBN 0 8039 7882-0
ISBN 0 8039 7883-9 (pbk)

Library of Congress catalog record available

Typeset by Type Study, Scarborough, North Yorkshire
Printed in Great Britain by The Cromwell Press Ltd,
Broughton Gifford, Melksham, Wilts

Contents

Notes on Contributors

Zygmunt Bauman is Emeritus Professor of Sociology at the University of Leeds. His recent publications include: *Mortality, Immortality & Other Life Strategies* (Polity), *Postmodern Ethics* (Blackwell) and *Life in Fragments* (Blackwell).

Homi K. Bhabha is a Professor of English at the University of Chicago. His publications include: *The Location of Culture* (1994).

James Donald is Reader in Media Studies at the University of Sussex. His recent publications include: *Sentimental Education* (Verso), and the co-edited collections *Race, Culture & Difference* (Sage), and *Space and Place* (Lawrence and Wishart). He has edited the journals *Screen Education* and *New Formations*.

Paul du Gay is Lecturer in Sociology and Secretary of the Pavis Centre for Sociological and Social Anthropological Studies at the Open University. He is the author of *Consumption and Identity at Work* (Sage, 1996).

Simon Frith is Professor of English and Co-Director of the John Logie Baird Centre at the University of Strathclyde, Glasgow. His latest book is *Performing Rites: the Value of Popular Music* (Harvard, 1996).

Lawrence Grossberg is the Morris Davis Professor of Communication Studies at the University of North Carolina at Chapel Hill. He is editor of the international journal *Cultural Studies*. His most recent publications include: *We Gotta Get Out of This Place: Popular Conservatism and Postmodern Culture, Dancing in Spite of Myself: Essays in Cultural Studies* (forthcoming) and *'It's a Sin' and Other Essays on Popular Culture and Postmodernity* (forthcoming).

Stuart Hall is Professor of Sociology at the Open University. He has written widely in the areas of culture, politics and race. His recent publications include *Formations of Modernity* (1992) and *Modernity and its Futures* (1992).

Kevin Robins is Professor of Cultural Geography at the University of Newcastle upon Tyne and a researcher in the Centre for Urban and Regional Studies. He is the author of *Geografia dei Media* (Baskerville, 1993) and, with David Morley, of *Spaces of Identity* (Routledge, 1995).

Nikolas Rose is Professor of Sociology at Goldsmiths College, University of London. He is the author of *The Psychological Complex* (Routledge, 1985), *Governing the Soul* (Routledge, 1990) and *Inventing Our Selves* (Cambridge, 1996). His current research is on changing rationalities and technologies of political power and the government of conduct.

Marilyn Strathern is Professor of Social Anthropology at the University of Cambridge. *The Gender of the Gift* (1988) is a critique of anthropological theories of society and gender relations as they have been applied to Melanesia, while *After Nature: English Kinship in the Late Twentieth Century* (1992) comments on the cultural revolution at home. Her most recent publication is the co-authored *Technologies of Procreation* (1993).

Preface

The chapters in this volume originated in a series of seminars organized by the Sociology Research Group at the Open University as part of its 1993–94 research theme 'Cultural Identities'. The aim of the seminar series was to examine why questions of cultural identity have acquired increasing visibility and salience in recent years in social and cultural theory as well as in a number of different fields of research in the social sciences, cultural studies and the humanities. Bringing together contributions from different disciplines and theoretical traditions this collection aims both to illuminate and to move forward debates about 'cultural identity' and their meaning in contemporary social formations.

The Introduction to the volume identifies some of the main themes explored in the chapters that follow as well as offering explanations of its own as to why the question of identity has emerged in so compelling and at the same time so deconstructed and decentred a form. However, neither the Introduction nor the volume as a whole lays claim to providing a 'complete' account, even in schematic form. Nor should readers expect to find complete agreement amongst the contributors. Rather, the collection aims to open up a wide range of significant questions and possible lines of analysis.

We would like to thank everybody who contributed to the seminar series, particularly Henrie Lidchi who helped substantially in its organization and smooth running and Kenneth Thompson who chaired a number of sessions. Our thanks also to the Faculty of Social Sciences at the Open University whose financial support enabled the series to take place.

Finally, the chapter authors have borne stoically the successive rounds of alterations and amendments. Our thanks to them and to Pauline Turner for her marvellous secretarial support throughout the production process.

1

Introduction: Who Needs 'Identity'?

Stuart Hall

There has been a veritable discursive explosion in recent years around the concept of 'identity', at the same moment as it has been subjected to a searching critique. How is this paradoxical development to be explained? And where does it leave us with respect to the concept? The deconstruction has been conducted within a variety of disciplinary areas, all of them, in one way or another critical of the notion of an integral, originary and unified identity. The critique of the self-sustaining subject at the centre of post-Cartesian western metaphysics has been comprehensively advanced in philosophy. The question of subjectivity and its unconscious processes of formation has been developed within the discourse of a psychoanalytically influenced feminism and cultural criticism. The endlessly performative self has been advanced in celebratory variants of postmodernism. Within the anti-essentialist critique of ethnic, racial and national conceptions of cultural identity and the 'politics of location' some adventurous theoretical conceptions have been sketched in their most grounded forms. What, then, is the need for a further debate about 'identity'? Who needs it?

There are two ways of responding to the question. The first is to observe something distinctive about the deconstructive critique to which many of these essentialist concepts have been subjected. Unlike those forms of critique which aim to supplant inadequate concepts with 'truer' ones, or which aspire to the production of positive knowledge, the deconstructive approach puts key concepts 'under erasure'. This indicates that they are no longer serviceable – 'good to think with' – in their originary and unreconstructed form. But since they have not been superseded dialectically, and there are no other, entirely different concepts with which to replace them, there is nothing to do but to continue to think with them – albeit now in their detotalized or deconstructed forms, and no longer operating within the paradigm in which they were originally generated (cf. Hall, 1995). The line which cancels them, paradoxically, permits them to go on being read. Derrida has described this approach as thinking at the limit, as thinking in the interval, a sort of double writing. 'By means of this double, and precisely stratified, dislodged and dislodging writing, we must also mark the interval between inversion, which brings low what was high, and the irruptive emergence of a new 'concept', a concept that can no longer be and never could be, included in the previous regime' (Derrida, 1981). Identity is such a concept – operating 'under erasure' in the interval between reversal and emergence; an idea which cannot be thought in the old way, but without which certain key questions cannot be thought at all.

A second kind of answer requires us to note where, in relation to what set of problems, does the *irreducibility* of the concept, identity, emerge? I think the answer here lies in its centrality to the question of agency and politics. By politics, I mean both the significance in modern forms of political movement of the signifier 'identity', its pivotal relationship to a politics of location – but also the manifest difficulties and instabilities which have characteristically affected all contemporary forms of 'identity politics'. By 'agency' I express no desire whatsoever to return to an unmediated and transparent notion of the subject or identity as the centred author of social practice, or to restore an approach which 'places its own point of view at the origin of all historicity – which, in short, leads to a transcendental consciousness' (Foucault, 1970, p. xiv). I agree with Foucault that what we require here is 'not a theory of the knowing subject, but rather a theory of discursive practice'. However, I believe that what this decentring requires – as the evolution of Foucault's work clearly shows – is not an abandonment or abolition of 'the subject' but a reconceptualization – thinking it in its new, displaced or decentred position within the paradigm. It seems to be in the attempt to rearticulate the relationship between subjects and discursive practices that the question of identity recurs – or rather, if one prefers to stress the process of subjectification to discursive practices, and the politics of exclusion which all such subjectification appears to entail, the question of *identification*.

Identification turns out to be one of the least well-understood concepts – almost as tricky as, though preferable to, 'identity' itself; and certainly no guarantee against the conceptual difficulties which have beset the latter. It is drawing meanings from both the discursive and the psychoanalytic repertoire, without being limited to either. This semantic field is too complex to unravel here, but it is useful at least to establish its relevance to the task in hand indicatively. In common sense language, identification is constructed on the back of a recognition of some common origin or shared characteristics with another person or group, or with an ideal, and with the natural closure of solidarity and allegiance established on this foundation. In contrast with the 'naturalism' of this definition, the discursive approach sees identification as a construction, a process never completed – always 'in process'. It is not determined in the sense that it can always be 'won' or 'lost', sustained or abandoned. Though not without its determinate conditions of existence, including the material and symbolic resources required to sustain it, identification is in the end conditional, lodged in contingency. Once secured, it does not obliterate difference. The total merging it suggests is, in fact, a fantasy of incorporation. (Freud always spoke of it in relation to 'consuming the other' as we shall see in a moment.) Identification is, then, a process of articulation, a suturing, an over-determination not a subsumption. There is always 'too much' or 'too little' – an over-determination or a lack, but never a proper fit, a totality. Like all signifying practices, it is subject to the 'play', of *différance*. It obeys the logic of more-than-one. And since as a process it operates across difference, it entails discursive work, the binding and marking of symbolic boundaries, the production of 'frontier-effects'. It requires what is left outside, its constitutive outside, to consolidate the process.

From its psychoanalytic usage, the concept of identification inherits a rich semantic legacy. Freud calls it 'the earliest expression of an emotional tie with another person' (Freud, 1921/1991) In the context of the Oedipus complex, however, it takes the parental figures as both love-objects and objects of rivalry, thereby inserting ambivalence into the very centre of the process. 'Identification is, in fact, ambivalent from the very start' (1921/1991: 134). In 'Mourning and Melancholia', it is not that which binds one to an object that exists, but that which binds one to an abandoned object-choice. It is, in the first instance, a 'moulding after the other' which compensates for the loss of the libidinal pleasures of primal narcissism. It is grounded in fantasy, in projection and idealization. Its object is as likely to be the one that is hated as the one that is adored; and as often taken back into the unconscious self as 'taking one out of oneself'. It is in relation to identification that Freud elaborated the critical distinction between 'being' and 'having' the other. 'It behaves like a derivative of the first, oral phase of organization of the libido, in which the object that we long for is assimilated by eating and is in that way annihilated as such' (1921/1991: 135). 'Identifications viewed as a whole', Laplanche and Pontalis (1985) note 'are in no way a coherent relational system. Demands coexist within an agency like the super-ego, for instance, which are diverse, conflicting and disorderly. Similarly, the ego-ideal is composed of identifications with cultural ideals that are not necessarily harmonious' (p. 208).

I am not suggesting that all these connotations should be imported wholesale and without translation into our thinking around 'identity', but they are cited to indicate the novel repertoires of meaning with which the term is now being inflected. The concept of identity deployed here is therefore not an essentialist, but a strategic and positional one. That is to say, directly contrary to what appears to be its settled semantic career, this concept of identity does *not* signal that stable core of the self, unfolding from beginning to end through all the vicissitudes of history without change; the bit of the self which remains always-already 'the same', identical to itself across time. Nor – if we translate this essentializing conception to the stage of cultural identity – is it that 'collective or true self hiding inside the many other, more superficial or artificially imposed "selves" which a people with a shared history and ancestry hold in common' (Hall, 1990) and which can stabilize, fix or guarantee an unchanging 'oneness' or cultural belongingness underlying all the other superficial differences. It accepts that identities are never unified and, in late modern times, increasingly fragmented and fractured; never singular but multiply constructed across different, often intersecting and antagonistic, discourses, practices and positions. They are subject to a radical historicization, and are constantly in the process of change and transformation. We need to situate the debates about identity within all those historically specific developments and practices which have disturbed the relatively 'settled' character of many populations and cultures, above all in relation to the processes of globalization, which I would argue are coterminous with modernity (Hall, 1996) and the processes of forced and 'free' migration which have become a global phenomenon of the so-called 'post-colonial' world. Though they seem to invoke an origin in a historical past with which they continue to correspond, actually identities are about questions of using the resources of history, language and culture in the process of becoming rather than being: not 'who we are' or 'where we came from', so much as what we might become, how we have been represented and how that bears on how we might represent ourselves. Identities are therefore constituted within, not outside representation. They relate to the invention of tradition as much as to tradition itself, which they oblige us to read not as an endless reiteration but as 'the changing same' (Gilroy, 1994): not the so-called return to roots but a coming-to-terms-with our 'routes'. They arise from the narrativization of the self, but the necessarily fictional nature of this process in no way undermines its discursive, material or political effectivity, even if the belongingness, the 'suturing into the story' through which identities arise is, partly, in the imaginary (as well as the symbolic) and therefore, always, partly constructed in fantasy, or at least within a fantasmatic field.

Precisely because identities are constructed within, not outside, discourse, we need to understand them as produced in specific historical and institutional sites within specific discursive formations and practices, by specific enunciative strategies. Moreover, they emerge within the play of specific modalities of power, and thus are more the product of the marking of difference and exclusion, than they are the sign of an identical, naturally-constituted unity – an 'identity' in its traditional meaning (that is, an all-inclusive sameness, seamless, without internal differentiation).

Above all, and directly contrary to the form in which they are constantly invoked, identities are constructed through, not outside, difference. This entails the radically disturbing recognition that it is only through the relation to the Other, the relation to what it is not, to precisely what it lacks, to what has been called its *constitutive outside* that the 'positive' meaning of any term – and thus its 'identity' – can be constructed (Derrida, 1981; Laclau, 1990; Butler, 1993). Throughout their careers, identities can function as points of identification and attachment only *because* of their capacity to exclude, to leave out, to render 'outside', abjected. Every identity has at its 'margin', an excess, something more. The unity, the internal homogeneity, which the term identity treats as foundational is not a natural, but a constructed form of closure, every identity naming as its necessary, even if silenced and unspoken other, that which it 'lacks'. Laclau (1990) argues powerfully and persuasively that 'the constitution of a social identity is an act of power' since,

> If . . . an objectivity manages to partially affirm itself it is only by repressing that which threatens it. Derrida has shown how an identity's constitution is always based on excluding something and establishing a violent hierarchy between the two resultant poles – man/woman, etc. What is peculiar to the second term is thus reduced to the function of an accident as opposed to the essentiality of the first. It is the same with the black–white relationship, in which white, of course, is equivalent to 'human being'. 'Woman' and 'black' are thus 'marks' (i.e. marked terms) in contrast to the unmarked terms of 'man' and 'white'. (Laclau, 1990: 33)

So the 'unities' which identities proclaim are, in fact, constructed within the play of power and exclusion, and are the result, not of a natural and inevitable or primordial totality but of the naturalized, overdetermined process of 'closure' (Bhabha, 1994; Hall, 1993).

If 'identities' can only be read against the grain – that is to say, specifically *not* as that which fixes the play of difference in a point of origin and stability, but as that which is constructed in or through *différance* and is constantly destabilized by what it leaves out, then how can we understand its meaning and how can we theorize its emergence? Avtar Brah (1992: 143), in her important article on 'Difference, diversity and differentiation', raises an important series of questions which these new ways of conceptualizing identity have posed:

> Fanon notwithstanding, much work is yet to be undertaken on the subject of how the racialized 'other' is constituted in the psychic domain. How is post-colonial gendered and racialized subjectivity to be analyzed? Does the privileging of 'sexual difference' and early childhood in psychoanalysis limit its explanatory value in helping us to understand the psychic dimensions of social phenomena such as racism? How do the 'symbolic order' and the social order articulate in the formation of the subject? In other words, how is the link between social and psychic reality to be theorized?' (1992: 142.)

What follows is an attempt to begin to respond to this critical but troubling set of questions.

In some recent work on this topic, I have made an appropriation of the term identity which is certainly not widely shared and may not be well understood. I use 'identity' to refer to the meeting point, the point of *suture*, between on the one hand the discourses and practices which attempt to 'interpellate', speak to us or hail us into place as the social subjects of particular discourses, and on the other hand, the processes which produce subjectivities, which construct us as subjects which can be 'spoken'. Identities are thus points of temporary attachment to the subject positions which discursive practices construct for us (see Hall, 1995). They are the result of a successful articulation or 'chaining' of the subject into the flow of the discourse, what Stephen Heath, in his path-breaking essay on 'Suture' called 'an intersection' (1981: 106). 'A theory of ideology must begin not from the subject but as an account of su-turing effects, the effecting of the join of the subject in structures of meaning.' Identities are, as it were, the positions which the subject is obliged to take up while always 'knowing' (the language of conscious-ness here betrays us) that they are representations, that representation is always constructed across a 'lack', across a division, from the place of the Other, and thus can never be adequate – identical – to the subject processes which are invested in them. The notion that an effective su-turing of the subject to a subject-position requires, not only that the subject is 'hailed', but that the subject invests in the position, means that suturing has to be thought of as an *articulation*, rather than a one-sided process, and that in turn places *identification*, if not identities, firmly on the theoretical agenda.

The references to the term which describes the hailing of the subject by discourse – interpellation – remind us that this debate has a signifi-cant and uncompleted pre-history in the arguments sparked off by Althusser's 'Ideological state apparatuses' essay (1971). This essay intro-duced the notion of interpellation, and the speculary structure of ideol-ogy in an attempt to circumvent the economism and reductionism of the classical Marxist theory of ideology, and to bring together within one explanatory framework both the materialist function of ideology in re-producing the social relations of production (Marxism) and (through its borrowings from Lacan) the symbolic function of ideology in the consti-tution of subjects. Michele Barrett, in her recent discussion of this debate, has gone a considerable way to demonstrating 'the profoundly divided and contradictory nature of the argument Althusser was begin-ning to make' (Barrett, 1991: 96; see also Hall, 1985: 102: 'The two sides of the difficult problem of ideology were fractured in that essay and, ever since, have been assigned to different poles'). Nevertheless, the ISAs essay, as it came to be known, has turned out to be a highly significant, even if not successful, moment in the debate. Jacqueline Rose, for ex-ample, has argued in *Sexuality in the Field of Vision* (1986), that 'the question of identity – how it is constituted and maintained – is therefore the central issue through which psychoanalysis enters the political field'.

This is one reason why Lacanian psychoanalysis came into English intellectu-al life, via Althusser's concept of ideology, through the two paths of feminism and the analysis of film (a fact often used to discredit all three). Feminism because the issue of how individuals recognize themselves as male or female, the demand that they do so, seems to stand in such fundamental relation to the forms of inequality and subordination which it is feminism's objective to change. Film because its power as an ideological apparatus rests on the mechanisms of identification and sexual fantasy which we all seem to participate in, but which – outside the cinema – are for the most part only ever admitted on the couch. If ideology is effective, it is because it works at the most rudimentary levels of psychic identity and the drives. (Rose, 1986: 5)

However, if we are not to fall directly from an economistic reductionism into a psychoanalytic one, we need to add that, if ideology is effective, it is because it works at *both* 'the rudimentary levels of psychic identity and the drives' *and* at the level of the discursive formation and practices which constitute the social field; and that it is in the articulation of these mutually constitutive but not identical fields that the real conceptual problems lie. The term identity – which arises precisely at the point of intersection between them – is thus the site of the difficulty. It is worth adding that we are unlikely ever to be able to square up these two constituents as equivalents – the unconscious itself acting as the bar or cut between them which makes it 'the site of a perpetual postponement or deferral of equivalence' (Hall, 1995) but which cannot, for that reason, be given up.

Heath's essay (1981) reminds us that it was Michael Pêcheux who tried to develop an account of discourse within the Althusserian perspective, and who in effect, registered the unbridgeable gap between the first and the second halves of Althusser's essay in terms of 'the heavy absence of a conceptual articulation elaborated between *ideology* and the *unconscious*, (quoted in Heath, 1981: 106). Pêcheux tried 'to describe with reference to the mechanisms of the setting in position of its subjects' (Heath, 1981: 101–2), using the Foucauldian notion of discursive formation as that which 'determines what can and must be said'. As Heath put Pêcheux's argument:

Individuals are constituted as subjects through the discursive formation, a process of subjection in which [drawing on Althusser's loan from Lacan concerning the speculary character of the constitution of subjectivity] the individual is identified as subject to the discursive formation in a structure of misrecognition (the subject thus presented as the source of the meanings of which it is an effect). Interpellation names the mechanism of this structure of misrecognition, effectively the term of the subject in the discursive and the ideological, the point of their correspondence (1981: 101–2).

Such 'correspondence', however, remained troublingly unresolved. Interpellation, though it continues to be used as a general way of describing the 'summoning into place' of the subject, was subjected to Hirst's famous critique. It depended, Hirst argued, on a recognition which, in effect, the subject would have been required to have the capacity to perform *before* it had been constituted, within discourse, as a subject. 'This something which is not a subject must already have the faculties necessary to support the recognition that will constitute it as a subject' (Hirst, 1979: 65). This argument has proved very persuasive to many of Althusser's subsequent readers, in effect bringing the whole field of investigation to an untimely halt.

The critique was certainly a formidable one, but the halting of all further inquiry at this point may turn out to have been premature. Hirst's critique was effective in showing that all the mechanisms which constituted the subject in discourse as an interpellation, (through the speculary structure of misrecognition modelled on the Lacanian mirror phase), were in danger of presupposing an already constituted subject. However, since no one proposed to renounce the idea of the subject as constituted in discourse as an effect, it still remained to be shown by what mechanism which was not vulnerable to the charge of presupposition this constitution could be achieved. The problem was postponed, not resolved. Some of the difficuties, at least, seemed to arise from accepting too much at face value, and without qualification, Lacan's somewhat sensationalist proposition that *everything* constitutive of the subject not only happens through this mechanism of the resolution of the Oedipal crisis, but happens in the same moment. The 'resolution' of the Oedipal crisis, in the over-condensed language of the Lacanian hot-gospellers, *was* identical with, and occurred through the equivalent mechanism as, the submission to the Law of the Father, the consolidation of sexual difference, the entry into language, the formation of the unconscious as well – after Althusser – as the recruitment into the patriarchal ideologies of late capitalist western societies! The more complex notion of a subject-in-process is lost in these polemical condensations and hypothetically aligned equivalences. (Is the subject racialized, nationalized and constituted as a late-liberal entrepreneurial subject in this moment too?)

Hirst, too, seems to have assumed what Michele Barrett calls 'Althusser's Lacan'. However, as he puts it, 'the complex and hazardous process of formation of a human adult from "a small animal" does not necessarily correspond to Althusser's mechanism of ideology . . . *unless the Child* . . . remains in Lacan's mirror phase, or unless we fill the child's cradle with anthropological assumptions' (Hirst, 1979). His response to this is somewhat perfunctory. 'I have no quarrel with Children, and I do not wish to pronounce them blind, deaf or dumb, merely to deny that they posses the capacities of *philosophical* subjects, that they have the attributes of "knowing" subjects independent of their formation and training as social beings.' What is at issue here is the capacity for self-recognition. But it is an unwarrantable assumption to make, that 'recognition' is a purely cognitive let alone 'philosophical' attribute, and unlikely that it should appear in the child at one fell swoop, in a before/after fashion. The stakes here seem, unaccountably, to have been pitched very high indeed. It hardly requires us to endow the individual 'small animal' with the full philosophical apparatus to account for why it may have the capacity to 'misrecognize' itself in the look from the place of the other which is all we require to set the passage between the Imaginary and the Symbolic in motion in Lacan's terms. After all, following Freud, the basic cathexing of the zones of bodily activity and the apparatus of sensation, pleasure and pain must be already 'in play' in however embryonic a form in order for any relation of any kind to be established with the external world. There is already a relation to a source of pleasure – the relation to the Mother in the Imaginary – so there must be already something which is capable of 'recognizing' what pleasure is. Lacan himself noted in his essay on 'The Mirror Stage' that 'The child, at an age when he is for a time, however short, outdone by the chimpanzee in instrumental intelligence, can nevertheless already recognize his own image in a mirror.' What is more, the critique seems to be pitched in a rather binary, before/after, either/or logical form. The mirror stage is not the *beginning* of something, but the *interruption* – the loss, the lack, the division – which initiates the process that 'founds' the sexually differentiated subject (and the unconscious) and this depends not alone on the instantaneous formation of some internal cognitive capacity, but on the dislocating rupture of the look from the place of the Other. For Lacan, however, this is already a fantasy – the very image which places the child divides its identity into two. Furthermore, that moment only has meaning in relation to the supporting presence and the look of the mother who guarantees its reality for the child. Peter Osborne notes (1995) that in *The Field Of The Other* Lacan (1977) describes the 'parent holding him up before the mirror', with the child looking towards the Mother for confirmation, the child seeing her as a 'reference point . . . not his ego ideal but his ideal ego' (p. 257). This argument, Osborne suggests, 'exploits the indeterminacy inherent in the discrepancy between the temporality of Lacan's description of the child's encounter with its bodily image in the mirror as a "stage" and the punctuality of his depiction of it as a scene, the dramatic point of which is restricted to the relations between two "characters" alone: the child and its bodily image'. However, as Osborne says, either it represents a critical addition to the 'mirror stage' argument – in which case, why is it not developed? Or it introduces a different logic whose implications remain unaddressed in Lacan's subsequent work.

The notion that nothing of the subject is there until the Oedipal drama is an exaggerated reading of Lacan. The assertion that subjectivity is not fully constituted until the Oedipal crisis has been 'resolved' does not require a blank screen, *tabula rasa*, or a before/after conception of the subject, initiated by a sort of *coup de théâtre*, even if – as Hirst rightly noted – it leaves unsettled the problematic relationship between 'the individual' and the subject. (What *is* the individual 'small animal' that is not yet a subject?).

One could add that Lacan's is only one of the many accounts of the formation of subjectivity which takes account of unconscious psychic processes and the relation to the other, and the debate may look different now that the 'Lacanian deluge' is somewhat receding and in the absence of the early powerful impulsion in that direction which we were given by Althusser's text. In his thoughtful recent discussion of the Hegelian

origins of this concept of 'recognition' referred to above, Peter Osborne
has criticized Lacan for 'the way in which the child's relation to the image
is absolutized by being abstracted from the context of its relations to
others (particularly, the mother)', while being made ontologically constitutive of 'the symbolic matrix in which the I is precipitated in a primordial
form . . .' and considers several other variants (Kristeva, Jessica Benjamin, Laplanche) which are not so confined within the alienated
misrecognition of the Lacanian scenario. These are useful pointers
beyond the impasse in which this discussion, in the wake of 'Althusser's
Lacan', has left us, with the threads of the psychic and the discursive
spinning loose in our hands.

Foucault, I would argue, also approaches the impasse with which
Hirst's critique of Althusser leaves us, but so to speak from the opposite
direction. Ruthlessly attacking 'the great myth of interiority', and driven
both by his critque of humanism and the philosophy of consciousness,
and by his negative reading of psychoanalysis, Foucault also undertakes a
radical historicization of the category of the subject. The subject is
produced 'as an effect' through and within discourse, within specific
discursive formations, and has no existence, and certainly no transcendental continuity or identity from one subject position to another. In
his 'archaeological' work (*Madness and Civilization, The Birth of the Clinic,
The Order of Things, The Archaeology of Knowledge*), discourses construct
subject positions through their rules of formation and 'modalities of
enunciation'. Powerfully compelling and original as these works are, the
criticism levelled against them in this respect at least seems justified. They
offer a formal account of the construction of subject positions within
discourse while revealing little about why it is that certain individuals
occupy some subject positions rather than others. By neglecting to
analyse how the social positions of individuals interact with the construction of certain 'empty' discursive subject positions, Foucault reinscribes
an antinomy between subject positions and the individuals who occupy
them. Thus his archaeology provides a critical, but one-dimensional,
formal account of the subject of discourse. Discursive subject positions
become *a priori* categories which individuals seem to occupy in an
unproblematic fashion. (McNay, 1994: 76–7). McNay cites Brown and
Cousins's key observation that Foucault tends here to elide 'subject
positions of a statement with individual capacities to fill them' (Brown
and Cousins, 1980: 272) – thus coming up against the very difficulty which
Althusser failed to resolve, by a different route.

The critical shift in Foucault's work from an archaeological to a
genealogical method does many things to render more concrete the
somewhat 'empty formalism' of the earlier work, especially in the
powerful ways in which power, which was missing from the more formal
account of discourse, is now centrally reintroduced and the exciting
possibilities opened up by Foucault's discussion of the double-sided
character of subjection/subjectification (*assujettisement*). Moreover, the

centring of questions of power, and the notion that discourse itself is a regulative and regulated formation, entry into which is 'determined by and constitutive of the power relations that permeate the social realm' (McNay, 1994: 87), brings Foucault's conception of the discursive formation closer to some of the classical questions which Althusser tried to address through the concept of 'ideology' – shorn, of course, of its class reductionism, economistic and truth-claiming overtones.

In the area of the theorization of the subject and identity, however, certain problems remain. One implication of the new conceptions of power elaborated in this body of work is the radical 'deconstruction' of the body, the last residue or hiding place of 'Man', and its 'reconstruction' in terms of its historical, genealogical and discursive formations. The body is constructed by, shaped and reshaped by the intersection of a series of disciplinary discursive practices. Genealogy's task, Foucault proclaims, 'is to expose the body totally imprinted by history and the processes of history's destruction of the body' (1984: 63). While we can accept this, with its radically 'constructivist' implications (the body becomes infinitely malleable and contingent) I am not sure we can or ought to go as far as his proposition that 'Nothing in man – not even his body – is sufficiently stable to serve as a basis for self-recognition or for understanding other men.' This is not because the body *is* such a stable and true referent for self-understanding, but because, though this may be a 'misrecognition', it is precisely how the body has served *to function as the signifier of the condensation of subjectivities in the individual* and this function cannot simply be dismissed because, as Foucault effectively shows, it is not true.

Further, my own feeling is that, despite Foucault's disclaimers, his invocation of *the body* as the point of application of a variety of disciplinary practices tends to lend this theory of disciplinary regulation a sort of 'displaced or misplaced concreteness' – a residual materiality – and in this way operates discursively to 'resolve' or appear to resolve the unspecified relationship between the subject, the individual and the body. To put it crudely, it pins back together or 'sutures' those things which the theory of the discursive production of subjects, if taken to its limits, would irretrievably fracture and disperse. I think 'the body' has acquired a totemic value in post-Foucauldian work precisely because of this talismanic status. It is almost the only trace we have left in Foucault's work of a 'transcendental signifier'.

The more well-established critique, however, has to do with the problem which Foucault encounters with theorizing resistance within the theory of power he deploys in *Discipline and Punish* and *The History of Sexuality*; the entirely self-policing conception of the subject which emerges from the disciplinary, confessional and pastoral modalities of power discussed there, and the absence of any attention to what might in any way interrupt, prevent or disturb the smooth insertion of individuals into the subject positions constructed by these discourses. The submission of the body through 'the soul' to the normalizing regimes of truth constitutes a powerful way of rethinking the body's so-called 'materiality' (which has been productively taken up by Nikolas Rose, and the 'govern-mentality' school, as well as, in a different mode, by Judith Butler in *Bodies That Matter*, 1993). But it is hard not to take Foucault's own formulation seriously, with all the difficulties it brings in its train: namely, that the subjects which are constructed in this way are 'docile bodies'. There is no theorized account of how or why bodies should not always-for-ever turn up, in place, at the right time (exactly the point from which the classical Marxist theory of ideology started to unravel, and the very difficulty which Althusser reinscribed when he normatively defined the function of ideology as 'to reproduce the social relations of production'). Further-more, there is no theorization of the psychic mechanism or interior processes by which these automatic 'interpellations' might be produced, or – more significantly – fail or be resisted or negotiated. Powerful and productive as this work undoubtedly is, then, it remains the case that here 'Foucault steps too easily from describing disciplinary power as a *tendency* within modern forms of social control, to positing disciplinary power as a fully installed monolithic force which saturates all social relations. This leads to an overestimation of the efficacy of disciplinary power and to an impoverished understanding of the individual which cannot account for experiences that fall outside the realm of the "docile" body' (McNay, 1994: 104.)

That this became obvious to Foucault, even if it is still refused as a critique by many of his followers, is apparent from the further and distinctive shift in his work marked by the later (and incomplete) volumes of his so-called 'History of Sexuality' (*The Use of Pleasure*, 1987; *The Care of the Self*, 1988, and as far as we can gather, the unpublished – and from the point of view of the critique just passed, the critical – volume on 'The Perversions'). For here, without moving very far from his insightful work on the productive character of normative regulation (no subjects outside the Law, as Judith Butler puts it), he tacitly recognizes that it is not enough for the Law to summon, discipline, produce and regulate, but there must also be the corresponding production of a response (and thus the capacity and apparatus of subjectivity) from the side of the subject. In the critical Introduction to *The Use of Pleasure* Foucault lists what by now we would expect of his work – 'the correlation between fields of know-ledge, types of normativity and forms of subjectivity in particular cul-tures' – but now critically adds

> the practices by which individuals were led to focus attention on themselves, to decipher, recognize and acknowledge themselves as subjects of desire, bring-ing into play between themselves and themselves a certain relationship that allows them to discover, in desire, the truth of their being, be it natural or fallen. In short, with this genealogy, the idea was to investigate how individuals were led to practice, on themselves and on others, a hermeneutics of desire. (1987: 5)

Foucault describes this – correctly, in our view – as 'a third shift, in order to analyze what is termed "the subject". It seemed appropriate to look for the forms and modalities of the relation to self by which the individual constitutes and recognizes himself *qua* subject.' Foucault, of course, would not commit anything so vulgar as actually to deploy the term 'identity', but I think, with 'the relation to self' and the constitution and recognition of 'himself' (*sic*) qua subject we are approaching something of the territory which, in the terms established earlier, belongs to the problematic of 'identity'.

This is not the place to trace through the many productive insights which flow from Foucault's analysis of the truth-games, the elaboration of ethical work, of the regimes of self-regulation and self-fashioning, of the 'technologies of the self' involved in the constitution of the desiring subject. There is certainly no single switch to 'agency', to intention and volition, here (though there are, very centrally, the practices of freedom which prevent this subject from ever being simply a docile sexualized body).

But there is the *production* of self as an object in the world, the practices of self-constitution, recognition and reflection, the relation to the rule, alongside the scrupulous attention to normative regulation, and the constraints of the rules without which no 'subjectification' is produced. This is a significant advance, since it addresses for the first time in Foucault's major work the existence of some interior landscape of the subject, some interior mechanisms of assent to the rule, as well as its objectively disciplining force, which saves the account from the 'behaviourism' and objectivism which threatens certain parts of *Discipline and Punish*. Often, in this work, the ethics and practices of the self are most fully described by Foucault as an 'aesthetics of existence', a deliberate stylization of daily life; and its technologies are most effectively demonstrated in the practices of self-production, in specific modes of conduct, in what we have come from later work to recognize as a kind of *performativity*.

What I think we can see here, then, is Foucault being pushed, by the scrupulous rigour of his own thinking, through a series of conceptual shifts at different stages in his work, towards a recognition that, since the decentring of the subject is not the destruction of the subject, and since the 'centring' of discursive practice cannot work without the constitution of subjects, the theoretical work cannot be fully accomplished without complementing the account of discursive and disciplinary regulation with an account of the practices of subjective self-constitution. It has never been enough – in Marx, in Althusser, in Foucault – to elaborate a theory of how individuals are summoned into place in the discursive structures. It has always, also, required an account of how subjects are constituted; and in this work, Foucault has gone a considerable way in showing this, in reference to historically-specific discursive practices, normative self-regulation and technologies of the self. The question which remains is whether we also require to, as it were, close the gap between the two: that is to say, a theory of what the mechanisms are by which individuals as subjects identify (or do not identify) with the 'positions' to which they are summoned; as well as how they fashion, stylize, produce and 'perform' these positions, and why they never do so completely, for once and all time, and some never do, or are in a constant, agonistic process of struggling with, resisting, negotiating and accommodating the normative or regulative rules with which they confront and regulate themselves. In short, what remains is the requirement to think this relation of subject to discursive formations *as an articulation* (all articulations are properly relations of 'no necessary correspondence', i.e. founded on that contingency which 'reactivates the historical' cf. Laclau, 1990: 35).

It is therefore all the more fascinating that, when finally Foucault *does* make the move in this direction (in work which was then tragically cut short), he was prevented, of course, from going to one of the principal sources of thinking about this neglected aspect – namely, psychoanalysis; prevented from moving in that direction by his own critique of it as simply another network of disciplinary power relations. What he produces instead is a discursive *phenomenology* of the subject (drawing perhaps on earlier sources and influences whose importance for him have been somewhat underplayed) and a genealogy of the *technologies of the self*. But it is a phenomenology which is in danger of being overwhelmed by an overemphasis on intentionality – precisely because it cannot engage with *the unconscious*. For good or ill, that door was already foreclosed.

Fortunately it has not remained so. In *Gender Trouble* (1990) and more especially in *Bodies That Matter* (1993), Judith Butler has taken up, through her concern with 'the discursive limits of "sex"' and with the politics of feminism, the complex transactions between the subject, the body and identity, through the drawing together in one analytic framework insights drawn from a Foucauldian and a psychoanalytic perspective. Adopting the position that the subject is discursively constructed and that there is no subject before or outside the Law, Butler develops a rigorously argued case that

> sex is, from the start, normative; it is what Foucault has called a 'regulatory ideal'. In this sense, then, sex not only functions as a norm, but is part of a regulatory practice that produces (through the repetition or iteration of a norm which is without origin) the bodies it governs, that is, whose regulatory force is made clear as a kind of productive power, the power to produce – demarcate, circulate, differentiate – the bodies it controls . . . 'sex' is an ideal construct which is forcibly materialized through time. (Butler, 1993: 1)

Materialization here is rethought as an effect of power. The view that the subject is produced in the course of its materialization is strongly grounded in a performative theory of language and the subject, but performativity is shorn of its associations with volition, choice and intentionality and (against some of the misreadings of *Gender Trouble*) re-read 'not as the act by which a subject brings into being what she/he names

but rather as that reiterative power of discourse to produce the phenomena that it regulates and constrains' (Butler, 1993: 2).

The decisive shift, from the viewpoint of the argument being developed here, however, is 'a linking of this process of "assuming" a sex
with the question of *identification*, and with the discursive means by which
the heterosexual imperative enables certain sexed identifications and
forecloses and/or disavows other identifications' (Butler, 1993: 5). This
centring of the question of identification, together with the problematic of
the subject which 'assumes a sex', opens up a critical and reflexive
dialogue in Butler's work between Foucault and psychoanalysis which is
enormously productive. It is true that Butler does not provide an
elaborate theoretical meta-argument for the way the two perspectives, or
the relation between the discursive and the psychic, are 'thought'
together in her text beyond a suggestive indication: 'There may be a way
to subject psychoanalysis to a Foucauldian redescription even as Foucault
himself refused that possibility.' At any rate

> this text accepts as a point of departure Foucault's notion that regulatory power
> produces the subjects it controls, that power is not only imposed externally but
> works as the regulatory and normative means by which subjects are formed.
> The return to psychoanalysis, then, is guided by the question of how certain
> regulatory norms form a 'sexed' subject in terms that establish the indis-
> tinguishability of psychic and bodily formation. (1993: 23)

However, Butler's relevance to the argument is made all the more
pertinent because it is developed in the context of the discussion of
gender and sexuality, framed by feminism, and so is directly recurrent
both to the questions of identity and identity politics, and to the questions
which Avtar Brah's work posed earlier about the paradigmatic function of
sexual difference in relation to other axes of exclusion. Here Butler makes
a powerful case that all identities operate through exclusion, through the
discursive construction of a constitutive outside and the production of
abjected and marginalized subjects, apparently outside the field of the
symbolic, the representable – 'the production of an "outside", a domain
of intelligible effects' (1993: 22) – which then returns to trouble and
unsettle the foreclosures which we prematurely call 'identities'. She
deploys this argument with effect in relation to the sexualizing and the
racializing of the subject – an argument which requires to be developed if
the constitution of subjects in and through the normalizing regulatory
effects of racial discourse is to acquire the theoretical development
hitherto reserved for gender and sexuality (though, of course, her most
well-worked example is in relation to the production of these forms of
sexual abjection and lived unintelligibility usually 'normalized' as pathological or perverse).

As James Souter (1995) has pointed out, 'Butler's internal critique of
feminist identity politics and its foundationalist premises questions the
adequacy of a representational politics whose basis is the presumed
universality and unity of its subject – a seamless category of women.'

Paradoxically, as in all other identities treated politically in a foundational manner, this identity 'is based on excluding "different" women . . . and by normatively prioritizing heterosexual relations as the basis for feminist politics'. This 'unity', Souter argues, is a 'fictive unity', 'produced and restrained by the very structures of power through which emancipation is sought'. Significantly, however, as Souter also argues, this does *not* lead Butler to argue that all notions of identity should therefore be abandoned because they are theoretically flawed. Indeed, she takes the speculary structure of identification as a critical part of her argument. But she acknowledges that such an argument *does* suggest 'the necessary limits of identity politics'.

> In this sense, identifications belong to the imaginary; they are phantasmatic efforts of alignment, loyalty, ambiguous and cross-corporeal cohabitations, they unsettle the I; they are the sedimentation of the 'we' in the constitution of any I, the structuring present of alterity in the very formulation of the I. Identifications are never fully and finally made; they are incessantly reconstituted, and, as such, are subject to the volatile logic of iterability. They are that which is constantly marshalled, consolidated, retrenched, contested and, on occasion, compelled to give way. (1993: 105)

The effort, now, to think the question of the distinctiveness of the logic within which the racialized and ethnicized body is constituted discursively, through the regulatory normative ideal of a 'compulsive Eurocentrism' (for want of a different word), cannot be simply grafted on to the arguments briefly sketched above. But they have received an enormous and original impetus from this tangled and unconcluded argument, which demonstrates beyond the shadow of a doubt that the question, and the theorization, of identity is a matter of considerable political significance, and is only likely to be advanced when both the necessity and the 'impossibility' of identities, and the suturing of the psychic and the discursive in their constitution, are fully and unambiguously acknowledged.

References

Althusser, L. (1971) *Lenin and Philosophy and Other Essays*, London: New Left Books.
Barrett, M (1991) *The Politics of Truth*, Cambridge: Polity.
Bhabha, H. (1994) 'The Other Question', in *The Location Of Culture*, London: Routledge.
Brah, A. (1992) 'Difference, diversity and differentiation', in J. Donald and A. Rattansi (eds), *Race, Culture and Difference*, London: Sage (126–45).
Brown, B. and Cousins, M. (1980) 'The linguistic fault', *Economy and Society*, 9(3).
Butler, J. (1990) *Gender Trouble*, London: Routledge.
Butler, J. (1993) *Bodies That Matter*, London: Routledge.
Derrida, J. (1981) *Positions*, Chicago: University of Chicago Press.
Foucault, M. (1970) *The Order of Things*, London: Tavistock.
Foucault, M. (1972) *The Archaeology of Knowledge*, London: Tavistock.
Foucault, M. (1977) *Discipline and Punish*, Harmondsworth: Penguin.
Foucault, M. (1981) *The History of Sexuality Volume 1*, Harmondsworth: Penguin.
Foucault, M. (1987) *The Use of Pleasure*, Harmondsworth: Penguin.
Foucault, M. (1988) *The Care of the Self*, Harmondsworth: Penguin.

Foucault, M. (1984) 'Nietzsche, genealogy, history', in P. Rabinow (ed.), *The Foucault Reader*, Harmondsworth: Penguin.

Freud, S (1921/1991) *Group psychology and the analysis of the ego*, in *Civilization, Society and Religion, Vol. 12 Selected Works*, Harmondsworth: Penguin.

Gilroy, P. (1994) *The Black Atlantic: Modernity and Double Consciousness*, London: Verso.

Hall, S. (1985) 'Signification, representation and ideology: Althusser and the post-structuralist debates', *Critical Studies in Mass Communication*, 2(2).

Hall, S. (1990) 'Cultural identity and diaspora', in J. Rutherford (ed.), *Identity*, London: Lawrence & Wishart.

Hall, S. (1993) 'Cultural identity in question', in S. Hall, D. Held and T. McGrew (eds), *Modernity and its Futures*, Cambridge: Polity.

Hall, S. (1995) 'Fantasy, identity, politics', in E. Carter, J. Donald and J. Squites (eds), *Cultural Remix: Theories of Politics and the Popular*, London: Lawrence & Wishart.

Hall, S. (1996) 'When was the post-colonial?', in L. Curti and I. Chambers (eds), *The Post-Colonial in Question*, London: Routledge.

Heath, S. (1981) *Questions of Cinema*, Basingstoke: Macmillan.

Hirst, P. (1979) *On Law and Ideology*, Basingstoke: Macmillan.

Laclau, E. (1990) *New Reflections on the Revolution of Our Time*, London: Verso.

Lacan, J. (1977) *Ecrits*, London: Tavistock.

Lacan, J. (1977) *The Four Fundamental Concepts of Psychoanalysis*, London: Hogarth Press.

Laplanche, J. and Pontalis, J.-B. (1985) *The Language of Psychoanalysis*, London: Hogarth Press.

McNay, L. (1994) *Foucault: A Critical Introduction*, Cambridge: Polity Press.

Osborne, P. (1995) *The Politics of Time*, London: Verso.

Rose, J. (1986) *Sexuality in the Field of Vision*, London: Verso.

Souter, J. (1995) 'From *Gender Trouble* to *Bodies That Matter*', unpublished manuscript.

2

From Pilgrim to Tourist – or a Short History of Identity

Zygmunt Bauman

'Identity continues to be the problem it was throughout modernity', says Douglas Kellner, and adds that 'far from identity disappearing in contemporary society, it is rather reconstructed and redefined' – though just a few paragraphs later he casts doubts on the feasibility of the selfsame 'reconstruction and redefinition', pointing out that 'identity today becomes a freely chosen game, a theatrical presentation of the self' and that 'when one radically shifts identity at will, one might lose control.'[1] Kellner's ambivalence reflects the present ambivalence of the issue itself. One hears today of identity and its problems more often than ever before in modern times. And yet one wonders whether the current obsession is not just another case of the general rule of things being noticed only *ex post facto*; when they vanish, go bust or fall out of joint.

I propose that while it is true that identity 'continues to be the problem', this is *not* 'the problem it was throughout modernity'. Indeed, if the *modern* 'problem of identity' was how to construct an identity and keep it solid and stable, the *postmodern* 'problem of identity' is primarily how to avoid fixation and keep the options open. In the case of identity, as in other cases, the catchword of modernity was creation; the catchword of postmodernity is recycling. Or one may say that if the 'media which was the message' of modernity was the photographic paper (think of the relentlessly swelling family albums, tracing page by yellowing page the slow accretion of irreversible and non-erasable identity-yielding events), the ultimately postmodern medium is the videotape (eminently erasable and re-usable, calculated not to hold anything for ever, admitting today's events solely on condition of effacing yesterday's ones, oozing the message of universal 'until-further-noticeness' of everything deemed worthy of recording). The main identity-bound anxiety of modern times was the worry about durability; it is the concern with commitment-avoidance today. Modernity built in steel and concrete; postmodernity, in bio-degradable plastic.

Identity as such is a modern invention. To say that modernity led to the 'disembedding' of identity, or that it rendered the identity 'unencumbered', is to assert a pleonasm, since at no time did identity 'become' a problem; it was a 'problem' from its birth – was *born as a problem* (that is, as something one needs do something about – as a task), could exist only as a problem; it was a problem, and thus ready to be born, precisely because of that experience of under-determination and free-floatingness which came to be articulated *ex post facto* as 'disembeddedment'. Identity would not have congealed into a visible and graspable entity in any other but the 'disembedded' or 'unencumbered' form.

One thinks of identity whenever one is not sure of where one belongs; that is, one is not sure how to place oneself among the evident variety of behavioural styles and patterns, and how to make sure that people around would accept this placement as right and proper, so that both sides would know how to go on in each other's presence. 'Identity' is a name given to the escape sought from that uncertainty. Hence 'identity', though ostensibly a noun, behaves like a verb, albeit a strange one to be sure: it appears only in the future tense. Though all too often hyposta-sized as an attribute of a material entity, identity has the ontological status of a project and a postulate. To say 'postulated identity' is to say one word too many, as neither there is nor can there be any other identity but a postulated one. Identity is a critical projection of what is demanded and/or sought upon what is; or, more exactly still, an oblique assertion of the inadequacy or incompleteness of the latter.

Identity entered modern mind and practice dressed from the start as an individual task. It was up to the individual to find escape from uncertainty. Not for the first and not for the last time, socially created problems were to be resolved by individual efforts, and collective maladies healed by private medicine. Not that the individuals were left to their own initiative and that their acumen was trusted; quite the contrary – putting the individual responsibility for self-formation on the agenda spawned the host of trainers, coaches, teachers, counsellors and guides all claiming to hold superior knowledge of what identities could be acquired and held. The concepts of identity-building and of culture (that is, of the idea of the individual incompetence, of the need of collective breeding and of the importance of skilful and knowledgeable breeders) were and could only be born together. The 'disembedded' identity simultaneously ushered in the individual's freedom of choice and the individual's dependency on expert guidance.

Modern life as pilgrimage

The figure of the pilgrim was not a modern invention; it is as old as Christianity. But modernity gave it a new prominence and a seminally novel twist.

When Rome lay in ruins – humbled, humiliated and sacked and pillaged by Alaric's nomads – St Augustine jotted down the following observation: '[I]t is recorded of Cain that he built a city, while Abel, as though he were a merely a pilgrim on earth, built none.' 'True city of the saints is in heaven'; here on earth, says St Augustine, Christians wander 'as on pilgrimage through time looking for the Kingdom of eternity'.[2]

For pilgrims through time, the truth is elsewhere; the true place is always some distance, some time away. Wherever the pilgrim may be now, it is not where he ought to be, and not where he dreams of being. The distance between the true world and this world here and now is made of the mismatch between what is to be achieved and what has been. The glory and gravity of the future destination debases the present and makes light of it. For the pilgrim, what purpose may the city serve? For the pilgrim, only streets make sense, not the houses – houses tempt one to rest and relax, to forget about the destination. Even the streets, though, may prove to be obstacles rather than help, traps rather than thorough-fares. They may misguide, divert from the straight path, lead astray. 'Judeo-Christian culture,' writes Richard Sennett, 'is, at its very roots, about experiences of spiritual dislocation and homelessness. . . . Our faith began at odds with place.'[3]

'We are pilgrims through time' was, under the pen of St Augustine not an exhortation, but a statement of fact. We are pilgrims whatever we do, and there is little we can do about it even if we wished. Earthly life is but a brief overture to the eternal persistence of the soul. Only few would wish, and have the ability, to compose that overture themselves, in tune with the music of heavenly spheres – to make their fate into a consciously embraced destiny. These few would need to escape the distractions of the town. The desert is the habitat they must choose. The desert of the Christian hermit was set at a distance from the hurly-burly of family life, away from the town and the village, from the mundane, from the *polis*. The desert meant putting a distance between oneself and one's duties and obligations, the warmth and the agony of being with others, being looked at by others, being framed and moulded by their scrutiny, demands and expectations. Here, in mundane quotidianity, one's hands were tied, and so were one's thoughts. Here, horizon was tightly packed with huts, barns, copses, groves and church towers. Here, wherever one moved, one was *in a place*, and being in place meant staying put, doing what the place needed to be done. The desert, on the contrary, was a land not yet sliced into places, and for that reason it was the land of self-creation. The desert, said Edmond Jabès, 'is a space where one step gives way to the next, which undoes it, and the horizon means hope for a tomorrow which speaks.' 'You do not go to the desert to find identity, but to lose it, to lose your personality, to become anonymous. . . . And then something extraordinary happens: you hear silence speak.'[4] The desert is the archetype and the greenhouse of the raw, bare, primal and bottom-line freedom that is but the absence of bounds. What made the mediaeval hermits feel so close to God in the desert was the feeling of being themselves god-like: unbound by habit and convention, by the needs of their own bodies and other people's souls, by their past deeds and present actions. In the words of the present-day theorists, one would say that the hermits were the first to live through the experience of 'disembedded', 'unencumbered' selves. They were god-like, because whatever they did they did *ab nihilo*. Their pilgrimage to God was an exercise in self-construction (this is why the Church, wishing to be the sole connecting line to God, resented the hermits from the start – and soon went out of its way to force them into monastic orders, under the close supervision of rules and routine).

The Protestants, as Weber told us, accomplished a feat unthinkable for the lonely hermits of yore: they became *inner-worldly pilgrims*. They invented the way of embarking on pilgrimage without leaving home and of leaving home without becoming homeless. This they could do, however, only because the desert stretched and reached deep into their towns right up to their doorsteps. They did not venture into the desert; it was the world of their daily life which was turning more and more 'like the desert'. Like the desert, the world turned placeless; the familiar features had been obliterated, but the new ones which were meant to replace them were given the kind of permanence once thought as unique to the sand dunes. In the new post-Reformation city of modernity, the desert began on the other side of the door.

The Protestant, that pattern-setter (or is he but an allegory?) for the modern man, so Sennett tells us, was 'tempted by wilderness, by a place of emptiness which made no seductive demands of its own upon him'. In this he was not different from the hermit. The difference was that instead of travelling to the desert, the Protestant worked hard to make desert come to him – to remake the world in the likeness of the desert. 'Impersonality, coldness and *emptiness* are essential words in the Prot-estant language of environment; they express the desire to see the outside as null, lacking value.'[5] This is the kind of language in which one speaks of the desert: of nothingness waiting to become something, if only for a while; of meaninglessness waiting to be given meaning, if only a passing one; of the space without contours, ready to accept any contour offered, if only until other contours are offered; of a space not scarred with past furrows, yet fertile with expectations of sharp blades; of virgin land yet to be ploughed and tilled; of the land of the perpetual beginning; of the place-no-place whose name and identity is not-yet. In such a land, the trails are blazed by the destination of the pilgrim, and there are few other tracks to reckon with.

In such a land, commonly called modern society, pilgrimage is no longer a choice of the mode of life; less still is it a heroic or saintly choice. Living one's life as pilgrimage is no longer the kind of ethical wisdom revealed to, or initiated by, the chosen and the righteous. Pilgrimage is what one does of necessity, to avoid being lost in a desert; to invest the walking with a purpose while wandering the land with no destination. Being a pilgrim, one can do more than walk – one can walk *to*. One can look back at the footprints left in the sand and see them as a road. One can *reflect* on the road past and see it as a *progress towards*, an advance, a coming *closer to*; one can make a distinction between 'behind' and 'ahead', and plot the 'road ahead' as a succession of footprints yet to pockmark the land without features. Destination, the set purpose of life's pilgrimage, gives form to the formless, makes a whole out of the fragmentary, lends continuity to the episodic.

The desert-like world commands life to be lived as pilgrimage. But because life is a pilgrimage, the world at the doorsteps is desert-like, featureless, as its meaning is yet to be brought into it through the wandering which would transform it into the track leading to the finishing line where the meaning resides. This 'bringing in' of meaning has been called 'identity-building'. The pilgrim and the desert-like world he walks acquire their meanings *together*, and *through each other*. Both processes can and must go on because there is a distance between the goal (the meaning of the world and the identity of the pilgrim, always not-yet-reached, always in the future) and the present moment (the station of the wandering and the identity of the wanderer).

Both meaning and identity can exist only as *projects*, and it is the distance which enables projects to be. The 'distance' is what we call, in the 'objective' language of space, the experience which in 'subjective', psychological terms we speak about as dissatisfaction with, and denigration of, the here and now. The 'distance' and 'dissatisfaction' have the same referent, and both make sense within the life lived as pilgrimage.

'It is the difference in amount between the pleasure of satisfaction which is *demanded* and that which is actually *achieved* that provides the driving factor which will permit of no halting at any position attained, but, in the poet's words 'Presses ever forward unsubdued' (Faust),' observed Freud in *Beyond the Pleasure Principle*. Janine Chasseguet-Smirgel[6] offers an extended commentary on that seminal observation, tracing the beginning of self-development, identity-building etc. to the primary condition of delayed gratification, of the never-to-be-bridged distance between the ego-ideal and the realities of the present.

'Distance' translates as 'delay' . . . Passage through space is a function of time, distances are measured by the time needed to cancel them. 'Here' is the waiting, 'there' is the gratification. How far is it from here to there, from the waiting to gratification, from the void to meaning, from the project to identity? Ten years, twenty? As long as it takes to live one's vocation through? Time one can use to measure distances must be of the sort the rulers are – straight, in one piece, with equidistant markings, made of tough and solid material. And such was, indeed, the time of modern living-towards-projects. Like life itself, it was directional, continuous, and unbendable. It 'marched on' and 'passed by'. Both life and time were made to the measure of pilgrimage.

For the pilgrim, for the modern man, this meant in practical terms that he could-should-had-to select his point of arrival fairly early in life with confidence, certain that the straight line of life-time ahead will not bend, twist or warp, come to a halt or turn backwards. Delay of gratification, much as the momentary frustration it begot, was an energizing factor and the source of identity-building zeal in so far as it was coupled with the trust in the linearity and cumulativeness of time. The foremost strategy of life as pilgrimage, of life as identity-building, was 'saving for the future', but saving for the future made sense as strategy only in so far as one could be sure that the future would reward the savings with interest and the bonus once accrued will not be withdrawn, that the savings will not be devalued before the bonus-distribution date or declared invalid currency; that what is seen today as capital will be seen the same way tomorrow and the day after tomorrow. Pilgrims had a stake in solidity of the world they walked; in a kind of world in which one can tell life as a continuous story, a 'sense-making' story, such a story as makes each event the effect of the event before and the cause of the event after, each age a station on the road pointing towards fulfilment. The world of pilgrims – of identity-*builders* – must be orderly, determined, predictable, ensured; but above all, it must be a kind of world in which footprints are engraved for good, so that the trace and the record of past travels are kept and preserved. A world in which travelling may be indeed a pilgrimage. A world hospitable to the pilgrims.

The world inhospitable to pilgrims

The world is not hospitable to the pilgrims any more. The pilgrims lost their battle by winning it. They strove to make the world solid by making it pliable, so that identity could be *built at will*, but built *systematically*, floor by floor and brick by brick. They proceeded by turning the space in which identity was to be built into a desert. They found out that the desert, though comfortingly featureless for those who seek to make their mark, does not hold features well. The easier it is to emboss a footprint, the easier it is to efface it. A gust of wind will do. And deserts are windy places.

It soon transpired that the real problem is not how to build identity, but how to preserve it; whatever you may build in the sand is unlikely to be a castle. In a desert-like world it takes no great effort to blaze a trail – the difficulty is how to recognize it as a trail after a while. How to distinguish a forward march from going in circles, from eternal return? It becomes virtually impossible to patch the trodden stretches of sand into an itinerary – let alone into a plan for a lifelong journey.

The meaning of identity, points out Christopher Lasch, 'refers both to persons and to things. Both have lost their solidity in modern society, their definiteness and continuity.' The world constructed of durable objects has been replaced 'with disposable products designed for immediate obsolescence'. In such a world, 'identities can be adopted and discarded like a change of costume'.[7] The horror of the new situation is that all diligent work of construction may prove to be in vain; its allurement is the fact of not being bound by past trials, being never irrevocably defeated, always 'keeping the options open'. The horror and the allurement alike make life-as-pilgrimage hardly feasible as a strategy and unlikely to be chosen as one. Not by many, anyway. And not with great chance of success.

In the life-game of the postmodern consumers the rules of the game keep changing in the course of playing. The sensible strategy is therefore to keep each game short – so that a sensibly played game of life calls for the splitting of one big all-embracing game with huge stakes into a series of brief and narrow games with small ones. 'Determination to live one day at a time', 'depicting daily life as a succession of minor emergencies'[8] become the guiding principles of all rational conduct.

To keep the game short means to beware long-term commitments. To refuse to be 'fixed' one way or the other. Not to get tied to the place. Not to wed one's life to one vocation only. Not to swear consistency and loyalty to anything and anybody. Not to *control* the future, but to *refuse to mortgage* it: to take care that the consequences of the game do not outlive the game itself, and to renounce responsibility for such as do. To forbid the past to bear on the present. In short, to cut the present off at both ends, to sever the present from history, to abolish time in any other form but a flat collection or an arbitrary sequence of present moments; a *continuous present*.

Once disassembled and no more a vector, time no longer structures the space. On the ground, there is no more 'forward' and 'backward'; it is just the ability not to stand still that counts. *Fitness* – the capacity to move swiftly where the action is and be ready to take in experiences as they come – takes precedence over *health*, that idea of the standard of normalcy and of keeping that standard stable and unscathed. All delay, including 'delay of gratification', loses its meaning: there is no arrow-like time left to measure it.

And so the snag is no longer how to discover, invent, construct, assemble (even buy) an identity, but how to prevent it from sticking. Well constructed and durable identity turns from an asset into a liability. The hub of postmodern life strategy is not identity building, but avoidance of fixation.

What possible purpose could the strategy of pilgrim-style 'progress' serve in this world of ours? In this world, not only have jobs-for-life disappeared, but trades and professions which have acquired the confusing habit of appearing from nowhere and vanishing without notice can hardly be lived as Weberian 'vocations' – and to rub salt into the wound, the demand for the skills needed to practise such professions seldom lasts as long as the time needed to acquire them. Jobs are no longer protected, and most certainly no better than the stability of places where they are practised; whenever the word 'rationalization' is pronounced, one knows for sure that the disappearance of further jobs and places is in the pipeline. The stability and trustworthiness of the network of human relations fares little better. Ours is the age of Anthony Giddens's 'pure relationship' which 'is entered for its own sake, for what can be derived by each person' and so 'it can be terminated, more or less at will, by either partner at any particular point'; of 'confluent love' which 'jars with the "for-ever", "one-and-only" qualities of the romantic love complex' so that 'romance can no longer be equated with permanence'; of 'plastic sexuality', that is sexual enjoyment 'severed from its age-old integration with reproduction, kinship and the generations.'[9] One can hardly 'hook on' an identity to relationships which themselves are irreparably 'unhooked'; and one is solemnly advised not to try – as the strong commitment, the deep attachment (let alone loyalty, that tribute to the by now obsolete idea that attachment has consequences that bind, while commitment means obligations) may wound and scar when the time to detach the self from the partner arrives, as it almost certainly will. The game of life is fast and leaves no time to pause and think and draw elaborate designs. But again, adding impotence to bafflement, the rules of the game keep changing long before the game is finished. In this 'cosmic casino' of ours (as George Steiner put it), values to be cherished and actively pursued, rewards to be fought for and stratagems to be deployed to get them, are all calculated 'for maximal impact and instant obsolescence'. For *maximal impact*, since in a world over-saturated with information attention turns into the scarcest of resources and only a shocking message, and one more shocking than the last, stands a chance of catching it (until the next shock); and *instant obsolescence*, as the site of attention needs to be cleared as soon as it is filled, to make room for new messages knocking at the gate.

The overall result is the *fragmentation* of time into *episodes*, each one cut from its past and from its future, each one self-enclosed and self-contained. Time is no longer a river, but a collection of ponds and pools.

No consistent and cohesive life strategy emerges from the experience which can be gathered in such a world – none remotely reminiscent of the sense of purpose and the rugged determination of the pilgrimage. Nothing emerges from that experience but certain, mostly negative, rules of the thumb: do not plan your trips too long – the shorter the trip, the greater the chance of completing it; do not get emotionally attached to people you meet at the stopover – the less you care about them, the less it will cost you to move on; do not commit yourself too strongly to people, places, causes – you cannot know how long they will last or how long you will count them worthy of your commitment; do not think of your current resources as of capital – savings lose value fast, and the once-vaunted 'cultural capital' tends to turn in no time into cultural *liability*. Above all, do not delay gratification, if you can help it. Whatever you are after, try to get it *now*, you cannot know whether the gratification you seek today will be still be gratifying tomorrow.

I propose that in the same way as the pilgrim was the most fitting metaphor for the modern life strategy preoccupied with the daunting task of identity-building, the stroller, the vagabond, the tourist and the player offer jointly the metaphor for the postmodern strategy moved by the horror of being bound and fixed. None of the listed types/styles are postmodern inventions – they were known well before the advent of postmodern times. And yet in the same way that the modern conditions reshaped the figure of pilgrim they inherited from Christianity, the postmodern context gives new quality to the types known to its predecessors – and it does it in two crucial respects. First: the styles once practised by marginal people in marginal time-stretches and marginal places, are now practised by the majority in the prime time of their lives and in places central to their life-world; they have become now, fully and truly, lifestyles. Second: for some, if not for all – the types are not a matter of choice, not either/or – postmodern life is too messy and incoherent to be grasped by any one cohesive model. Each type conveys but a part of the story which never integrates into a totality (its 'totality' is *nothing* but the sum of its parts). In the postmodern chorus, all four types sing – sometimes in harmony, though much more often with cacophony as the result.

The pilgrim's successors

The stroller

Charles Baudelaire baptized Constantin Guy 'the painter of modern life' because Guy painted city streets scenes the way they were seen by the stroller (*flâneur*). Commenting on Baudelaire's observation, Walter Benjamin made *flâneur* into a household name of cultural analysis and the central symbolic figure of the modern city. All strands of modern life seemed to meet and tie together in the pastime and the experience of the stroller: going for a stroll as one goes to a theatre, finding oneself among strangers and being a stranger to them (*in* the crowd but *not* of the crowd), taking in those strangers as 'surfaces' – so that 'what one sees' exhausts 'what they are' – and above all seeing and knowing of them episodically; psychically, strolling means rehearsing human reality as a series of episodes, that is as events without past and with no consequences. It also means rehearsing meetings as mis-meetings, as encounters without impact: the fleeting fragments of other persons' lives the stroller spun off into stories at will – it was his perception that made them into actors, let alone the plot of the drama they play. The stroller was the past master of simulation – he imagined himself a scriptwriter and a director pulling the strings of other people's lives without damaging or distorting their fate. The stroller practised the 'as if' life and the 'as if' engagement with other people's life; he put paid to the opposition between 'appearance' and 'reality'; he was the creator without penalties attached to creation, the master who need not fear the consequences of his deeds, the bold one never facing the bills of courage. The stroller had all the pleasures of modern life without the torments attached.

Life-as-strolling was a far cry from the life-as-pilgrimage. What the pilgrim did in all seriousness, the stroller mocked playfully; in the process, he got rid of the costs and the effects alike. The stroller fitted ill the modern scene, but then he hid in its wings. He was the man of leisure and he did his strolling in time of leisure. The stroller and the strolling waited at the periphery for their hour to arrive. And it did arrive – or rather it was brought by the postmodern avatar of the heroic producer into playful consumer. Now the strolling, once the activity practised by marginal people on the margins of 'real life', came to be life itself, and the question of 'reality' need not be dealt with any more.

'Malls' in its original meaning refers to the tracts for strolling. Now most of the malls are *shopping* malls, tracts to stroll while you shop and to shop in while you stroll. The merchandisers sniffed out the attraction and seductive power of strollers' habits and set about moulding them into life. Parisian arcades have been promoted retrospectively to the bridgeheads of the times to come: the postmodern islands in the modern sea. Shopping malls make the world (or the carefully walled-off, electronically monitored and closely guarded part of it) safe for life-as-strolling. Or, rather, shopping malls are the worlds made by the bespoke designers to the measure of the stroller. The sites of mis-meetings, of encounters guaranteed to be episodic, of the present prised off from the past and the future, of surfaces glossing over surfaces. In these worlds, every stroller may imagine himself to be a director, though all strollers are the objects of direction. That direction is, as their own used to be, unobstrusive and invisible (though, unlike theirs, seldom inconsequential), so that baits feel like desires, pressures like intentions, seduction like decision-making; in the shopping malls, in life as shopping-to-stroll and strolling-to-shop, dependence dissolves in freedom, and freedom seeks dependence.

The malls initiated the postmodern promotion of the stroller, but also prepared the ground for further elevation (or is it purification?) of the stroller's life-model. The latter has been achieved in the *telecity* (Henning Bech's felicitous term), the city-as-the-stroller's-haunt, distilled to its pure essence, now entering the ultimate shelter of the totally private, secure, locked and burglar-proof world of the lonely nomad, where the physical presence of strangers does not conceal or interfere with their psychical out-of-reachedness. In its telecity version, the streets and the shopping malls have been cleansed of all that which from the stroller's point of view was sport-spoiling, an impurity, redundancy or waste – so that what has been retained can shine and be enjoyed in all its unsullied purity. In Bech's words, 'the screen mediated world of the telecity exists only by way of surfaces; and, tendentially, everything can and must be turned into an object for the gaze. . . . [T]here is, by way of "readings" of the

surface signs, opportunity for a much more intense and changing empathy in and out of identities, because of the possibilities of uninterfered
and continual watching. . . . Television is totally non-committal.'[10] The
ultimate freedom is screen directed, lived in the company of surfaces,
and called zapping.

The vagabond

The vagabond was the bane of early modernity, the bugbear that spur-
red the rulers and the philosophers into an ordering and legislating fren-
zy.[11] The vagabond was *masterless*, and being masterless (out of control,
out of frame, on the loose) was one condition modernity could not bear
and thus spent the rest of its history fighting. The Elizabethan legislators
were obsessed with the need to rule the vagrants out of the roads and
back to the parishes 'where they belonged' (but which they left precisely
because they *did not* belong any more). The vagabonds were the advanced troops or guerrilla units of the post-traditional chaos (construed
by the rulers, in the usual fashion of using a mirror to paint the image of
the Other, as *anarchy*), and they had to go if order (that is, space managed and monitored) was to prevail. It was the free-roaming vagabonds
who made the search for new, state-managed, societal-level order imperative and urgent.

What made vagabonds so terrifying was their apparent freedom to
move and so to escape the net of heretofore locally based control. Worse
than that still, the movements of the vagabond are unpredictable; unlike
the pilgrim the vagabond has no set destination. You do not know
where he will move to next, because he himself does not know nor care
much. Vagabondage has no advance itinerary – its trajectory is patched
together bit by bit, one bit a time. Each place is for the vagabond a stopover, but he never knows how long he will stay in any of them; this will
depend on the generosity and patience of the residents, but also on
news of other places arousing new hopes (the vagabond is pushed from
behind by hopes frustrated, and pulled forward by hopes untested). The
vagabond decides where to turn when he comes to the crossroads; he
chooses the next stay by reading the names on the road signs. It is easy
to control the pilgrim, so utterly predictable thanks to his self-
determination. To control the wayward and erratic vagabond is a daunting task (though this proved to be one of the few tasks modern ingenuity did resolve).

Wherever the vagabond goes, he is a stranger; he can never be 'the
native', the 'settled one', one with 'roots in the soil' (too fresh is the
memory of his arrival – that is, of his being elsewhere before). Enter-
taining a dream of going native can only end in mutual recrimination
and bitterness. It is better, therefore, not to grow too accustomed to the
place. And, after all, other places beckon, not tested yet, perhaps more

hospitable, certainly able to offer new chances. Cherishing one's out-of-placeness is a sensible strategy. It gives all decisions the 'until-further-notice' flavour. It allows one to keep the options open. It prevents mortgaging the future. If natives cease to amuse, one can always try to find the more amusing ones.

The early modern vagabond wandered through the settled places; he was a vagabond because in no place could he be settled as the other people had been. The settled were many, the vagabonds few. Post-modernity reversed the ratio. Now there are few 'settled' places left. The 'forever settled' residents wake up to find the places (places in the land, places in society and places in life), to which they 'belong', no longer existing or no longer accommodating; neat streets turn mean, factories vanish together with jobs, skills no longer find buyers, knowledge turns into ignorance, professional experience becomes liability, secure networks of relations fall apart and foul the place with putrid waste. Now the vagabond is a vagabond not because of the reluctance or difficulty of settling down, but because of the scarcity of settled places. Now the odds are that the people he meets in his travels are other vagabonds – vagabonds today or vagabonds tomorrow. The world is catching up with the vagabond, and catching up fast. The world is re-tailoring itself to the measure of the vagabond.

The tourist

Like the vagabond, the tourist used once to inhabit the margins of 'properly social' action (though the vagabond was marginal *man*, while tourism was marginal *activity*), and has now moved to its centre (in both senses). Like the vagabond, the tourist is on the move. Like the vagabond, he is everywhere he goes *in*, but nowhere *of* the place he is in. But there are also differences, and they are seminal.

First, the balance between 'push' and 'pull' factors in the case of the tourist shifts toward the 'pull' end. The tourist moves *on purpose* (or so he thinks). His movements are first of all 'in order to', and only secondarily (if at all) 'because of'. The purpose is new experience; the tourist is a conscious and systematic seeker of experience, of a new and different experience, of the experience of difference and novelty – as the joys of the familiar wear off and cease to allure. The tourists want to immerse themselves in a strange and bizarre element (a pleasant feeling, a tickling and rejuvenating feeling, like letting oneself be buffeted by sea waves) – on condition, though, that it will not stick to the skin and thus can be shaken off whenever they wish. They choose the elements to jump into according to how strange, but also how innocuous, they are; you recognize the favourite tourist haunts by their blatant, ostentatious (if painstakingly groomed) oddity, but also by the profusion of safety cushions and well marked escape routes. In the tourist's world, the strange is tame, domesticated, and no longer frightens; shocks come in a package deal with safety. This makes the world seem infinitely gentle, obedient to the tourist's wishes and whims, ready to oblige; but also a do-it-yourself world, pleasingly pliable, kneaded by the tourist's desire, made and remade with one purpose in mind: to excite, please and amuse. There is no other purpose to justify the presence of that world and the tourist's presence in it. The tourist's world is fully and exclusively structured by *aesthetic* criteria (ever more numerous writers who note the 'aestheticization' of the postmodern world to the detriment of its other, also moral, dimensions, describe – even if unaware of it – the world as seen by the tourist; the 'aestheticized' world is the world inhabited by tourists). Unlike in the life of the vagabond, tough and harsh realities resistant to aesthetic sculpting do not interfere here. One may say that what the tourist buys, what he pays for, what he demands to be delivered (or goes to court if delivery is delayed) is precisely the right not to be bothered, freedom from any but aesthetic spacing.

    Second, unlike the vagabond who has little choice but to reconcile himself to the state of homelessness, the tourist has a home; or should have, at any rate. Having a home is a part of the safety package: for the pleasure to be unclouded and truly engrossing, there must be somewhere a homely and cosy, indubitably 'owned' place to go to when the present adventure is over, or if the voyage proves not as adventurous as expected. 'The home' is the place to take off the armour and to unpack – the place where nothing needs to be proved and defended as everything is just there, obvious and familiar. It is the placidity of home that sends the tourist to seek new adventures, but it is the selfsame placidity which renders the search of adventures an uncloudedly pleasurable pastime: whatever has happened to my face here, in the tourist land, or whichever mask I put on it, my 'real face' is in safe keeping, immune, stain-resistant, unsullied. . . . The problem is, though, that as life itself turns into an extended tourist escapade, as tourist conduct becomes the mode of life and the tourist stance grows into the character, it is less and less clear which one of the visiting places is the home. The opposition 'here I am but visiting, there is my home' stays clear-cut as before, but it is not easy to point out where the 'there' is. 'There' is increasingly stripped of all material features; the 'home' it contains is not even *imaginary* (each mental image would be too specific, too constraining), but *postulated*; what is postulated is *having* a home, not a particular building, street, landscape or company of people. Jonathan Matthew Schwartz advises us 'to distinguish the *homesick* searching from the nostalgic yearning'; the latter is, at least ostensibly, past oriented, while the home in homesickness is as a rule 'in the future perfect tenses. . . . It is an urge to feel at home, to recognize one's surroundings and belong there.'[12] Homesickness means a dream of *belonging*; to be, for once, *of* the place, not merely *in*. And yet if the present is notoriously the destination of all future tense, the future tense of 'homesickness' is an exception. The value of home for the homesick lies precisely in its tendency to stay in the future tense for ever.

It cannot move to the present without being stripped of its charm and allure; when tourism becomes the mode of life, when the experiences ingested thus far whet the appetite for further excitement, when the threshold of excitement climbs relentlessly upwards and each new shock must be more shocking than the last one – the possibility of the home-dream ever coming true is as horrifying as the possibility of it never becoming real. Homesickness, as it were, is not the sole tourist's sentiment: the other is the fear of *home-boundedness*, of being tied to a place and barred from exit. 'Home' lingers at the horizon of the tourist life as an uncanny mix of shelter and prison. The tourist's favourite slogan is 'I need more space'. And the space is the last thing one would find at home.

The player

In play, there is neither inevitability nor accident (there is no accident in a world that knows no necessity or determination); nothing is fully predictable and controllable, but nothing is totally immutable and irrevocable either. The world of play is soft yet elusive; in it, the thing that matters most is how well one plays one's hand. Of course, there is such a thing as a 'stroke of luck' – when cards are stacked in one's favour or wind helps the ball into the net. But the 'stroke of luck' (or misfortune, as it were) does not lend the world the toughness it conspicuously lacks; it only signals the limits of how far playing one's cards right may go in making things certain, but shares in the no-necessity no-accident status of the player's calculations.

In play, the world itself is a player, and luck and misfortune are but the moves of the world-as-player. In the confrontation between the player and the world there are neither laws nor lawlessness, neither order nor chaos. There are just the moves – more or less clever, shrewd or tricky, insightful or misguided. The point is to guess the moves of the adversary and anticipate them, prevent or pre-empt – to stay 'one ahead'. The rules the player may follow can be no more than rules of thumb; heuristic, not algorithmic instructions. The player's world is the world of *risks*, of intuition, of precaution-taking.

Time in the world-as-play divides into a succession of games. Each game is made of conventions of its own; each is a separate 'province of meaning' – a little universe of its own, self-enclosed and self-contained. Each demands that disbelief be suspended – though in each game a different disbelief is to be suspended. Those who refuse to obey the conventions do not rebel against the game; they only opt out and cease to be players. But the 'game goes on', and whatever the quitters say and do after that does not influence it a bit. The walls of the game are impenetrable, the voices outside reach the inside only as a muted, inarticulate noise.

Each game has its beginning and its end. The worry of the player is that each game should indeed start from the beginning, from 'square one', as if no games were played before and none of the players has amassed wins or losses which would make mockery of the 'zero point' and transform what was to be a beginning into a continuation. For this reason, however, one must make sure that the game also has a clear, uncontested ending. It should not 'spill over' into the time after: as far as later games are concerned, no game played before must handicap, privilege or otherwise determine the players – *be of consequence*. Whoever does not like the outcome must 'cut their losses' and start from scratch – and be able to do just that.

To make sure that no game leaves lasting consequences, the player must remember (and so must his/her partners and adversaries), that 'this is *but* a game'. An important, though difficult to accept reminder, as the purpose of the game is to win and so the game allows no room for pity, compassion, commiseration or cooperation. The game is like war, yet that war which is a game must leave no mental scars and no nursed grudges: 'we are grown up people, let us part as friends' demands the player opting out of the game of marriage, in the name of the gamesmanship of future, however merciless, games. War that is a game absolves the conscience for its lack of scruples. The mark of postmodern adulthood is the willingness to embrace the game wholeheartedly, as children do.

What chance of morality? What chance of polity?

Each of the four types sketched above contains a solid dose of ambivalence of its own; in addition, they also differ from each other in a number of respects, and so blending them into one cohesive lifestyle is not an easy matter. No wonder there is quite a generous pinch of schizophrenia in each postmodern personality – which goes some way towards accounting for the notorious restlessness, fickleness and irresoluteness of practised life strategies.

There are, though, certain features which the four types share. The most seminal among them are their effects on popular moral and political attitudes, and indirectly on the status of morality and politics in a postmodern context.

Elsewhere I suggested that modernity was prominent for the tendency to shift moral responsibilities away from the moral self either towards socially constructed and managed supra-individual agencies, or through floating responsibility inside a bureaucratic 'rule of nobody'.[13] The overall result was, on the one hand, the tendency to substitute ethics, that is a law-like code of rules and conventions, for moral sentiments, intuitions and urges of autonomous selves; and, on the other, the tendency towards 'adiaphorization', that is exemption of a considerable part of human action from moral judgement and, indeed, moral significance. These processes are by no means a thing of the past – but it seems that their impact is somewhat less decisive than in the times of 'classic' modernity. I suggest that the context in which moral attitudes are forged (or not) is today that of life-politics, rather than social and system structures; that, in other words, the postmodern life strategies, rather than the bureaucratic mode of management of social processes and coordinating action, are the most consequential among the factors shaping the moral situation of postmodern men and women.

All four intertwining and interpenetrating postmodern life strategies have in common that they tend to render human relations fragmentary (remember the 'purity' of relations reduced to single function and service) and discontinuous; they are all up in arms against 'strings attached' and long-lasting consequences, and militate against the construction of lasting networks of mutual duties and obligations. They all favour and promote a distance between the individual and the Other and cast the Other primarily as the object of aesthetic, not moral, evaluation; as a matter of taste, not responsibility. In the effect, they cast individual autonomy in opposition to moral (as well as all the other) responsibilities and remove huge areas of human interaction, even the most intimate among them, from moral judgement (a process remarkably similar in its consequences to bureaucratically promoted adiaphorization). Following the moral impulse means assuming responsibility for the other, which in turn leads to an engagement with the fate of the other and commitment to her/his welfare. The disengagement and commitment-avoidance favoured by all four postmodern strategies has a backlash effect in the shape of the suppression of the moral impulse as well as disavowal and denigration of moral sentiments.

What has been said above may well seem jarringly at odds with the cult of interpersonal intimacy, also a prominent feature of postmodern consciousness. There is no contradiction here, though. The cult is no more than a psychological (illusory and anxiety-generating) compensation for the loneliness that inevitably envelops the aesthetically oriented subjects of desire; and it is, moreover, self-defeating, as the consequence-proof interpersonality reduced to 'pure relationships' can generate little intimacy and sustains no trustworthy bridges over the sandpit of estrangement. As Christopher Lasch noted a decade and a half ago, 'the culture of personal relations . . . conceals a thoroughgoing disenchantment with personal relations, just as the cult of sensuality implies a repudiation of sensuality in all but its most primitive forms'. Our society 'has made deep and lasting friendships, love affairs and marriages increasingly difficult to achieve'.[14]

Political disablement of postmodern men and women arises from the same source as the moral one. Aesthetic spacing, preferred by and dominant in all listed postmodern strategies, differs from other kinds of social spacing (like moral or cognitive) in that it does not choose as its points of reference and orientation the traits and qualities possessed by or ascribed to the objects of spacing, but the attributes of the spacing subject (like interest, excitement, satisfaction or pleasure). As Jean-François

Lyotard recently observed, 'the objects and the contents have become indifferent. The only question is whether they are "interesting"'.[15] The world turns into the pool of potentially interesting objects, and the task is to squeeze out of them as much interest as they may yield. The task and its successful accomplishment stand and fall, however, by the effort and ingenuity of the interest-seeker. There is little or nothing that can be done by, and about, the objects themselves.[16] Focusing on the interest-seeking subject blurs the contours of the world in which the interest is to be sought. Met (mis-met?) only perfunctorily, in passing, surface deep, the objects do not come into vision as entities in their own right, such as may need more vigour, improvement, or a different shape altogether; we do not ruminate on the way to rectify commodities displayed on the supermarket shelves – if we find them unsatisfactory, we pass them by, with our trust in the supermarket system unscathed, in the hope that products answering our interests will be found on the next shelf or in the next shop. Emancipation, says Lyotard, 'is no more situated as an alternative to reality, as an ideal set to conquer and force itself upon reality from outside'; in consequence, the militant practice has been replaced by a defensive one, one that is easily assimilated by the 'system' since it is now assumed that the latter contains all the bits and pieces from which the 'emancipated self' will be eventually assembled.[17] The 'system' has done all it possibly can. The rest is up to those who 'play it'.

Exaggerating the picture, but only slightly, one may say that in popular perception the duty of the postmodern citizen (much like the duty of the inmates of Rabelais's Abbey of Télème) is to lead an enjoyable life. To treat subjects as citizens, the state is obliged to supply the facilities deemed necessary for such life, and not to give occasion for doubt that performance of the duty is feasible. This does not necessarily mean that the life of so reduced citizens must be unmitigated bliss. Discontent does arise, sometimes so acute as to prompt action reaching beyond the ordinary preoccupation with self-care. This happens time and again, even regularly, whenever the limits of individual pursuit of 'the interesting' are brought into relief; whenever factors evidently beyond individual control (like for instance planning decisions about a new bypass, motorway, residential developments likely to attract 'outsiders', closing a hospital, 'rationalizing' a school or a college) interfere with the interest-content of the environment. And yet the momentary explosions of solidary action which may result do not alter the essential traits of postmodern relationships: their fragmentariness and discontinuity, narrowness of focus and purpose, shallowness of contact. Joint engagements come and go, and in each case, indeed, the emergent 'totality' is no more than 'the sum of its parts'. Besides, the diffuse grudges and grievances, as a rule spawning one-issue campaigns, do not add up, condense or show a propensity for reinforcing each other. On the contrary – vying with each other for the scarce resource of public attention, they divide as much as they unite. One may say that the bones of contention do not fit together to form a skeleton around which a non-fragmentary and continuous, shared engagement could be wrapped.

Stuart Hall has pithily summarized the resulting condition and the prospects it may or may not hold: 'We don't have alternative means by which adults can benefit from the ways in which people have released themselves from the bonds of traditionalist forms of living and thinking, and still exert responsibilities for others in a free and open way. We have no notion of democratic citizenship in this sense.'[18] Or perhaps we may have – imagine – such a notion; what we cannot imagine, having no time left for exercising imagination, is a network of relationships that would accommodate and sustain such a notion. It is, in the end, the old truth all over again: each society sets limits to the life strategies that can be imagined, and certainly to those which can be practised. But the kind of society we live in limits such strategy(ies) as may critically and militantly question its principles and thus open the way to new strategies, at present excluded because of their non-viability. . . .

Dedicated to Judith Adler

Notes

1 Douglas Kellner 'Popular culture and constructing postmodern identities', in Scott Lasch and Jonathan Friedman (eds), *Modernity and Identity*, Basil Blackwell, Oxford, 1992.

2 St Augustine *The City of God*, trans. Gerald S. Walsh et al., Image, New York, 1958.

3 Richard Sennett, *The Conscience of the Eye: The Design and Social Life of Cities*, Faber and Faber, London, 1993, p. 6.

4 Edmond Jabès *The Books of Questions*, Vol. II, trans. Rosemarie Waldrop, Wesleyan University Press, Hanover, 1991, p. 342: *The Book of Margins*, trans. Rosmarie Waldrop, Chicago University Press, Chicago 1993, p. xvi. Jabès quotes the words of Gabriel Bounoure: 'The desert, by its exclusion of housing, opens an infinite elsewhere to man's essential wandering. Here, no here makes sense' (*The Book of Margins*, p. 16).

5 Sennett, *Conscience of the Eye*, pp. 44, 46.

6 Janine Chasseguet-Smirgel, *The Ego-Ideal: A Psychoanalytic Essay on the Malady of the Ideal*, trans. Paul Barrows, Free Association Books, London, 1985.

7 Christopher Lasch, *The Minimal Self: Psychic Survival in Troubled Times*, Pan Books, London, 1985, pp. 32, 34, 38.

8 Ibid., pp. 57, 62.

9 Anthony Giddens, *The Transformation of Intimacy: Sexuality, Love and Eroticism in Modern Societies*, Cambridge, Polity Press, 1992, pp. 58, 137, 61, 52, 27.

10 Henning Bech, 'Living together in the (post)modern world'. Paper presented at the session on Changing Family Structure and the New Forms of Living Together, European Conference of Sociology, Vienna, 22–28 August 1992.

11 Cf. Zygmunt Bauman, *Legislators and Interpreters: on Modernity, Postmodernity and Intellectuals*, Cambridge, Polity Press, 1987, Chapter 3.

12 Jonathan Matthew Schwartz, *In Defense of Homesickness: Nine Essays on Identity and Locality*, Akademisk Forlag, Copenhagen, 1989, pp. 15, 32.

13 Cf. Zygmunt Bauman, *Modernity and the Holocaust*, Polity Press, Cambridge, 1993, Chapter 7; *Postmodern Ethics*, Basil Blackwell, Oxford, 1993.

14 Christopher Lasch, *Culture of Narcissism: American Life in an Age of Diminishing Expectations*, Warner Books, New York, 1979, pp. 102, 69.

15 Jean-François Lyotard, *Moralités postmodernes*, Galilée, Paris, 1993, pp. 32–3.

16 Says Lasch: 'Having no hope of improving their lives in any of the ways that matter, people have convinced themselves that what matters is psychic self-improvement: getting in touch with their feelings, eating health food, taking lessons in ballet or belly-dancing, immersing themselves in the wisdom of the East, jogging, learning how to "relate", overcoming the "fear of pleasure"' (*Culture of Narcissism*, p. 29). Let us add that the diffuse, unfocused feeling that not all is well with the programme tends to be articulated as an issue of therapy aimed at the hapless or inept self-improver – but is channelled away from the programme itself; if anything, the programme emerges from the test with reinforced authority.

17 Lyotard, *Moralités postmodernes*, pp. 66–8.

18 Stuart Hall, 'Thatcherism today', *New Statesman and Society*, 26 November 1993, p. 16.

3

Enabling Identity? Biology, Choice and the New Reproductive Technologies

Marilyn Strathern

Whether primacy is given to social ties or biological ones, it seems that the late twentieth century affords new possibilities for people who wish to be certain about how and why they are related. This is true both of legal redress (what the courts are prepared to countenance) and of technological intervention in the reproductive process. As possibilities, these instruments and techniques exist in a cultural environment of empowerment or enablement. If, then, one were to ask what might be new and what might be old in such pursuits of identity, one would have to consider what is being enabled. One would also have to consider the value put on 'enablement' itself. This chapter sketches some of the cultural paradoxes that the idea stimulates, and some of the resultant contradictions that seem to lie in what people are able to make of identity through kinship.

It was with an evident sense of novelty that in 1992, first a girl and then a boy were reported in the British press to have divorced their parents.[1] They were both exercising the power, under the 1989 Children Act, to take legal action on their own account, and did so from a desire to move away from their mother and to reside with their grandparent(s). A claim going through the Florida courts a couple of months earlier had attracted similar publicity. Whereas in the British cases the severance of the child's tie with the parent lay in the assertion of legal autonomy and rejection of the parental home, the Florida twelve-year-old, in the words of the *New York Times*,[2], asked the court 'to end the parental rights of his biological mother'. It was not just a question of where the boy should live but who would be recognized as a parent (he wanted his foster parents to adopt him). The case was widely interpreted as an example of a child wanting to 'choose' his or her parents.

One might conclude from the way the issues were being presented that desire is thus realized in the exercise of choice. This would make sense of the analogy with marriage and its undoing, 'divorce'.

Yet the analogy is an odd one. Divorce is the undoing of a choice, as the contract is usually construed, whereas the boy was contesting rights otherwise invested in what was seen as a biological tie and any exercise of choice (as to the parents) could only come after the severance. David Schneider, an anthropological veteran in kinship studies, sent me the *New York Times* report with the accompanying note: 'Do you think it's too late for me to divorce my mother (who has been dead about twenty years)?' If he found an adopting mother, he goes on, then what happens to his sons? Whose grandsons are they?

He might have found reassurance, at least as far as his property was concerned, in the writings of a fellow American, John Beckstrom.[3] They would reassure him that whatever his children in turn did to him, his identity would continue to be carried by them. Desire does not after all have to be subject to the vagaries of choice – it can be hard-wired in. Beckstrom argued that laws governing intestate succession 'should be structured to give a decedent's assets to those most able to perpetuate the individual's genes' (Dreyfuss and Nelkin, 1992: 325–6). Succession laws are after all, his argument went, designed to reflect the wishes of the property holder, and because organisms survive in order to ensure the continuity of their specific genetic heritage, then 'a genes-based distribution best mirrors an individual's real desires'. Here there does not even have to be a mediating concept of paternity. More usually, paternal identity is regarded as crucial, as in a British case when DNA fingerprinting was used to establish the inheritance claims of a biological 'son'.[4] A High Court ruling in 1991 has already prepared the way for such DNA testing to determine paternal liability for child maintenance.

I have here mixed fantasy with fact, and British with American cases, in order to bring out what seem contradictory appeals to choice and to genes – to what can be negotiated in the best interests of (in the divorce cases) a child, and what can be taken for granted about parents' continuity of identity in their children. Indeed what is taken for granted is being quite variously justified. When biological connection is contested as the basis for rights, it ceases to be taken for granted and what follows from its acknowledgement is opened up to choice. At the same time, it is only the rights that follow which are at issue; the biological tie itself is not being dissolved. And it is because this tie appears indissoluble that parents can, in Beckstrom's view, surreptitiously perpetuate themselves through their genes regardless of the wishes of the child and regardless of whether it will in future recognize them as parents. Nonetheless these seem rather contradictory ways of imagining relationships.

I should note that the examples are misleading in one respect. They seem to point to a gender difference – that it is possible to override the kinds of claims a mother might base on biological connection whereas in the father's case it is precisely his biological ties to his children that form the basis of claims (and liabilities). In fact one can equally easily find counter-examples. Imagined, for instance, as a contest between genetic and birthing motherhood, surrogacy disputes may in lay opinion turn on *which* biological criteria should prevail. Biology was by tradition the basis of maternity, and far from ignoring biological connection in the case of mothers, disputes may be construed in terms of whether one biological process has the superior claim over the other.[5] Or one could cite the American Supreme Court judge who in 1989 ruled against the paternity suit of a putative natural father, where blood tests indicated a 98.07 per cent 'probability of paternity', on the grounds that his case left un-challenged the relevant state law as to the conditions under which a child born to a married woman is presumed to be the child of her husband.[6] I should add that the judgment itself was contested, as was the place of tradition. Something of an altercation ensued between the ruling and dissenting judges over the value of what were at one point called 'historical traditions'. The ruling judge claimed that on his side he not only had general 'societal tradition' regarding the rights of the natural father but 'a more specific tradition' in legal precedent where cases had rested upon 'the historic respect – indeed, sanctity would not be too strong a term – traditionally accorded to the relationships that develop within the unitary family'. The dissenting judge objected that what the 'deeply rooted traditions of the country are is arguable' and that 'reasonable people can disagree about the content of particular tra-ditions'.

With the reference to biological maternity, I have introduced the term 'tradition'. Of course we might want to reserve the concept of tradition for what is taken for granted and is thus not open to discursive controversy. Clearly this does not apply to the term itself. There are things being taken for granted here, but when they are named as 'tradition' they cease to have that taken-for-granted status. What is of interest then is precisely the rhetorical place that tradition occupies in disputes such as these. Operating as a kind of value in itself, it joins an array of other values, notably in these examples, 'choice'. Thus may it contribute to the sense that quite contradictory foundations are being claimed for people's relationships to one another.

I do not propose to resolve these contradictions, nor to draw out of them some single thread of commonality. There are values here that I would want to call 'cultural' in the anthropological sense, but they are not simply reducible to what these different positions might have in common. Rather the phenomenon I wish to describe is exactly the way in which a diversity of possibilities is sustained. There is one very simple cultural gambit by which people reconcile diversity with the fact that what they value are their values. The idioms say it all.

The people who are uttering remarks of the kind just quoted imagine their society is *going somewhere*. That is, anything may be taken as a sign of a social trend. Whether one is defending tradition or promoting new freedoms, whether one sees more choice about one or less of it, the world is thought to be always on the move. As a consequence, other people's prejudices, opinions, assumptions can be seen as a movement towards or away from what one values oneself.

The effect of this cultural assumption is twofold. First, however disparate people's ideas or actions, they can always be understood as showing a trend towards something. The values any individual person holds in turn afford a measure of divergence or convergence. Second, the idea of trend itself subsumes a kind of journeying unity. Whatever diverse bits and pieces it is made up of, society as such is inevitably and for better or for worse going forward. Thus what a social scientist may discern as a social trend may also involve the valuing of society itself. In commenting on the social costs of genetic welfare, one writer in the field of policy studies and disability suggests that a vision of 'genetic intervention *is coming to displace* a social vision of the world' (Miringoff, 1991: 147, my emphasis).

Values traditional and modern

But what is this society and who are these people with their values? The examples I have plucked out of a burgeoning field of literature on the implications of what are known as the new reproductive and new genetic technologies; the field serves as an exemplar of a wider cultural universe. This universe is a universe of discourse I call Euro-American. The awkwardness of the hybrid term conveys its application as both wider and narrower than anything one might wish to attribute to the citizens of Northern Europe and North America. It belongs in any case in the first instance to their works rather than to their persons.

Their works often convey a reflexive anxiety to say something true about the world, through a mode at once factual, literate and literary, taking everything and taking nothing for real, and at seeming liberty to cull evidence from qualitatively different data. They are produced by the people who belong to the class which frames legislation; they define the words that go into the dictionaries, see themselves as defending public and personal liberties and contest at every turn the assumptions built into all their practices. Social engineering Zygmunt Bauman (1991) calls their unfinished business. In so far as they are known by their works, Euro-Americans have existed ever since the first of them voiced the desire to make the kind of society they desired, with the important proviso that such a society would not be a reflection of desire but would reflect the needs of the human beings for which it existed. Now where else are the signs of what those needs might be but in trends backwards or forwards?

It is hardly original to say that if Euro-Americans thereby invented modernity, they reinvented tradition as pre-modern. Modernism consists in, among other things, the difference between the modern and the traditional, hence the ironic concept of traditional society. No society to which moderns might apply the epithet 'traditional' could of course know itself that way. That is not just because its members do not articulate what is traditional as opposed to what else is true of themselves; it is also that they are highly unlikely to have made 'society' their project. Making society into a project – not the *polis*, or a kingdom or the state, but society – is where Euro-Americanism began. Now in so far as this enterprise was thought to bring a new threshold of awareness, along with the product came a new form of endeavour or ability: modernism. Traditional becomes the epithet applied to those in a state of existence before such awareness. To paraphrase Anthony Giddens (1991), the traditional is characteristically pre-modern, presenting along with all its institutions a society not open to self-awareness, its certainties unchallenged. What a likeable, even nostalgic, encompassment of other orders of being!

Now the most successful pursuits of modernity have been found in those modernist regimes (I refer to cultural regimes) that have negotiated tradition as a source of special values. Such values may be protected as the kind of raw material on which moderns build – like the traditional family that is also the basis upon which the individual citizen goes out into the enterprising world. The citizen must of course do his or her bit to ensure that those traditional values are also there as a future resource for others. In fact, as we have known from the Thatcher years, back to tradition may be the best way forward. One interesting consequence follows.

This friendly encompassment of tradition implies that any Euro-American can look around present circumstances and detect what is 'traditional' and what is not. Since the traditional is substantively equated with what has a history – hence the doubly loaded 'historical traditions' to which the disputing judges appealed – there may appear to have been more of it in the past. Yet there seems very widespread agreement that certain cultural forms (such as kinship and family life) are continuous with the past whereas others break with it (hence the 'new' in the new technologies).

Were one to take these substantives literally, one could be forgiven for imagining that the cumulative effect of time, the direction society is heading in, would end in a situation where there was no more tradition left and one lived in a thoroughly post-traditional society. Euro-Americans would not of course take them literally: they know that 'traditions' (in the plural) are invented as fast as they disappear. But in addition they also know that without being embedded in traditional values of some kind the best efforts of modernity will not lead to greater human happiness. In the same way as it is necessary for contracts to be embedded in non-contractual relations in order to work,[7] so in that view must the value put on innovation and change remain responsive to the human needs which older values enshrined. The point is nicely expressed in remarks made to Jeanette Edwards (1993) in Alltown – gametes, that is, eggs and sperm made newly thinkable as objects of reproductive medicine, should have names, that is, have their identity acknowledged as an identity embedded in other persons.

Society on the move, then, showing this or that trend, registers itself to Euro-Americans in terms of (among other things), a tension between what can be taken for traditional and what can be taken for modern. To be at both poles at once would seem impossible. But that is also one way of imagining what may otherwise be thought of as a contradiction.

Just such a contradiction is pointed up by Janet Dolgin (1990a, 1990b), a feminist commentator trained in the States in both law and anthropology, during her scrutiny of arguments surrounding women's claims to motherhood, particularly as they have been contested in the US courts. She points out that no headway can be made in untangling the basis of current law unless one does indeed recognize certain fundamental contradictions and tensions lying within it. 'The most fundamental', she says, is between one 'based on set roles and biological certainties and one based on negotiation and choice' (1990a: 104). And that in turn is inexplicable unless one realizes the historical trends that have been going on within the law. She appeals to an English jurist for illumination. 'Current understandings of the family . . . can be contextualized histori-cally and sociologically in light of a fundamental shift, described by Sir Henry Maine more than a hundred years ago, from a universe based on relations of *status* to a universe based on relations of *contract*' (1990a: 105, original emphasis). The difference between these universes may appear radical.

The case of the American boy who wished to divest his mother of her parental rights could be framed in terms of just such a difference. One could say that the mother's claims were vested in a position she held by status, while he was claiming that an implicit contract, as implied in the desire of parents to nurture and bring up their child, had been broken by her negligence, and he wished to embark on an explicit contractual arrangement of his own making. The argument Dolgin takes from Maine, however, is that the difference indicates two poles of a societal move-ment. Indeed the starting point of Maine's own interest was the direction in which he observed opinion and society moving: 'There are few general propositions concerning the age to which we belong [the date is 1861] which seem at first sight likely to be received with readier concurrence than the assertion that the society of our day is mainly distinguished from that of preceding generations by the largeness of the sphere which is occupied in it by Contract' (1870: 304).[8]

Dolgin adds a twentieth-century gloss. The movement from status to contract is also a movement from inherent value to market value. This is where society is going today: 'In substituting contract for status, society substitutes freedom for security and choice for familiarity' (1990a: 106).[9] As a consequence present-day law, in the process of this transformation, is shot through with ambivalence. It reflects no single-minded approach to reality, she observes, but simultaneously incorporates status-based and contract-based assumptions. Thus Dolgin shows how the conflicting arguments about surrogacy that arose in the notorious American case of Baby M validated both status and contract. The New Jersey Superior Court 'upheld the surrogacy contract, framed the case as involving primarily the best interests of the baby . . . decided that those interests required terminating the surrogate's parental rights, granted full custody to the contracting father, and ordered the adoption of the baby [by the commissioning mother]'; while the New Jersey Supreme Court 'invalidated the surrogacy contract, outlawed the payment of money to the surrogate, and voided both the termination of [the surrogate's] parental rights and the adoption of the baby' (Dolgin, 1990b: 535–6).

Dolgin offers a superb and detailed analysis. Yet perhaps we do not need Maine's historical view. Perhaps it is not necessary to say that there has been a movement 'from' status 'to' contract. In fact one could as well say that the difference between contract and status suggested by Maine was an invention of a world view already based on contract, that is, a world view based on certain definitions of human responsibility, including the one basic to the will to engineer society. It thus includes the notorious social contract as conceived by the Enlightenment, though Maine himself takes the phrase as an inexcusable liberty with the facts. (He also found it necessary to criticize earlier ideas of the 'social compact' which bound subjects to the traditional authority of the king.)

In sum, 'status' refers to pre-existing conditions, values inherent in previous positions and relationships, and thus to the kind of (natural) world with which human enterprise must deal, precisely to the extent that 'contract' stands for what persons agree upon, these days often understood as also implying by choice. Both carry obligation, but a different weight is put on the origin of the obligation. Deciding on which phenomena can be allocated to one or to the other category, then, would not be so dissimilar to differentiating the traditional from the modern.

In drawing this parallel, I do not want to suggest that status and contract can be read off *as* traditional and modern. On the contrary, appeals to tradition and modernity constitute a rhetorical range of their own.

Tradition may support quite diverse positions, but is recognizable in its appeal to past practice. Thus the two judgments Dolgin quoted from the Baby M case – and, as she observes, 'judicial positions more thoroughly at odds cannot be imagined' – could argue from the same traditionalist stance. Both upheld 'that whatever the legitimate demands of the marketplace, they should retire before the sacred prerogatives of institutions and impulses hallowed by fixed, eternal nature' (Dolgin, 1990b: 536). The opinion of the Superior Court judge was that the family offered by the commissioning couple and the maternity offered by the commissioning mother were everything the historic ideal required; the surrogate mother, on the other hand, was in breach of contract (itself evidence of her unreliability) and was required to honour her prior agreement. The Supreme Court by contrast declared that contract could not invalidate motherhood, and that the child's parents were her biological parents; on various technical grounds the contract was also declared invalid for contravening New Jersey law. In effect the courts simultaneously upheld the idea of contract as an agreement governed by fair dealing, while deciding on suitability for parenting in diverse but thoroughly status terms. Dolgin suggests that 'traditional' ideas about family life were at the root of both sets of judicial opinion.

Appeals to modernity on the other hand, while also being in the interests of maintaining good practice, are likely to be expressed as appeals to realism or enlightenment. In the case of the 98.07 per cent father, one of the dissenting judges said that the atmosphere surrounding the decision (to reject the biological father's claim) was one of make-believe. 'When and if the Court awakes to reality,' he said, 'it will find a world very different from the one it expects.' As he earlier observed: 'In this day and age . . . proving paternity by asking intimate questions . . . would be decidedly anachronistic. Who on earth would choose this method . . . when blood tests prove it with far more certainty and far less fuss.'[10] However while 'tradition' as such can be evoked fairly safely, 'modernity' has a much more ambivalent ring; it cannot be appealed to with such certain authority. Thus, despite his comments on dis-agreements over interpretation, the dissenting judge in fact goes out of his way to say that his own arguments had not overlooked 'tradition' either in considering previous judgments or in upholding interests and practices central to the defence of liberty. His protagonist, on the other hand, more hesitantly asserts that 'even in modern times paternity claims by the natural father have not been generally acknowledged'.

Indeed, status and contract, tradition and modernity, are not terms of comparable cultural standing in these contexts. Litigants may refer to the importance of validating or annulling 'contracts', but in the material presented here it is the commentator who sees these arguments ranged side by side with those that appeal to status. 'Status' is unlikely to be bandied about in quite the same way. Similarly, one could probably find innumerable verbal references to 'tradition' and the values it represents, but I wonder if people would actually promote claims on the grounds of modernity, or at least do so without equivocation. What commentators might consider as modern will often simply be phrased in terms of what people feel is contemporary or new in their lives, or else is evidence of a 'realistic' approach to the world. Some of the couples in south-east England, to whom Eric Hirsch (1993: 91) talked about aspects of the new reproductive technologies, saw everything on the move in this sphere. In reflecting on how one might decide what is best, one woman observed, 'It's difficult to say . . . Because what would be sound now, in ten years' time, the improvements in science and the improvements in technology, who's to say the barriers won't move.' A man spoke in similar vein: 'A lot of it really is to say, through these questions, are people's morals or understanding keeping up with the changes in medicine and . . . do people feel all these changes are for the good and are we ready for them? Medicine is racing well ahead.' These people are not quoted as referring to modernity, but were they to do so one suspects it would be tinged with just such hesitations that qualify enthusiasm for it. It is somehow not quite as sound a concept as tradition on which to base positive claims.

'Tradition' and 'contract' belong to an everyday as well as an analytical vocabulary, then, while their complements, 'status' and 'modernity', are either esoteric or ambivalent. The domains of values to which the two sets refer are in any case found in overlapping and cross-cutting combinations. But there is an interesting parallel between them.

In one sense, the terms are coeval. We have seen that arguments based on contract lie side by side with those based on status. Yet the pairing as such semantically encompasses the idea of a trend, away from one domain and towards the other, so that they also seem to contain within them a movement (*from* status and *to* contract). And here it would seem we cannot be at both ends of the continuum at the same time. I want to suggest that is exactly where we might be. The suggestion arises from an otherwise perplexing sensation. This is the sense that there seems both *more* 'status' and *more* 'contract' around in the world, or at least in arguments about them. Would it also follow then that one might have both *more* tradition and *more* modernity at the same time?

Choosing certainty

In commenting on information and communication technology, Hirsch (1992: 212) notes a paradoxical picture; from the perspective of this technology it would seem that 'the most radical changes are occurring in modern culture. But, from a second, complementary perspective, that of family relations and their associated consumption practices, a picture of continuity with the past is in evidence.' He is reminded, and reminds his reader, of Raymond Williams's aphorism about the willed coexistence of very new technology and very old social forms being a characteristic of 'our society'. It is evident, however, that this distinction between the old and new applies as well to the way people think about aspects of these domains internal to themselves ('technology', 'kinship') as it does to the relationship between them. Thus the family relations to which Hirsch refers are internally subject to the same tension that is also held to exist between them and other areas of social life. Kinship is not some pre-modern form of social life left over from the past, any more than tradition antedates modernity. It (kinship) is traditional and modern at the same time. So when people draw on kinship as a source of identity, they evoke both old and new forms of relating, as well as the tension between them. Similarly, technology comes with an ancient promise: that of innovation. Many of the claims made for what new technology can do (the example here is cyberspace) were made for electricity a hundred years ago (Marvin, cited in Gray and Driscoll, 1992: 41). The sense of being at both poles of a continuum at the same moment is not resolved through allocating some institutions to one end ('kinship') and some ('technology') to the other.

I suspect the same is true for the relationship between what is taken for granted and what is seen as open to choice (status and contract). As ways in which Euro-Americans imagine the world in which they live, these are not to be distributed between historical epochs or social institutions either. So trying to sort out the relative weight to be given to the pursuit of individual choice on the one hand or to the claiming of pre-existing obligation and liability on the other, or to be given to the way natural facts are called on now to support values associated with innovation, now to uphold values regarded as long cherished, will not work. Such an adjudication would fail to register a most significant cultural feature of present life: *there is more of everything.*[11]

This is said somewhat tongue in cheek. Or rather I am deliberately participating in Euro-American slang – the short-cut way in which quantitative idioms are used for qualitative differences. One aspect of this convention is the close association between the notion of increase (in population, human capability, time) and the notion of movement forward in history,[12] just as the people who spoke to Hirsch (see above) indicated. Temporal increase (as each day passes, more has happened in the world) can be represented as a movement from one condition to another ('more' individualism, as Maine asserted, leads to the shift from status to contract). But equally well, of course, we observe that traditions supposedly left behind are also being brought forward at the same time, so the sense I want to convey is a kind of exaggeration that seems to take everything in its stride: not just that there is more essentialist thinking around (for instance, the essentialism crucial to the novel idea of 'genetic welfare' [Miringoff, 1991]), but that at the same time there is more relational thinking around (families we choose [Weston, 1991]). There is both 'more' nature and 'more' culture in people's discourses. I would even say that what lay people regard as science seemingly produces both more certainties and more uncertainties. And because that exaggeration encompasses everything it also encompasses reflexivity itself: how persons are 'constructed' has become a project not simply of social science reflection but of commercial management strategies desirous of investing in uncertain futures.[13] One might be driven to think that 'Societies running in the fast-forward mode cannot any longer be studied' (Chakrabarty, 1992: 49).[14]

What contributes to this? Why does this Euro-American have the sense that wherever society is going it is faster than it used to be? Is this simply its own exaggeration – that is, if everything is exaggerated then a sense of movement is too? From whence the exaggeration, then? There can be no single source to point to, but there is an enabling factor. This is the cultural place that is given to enablement itself. Euro-Americans imagine that they can do 'more' things than they once did, crystallized in the hypostatization of technology as 'enabling'. Technology has always had this capacity, so to speak, and in this its characteristic remains thoroughly and traditionally embedded in earlier expectations. At the same time technology contributes to the way in which late twentieth-century Euro-Americans perceive an overall enhancement of human ability. Reproductive and genetic technologies provide ample illustration.

It has not taken commentators long to point out that the same reproductive technologies – such as IVF and embryo transfer – that enable families to achieve their traditional goals by having children of their own also lay the grounds for innovation and unconventional arrangements. The virgin birth furore over artificial insemination was an example of this.[15] Those who became worried about the way women were seeking pregnancy suddenly saw how the means to overcome physical impairment could be used for quite unanticipated social ends. Procedures that may enable persons to fulfil their desires do not determine the kinds of choices into which such desires may be channelled.

Choice is a significant value to which Euro-Americans give weight in setting up families, and IVF and associated procedures widen the choice that is available to potential parents, regardless of their fertility, as does gamete donation in surrogacy arrangements. Couples may thus be enabled to preserve aspects of a biological connection to a child even where they cannot provide the whole. We may call these ties based on status. Choice is also an arbiter in what is closer to a kind of implicit contract: the unfolding of social ties as they develop within a family. It is overtly manifest in how people 'choose' to keep up with their kin, whom they regard as their intimates, how far away from their family they try to escape. A (British) colleague claims that her family was in any case never a family by blood and cannot understand why such fuss is made of genetic relationships. Her family, she says, is a family founded on choice. She also adds that in turn people often do not understand the strength of her feeling of obligation – in their view her family are only friends, not family! She might have been reassured then by an editorial in the *New York Times* that asserted, 'Friendship, not kinship, is the tie that binds.'[16] The writer claims an adopted array of cousins, uncles and aunts who are her elective family: 'What binds us is friendship.' Now there are no particular technologies involved here, any more than in the case of the children who 'divorced' their parents. I would suggest, however, that developments in reproductive technology have made newly explicit the possibility of choosing whom and what one desires to call family. In opening up ways of thinking, they offer a cultural enablement of a kind.

The climate of enablement that depicts a world where choices may be put into effect may lead to 'more' traditionalization of family life (more status: preserving some element of a biological tie in ways that were never possible before) or else to more de-traditionalization (more contract: creating a general climate in which desire is seen. to be legitimate and determining). This particular de-traditionalizing is also re-traditionalizing in another guise. As Janet Finch (1989) has observed, there always

was a strong elective component to the enactment of family relationships, and those families that base themselves on choice (symbolized by
'friendship') claim traditional virtues in attending to the quality of
interpersonal relations. It was the failure of the parents in question to
honour the relational side of the bargain, so to speak, that led to the
child-divorces I referred to at the beginning. If I suggest that new
technologies have created a context in which such non-technological
negotiations make cultural sense, I would also suggest that the enablement is most evident when the principal role of 'technology' is seen
to be that of facilitator.

It does not always appear so. Technological procedures may bring
painful choices for practitioners in the field of reproductive medicine, as
Frances Price (1993) has observed. Writing about genetic technologies
for a popular audience, the Nuffield Professor of Clinical Medicine at
Oxford put this dilemma:

> New problems are arising as a result of the application of DNA technology to
> genetic screening. For example, pre-natal diagnosis of genetic disease often
> requires that we are *absolutely certain* about the biological parentage of the
> fetus. Indeed, it may be necessary to run paternity tests on fetal material to
> ensure that a particular diagnosis is correct. *What are we to do* if we demon-
> strate non-paternity? Who should be told and what is the doctor's decision
> when he or she knows that information of this type may have a disastrous
> effect on a family? As our diagnostic technology becomes more sophisticated
> there will be many other examples of sensitive information acquired by
> chance. (Weatherall, 1991: 29, my emphasis)

In short, being absolutely certain about paternity brings with it
uncertainty about how best to handle the information. Yet even here
there is one sense in which the role of technology remains that of
facilitator. The technology that is enabling of genetic certainty is not
disabling of that; it simply brings to light a pre-existing state, the
information already contained by 'the genes'.[17] Disability and uncertainty come afterwards, in how to use the information. The case is a
classic one – not too much technology, but too much knowledge.

Knowledge that comes from such testing gives a modern way (genetic
identification) of being certain about a traditional category of parentage
(biological fatherhood); but it is also a traditional way (establishing
biological connection) of defining a thoroughly modern kind of parentage (scientifically certain fatherhood). The need to know the genetic
connection originally arose in the context of social arrangements that
turned on what were regarded as the foundations for family life; the
need to know the father arises now in the context, among others, of
medical concern to provide persons with as good as possible genetic
foundation to their lives. There are several displacements going on here,
but taken together the end result seems simultaneously more certainty
and more uncertainty.[18]

Perhaps it was always a condition of modernist Euro-American knowledge practices that uncertainties increase as fast as certainties are established: each horizon exposes more terrain, one of the sources of the sense of movement to which I referred earlier. Knowledge applied to social matter precipitates inevitable questions about how to choose this or that course of action on the basis of the information being conveyed, thereby recreating the division into what we can choose and what we have to take for granted. Yet the incremental effect seems given. And if it is a given, does it lie then in something we, as Euro-Americans, do take for granted – not in what we *think* we assume but in what we do assume?

We think we take 'tradition' for granted because that is its substantive status. In fact, as naming it makes plain, tradition emerges as a highly labile, sometimes contested and certainly explicit, category. That does not mean the Euro-Americans take nothing for granted. It might mean that what Euro-Americans most obviously take for granted is elsewhere altogether. I suspect that above all they take for granted, quite simply, that *given the technology* they can do anything. If technology is society made durable,[19] it is at the same time ability made effective. The enabling effect of 'technology' is a guarantee of that. Choice comes afterwards. Sever ourselves from our disabilities, and then we shall see how we want to live, and how we want to create the certain identity we feel, like children severing themselves from unsatisfactory parents.

The analogy is not too far fetched. In reporting on the kinds of expectation to which the Human Genome Project has given rise in the public at large, Nancy Wexler talks of the effort still required when tests use linked DNA markers. 'A major problem in presymptomatic and prenatal testing using linked DNA markers is that the whole family must be involved' (1992: 227). By contrast, she then goes on to say, when 'we have the gene in hand and can detect directly the specific mutation in the gene, we will only need to look at an individual's DNA'. In the meanwhile practitioners are faced with the cumbersome method of investigating entire families – in her words a 'tedious way of doing diagnostic testing, but until the gene itself can be found it is the only way' (ibid.).[20] The family that provides information is thus also a disability in the trouble it affords, including the new troubles that will come with relaying information back to it, as we have seen.[21] But technology will in the end enable us to sever ourselves from our disabilities!

If I conclude on a sceptical note, it is not because there are no benefits and advantages to be weighed up here. Rather it is to observe how much value Euro-Americans place on their ability to do things, including doing things to their sense of identity. But then again, they enhance their abilities only to enhance their critiques of them at the same time. There will always be more of both. Thus their odd idioms and curious habits of thought will lead them to ask where valuing this particular value – enablement – will lead them.

50   *Questions of Cultural Identity*

Acknowledgements

I am grateful to the members of the Faculty of Social Sciences at the Open University whose questions on another paper stimulated the formulation of this one. An earlier version of the present text was first given to the Centre for the Study of Cultural Values at the University of Lancaster, who have published it as a lecture (Occasional Papers Series, 1994).

Notes

1 Press headlines ran 'Girl, 11, first in England to "divorce" parents' (*Independent*, 12 November 1992); 'Boy "divorces" mother without her knowledge' (*Independent*, 31 December 1992). These were not isolated cases; the 'first' refers to the first successful actions to have been reported.

2 25 September 1992. An editorial comment a few days later (29 September) is headed 'Gregory needed the divorce'. He is thought to have been the first minor granted 'the right to sue to sever the parental rights of his natural parents'. A further British case of a girl seeking a residence order to live with foster parents was also going through the courts in late 1992, but no question about adoption was raised.

3 His book published in 1985, *Sociology and the Law*, is discussed by Dreyfuss and Nelkin (1992).

4 *Independent* (12 August 1992); the genetic information outlived the carrier of it. The cremation of the father in question was held up in order for his son to obtain the material that would establish his claims.

5 And hence who is the surrogate. See the discussion in Morgan (1989).

6 Details also sent to me by David Schneider. The case is reported in the *Supreme Court Reporter* (US) cited as 109 S Ct 2333 (1989). The remarks are quoted at pp. 2342, 2349.

7 Marcel Mauss's 1925 remarks on the matter expounded in *The Gift* are rediscovered in feminist critiques of 'classical liberal theory' (see Nelson and Nelson, 1989).

8 Fitzpatrick (1992) comments that this was a book written backwards; that is, from contract to status.

9 'Familiarity' in a double sense. Cf. Maine's (1870: 168) observation apropos what he calls the movement of progressive societies: 'Through all its course it has been distinguished by the gradual dissolution of family dependency and the growth of individual obligation in its place. The Individual is steadily substituted for the Family, as the unit of which civil laws take account.' Relations of persons formerly summed up in relations of family, he adds, now arise from 'the free agreement of Individuals' (1870: 169). It is interesting to compare Ruth Chadwick's (1994) account of the coexisting (and disputed) values of individualism and communitarianism in family law.

10 *Supreme Court Reporter* (US) *op. cit.*: both citations at 1989: 2359. The reference to modern times is at 1989: 2343.

11 Or, the same point, less of everything (more of the same): 'There seems to be a direct relation between the exuberant and expanding freedom of the "competent consumer" and the remorseless shrinking of the world inhabited by the disqualified one' (Bauman, 1991: 9).

12 Strathern (1992: Chapter 2).

13 I am grateful for permission to refer to Emily Martin's 'Biopolitics: the anthropology of the new genetics and immunology'. Paper given to AAA meeting, New Orleans, 1990.

14 A similar remark is echoed in Strathern (1992), where the speeding up is likened to the greenhouse effect. Teresa Brennan roots such speed in capitalist relations. All natural resources, she argues, are variable capital and there is no check on the speed with which variable capital can be used up: technology assists (and is the means by which the production of profit is speeded up (1993: 123).

15 Made explicit by a symposium on the so-called 'Virgin birth syndrome', London Hospital Medical College, organized in 1991 by fertility practitioners concerned about requests to provide treatment for women not because the traditional method of sexual intercourse had failed but because they wanted to bypass such methods altogether.

16 10 November 1992; 'An acquired family' is the heading. (A further commentary on the Florida boy refers to him as getting 'a new family' in court.)

17 I am grateful to Sarah Franklin for this observation, and for several conversations on genetic technology.

18 Pnina Werbner ('Allegories of sacred imperfection: time travel, global travel and the aesthetics of misinterpretation in *The Satanic Verses*', Manchester, mss) epitomizes this in terms of the certainties of modernity and uncertainties of modernism.

19 From the title of Bruno Latour's chapter in *A Sociology of Monsters* (1991).

20 Wexler, Professor of Clinical Psychology, Neurology and Psychiatry at Columbia, is a pioneer in the population analyses that led among other things to the localization of the gene for Huntington's disease. The issue is that particular patterns of markers prognosticate the disease in particular families.

21 And as Wexler herself forcefully comments upon; she argues at length that we are going to need to figure out how to offer genetic information to people at large in advance of 'the deluge of new tests' the human genome programme will bring (1992: 227).

References

Bauman, Zygmunt (1991) *Postmodernity: Chance or Menace*, Lancaster: Centre for the Study of Cultural Values.

Brennan, Theresa (1993) *History after Lacan*, London: Routledge.

Chadwick, Ruth (1994) 'Moral reasoning in family law: a response to Katherine O'Donovan', in D. Morgan and G. Douglas (eds), *Constituting Families: a Study in Governance*, Stuttgart: Steiner.

Chakrabarty, Dipesh (1992) 'The death of history? Historical consciousness and the culture of late capitalism', *Public Culture*, 4: 47–65.

Dolgin, Janet (1990a) 'Status and contract in feminist legal theory of the family: a reply to Bartlett', *Women's Rights Law Reporter*, 12: 103–13.

Dolgin, Janet (1990b) 'Status and contract in surrogate motherhood: an illumination of the surrogacy debate', *Buffalo Law Review*, 38: 515–50.

Dreyfuss, Rochelle Cooper and Nelkin, Dorothy (1992) 'The jurisprudence of genetics', *Vanderbilt Law Review*, 45: 313–48.

Edwards, Jeanette (1993) 'Explicit connections: ethnographic enquiry in north-west England', in Jeanette Edwards, Eric Hirsch, Sarah Franklin, Frances Price and Marilyn Strathern (eds), *Technologies of Procreation: Kinship in the Age of Assisted Conception*, Manchester: Manchester University Press.

Finch, Janet (1989) *Family Obligations and Social Change*, Cambridge: Polity Press.

Fitzpatrick, Peter (1992) *The Mythology of Modern Law*, London: Routledge.

Giddens, Anthony (1991) *Modernity and Self-identity: Self and Society in the Late Modern Age*, Cambridge: Polity Press.

Gray, Chris Hables and Driscoll, Mark (1992) 'What's real about virtual reality? Anthropology of, and in, cyberspace', *Visual Anthropology Review*, 8: 39–49.

Hirsch, Eric (1992) 'The long term and the short term of domestic consumption: an ethnographic case study', in R. Silverstone and E. Hirsch (eds), *Consuming Technologies: Media and Information in Domestic Spaces*, London: Routledge.

Hirsch, Eric (1993) 'Negotiated limits: interviews in south-east England', in Jeanette Edwards, Eric Hirsch, Sarah Franklin, Frances Price and Marilyn Strathern (eds), *Technologies of Procreation: Kinship in the Age of Assisted Conception*, Manchester: Manchester University Press.

Latour, Bruno (1991) 'Technology is society made durable', in John Law (ed.), *A Sociology of Monsters: Essays on Power, Technology and Domination*, London: Routledge.

Maine, Henry Summer (1870) *Ancient Law: Its Connection with the Early History of Society, and Communications in the Late Nineteenth Century* (1861), Oxford: Oxford University Press.

Miringoff, Marque-Luisa (1991) *The Social Costs of Genetic Welfare*, New Brunswick, NJ: Rutgers University Press.

Morgan, Derek (1989) 'Surrogacy: an introductory essay', in Robert Lee and Derek Morgan (eds), *Birthrights: Law and Ethics at the Beginnings of Life*, London: Routledge.

Nelson, Hilde and Nelson, James (1989) 'Cutting motherhood in two: some suspicions concerning surrogacy', *Hypatia*, 4: 85–94.

Price, Frances (1993) 'Beyond expectation: clinical practice and clinical concern', in Jeanette Edwards, Eric Hirsch, Sarah Franklin, Frances Price and Marilyn Strathern (eds), *Technologies of Procreation: Kinship in the Age of Assisted Conception*, Manchester: Manchester University Press.

Strathern, Marilyn (1992) *After Nature: English Kinship in the Late Twentieth Century*, Cambridge: Cambridge University Press.

Weatherall, David (1991) 'Manipulating human nature', *Science and Public Affairs* (occasional publication of Royal Society and BAAS): 24–31.

Weston, Kath (1991) *Families We Choose: Lesbians, Gays, Kinship*, New York: Columbia University Press.

Wexler, Nancy (1992) 'Clairvoyance and caution: repercussions from the human genome project', in David J. Kevles and Leroy Hood (eds), *The Code of Codes: Scientific and Social Issues in the Human Genome Project*, Cambridge, MA: Harvard University Press.

4

Culture's In-Between

Homi K. Bhabha

A recent change in the writing of cultural criticisms has left the prose plainer, less adorned with the props of the argument's staging. Where once 'scare quotes' festooned the text with the frequency of garlands at an Indian wedding, there is now a certain sobriety to semiotic and post-structuralist celebrations. The 'isms' and 'alities' – those tails that wagged the dogma of critical belief – no longer wave new paradigms or problematics into being. The death of the author, or the interment of intention, are occurrences that arouse no more scandal than the sight of a hearse in a Palermo suburb. Critical practices that sought to detotalize social reality by demonstrating the micrologies of power, the diverse enunciative sites of discourse, the slippage and sliding of signifiers, are suddenly disarmed.

Having relaxed our guard, hoping perhaps that the intellectual modes we sought to foster had passed into the common discourse of criticism, we are now caught with our pants down. Deprived of our stagecraft, we are asked to face the full frontal reality of the idea of 'Culture' itself – the very concept whose mastery we thought we had dissolved in the language of signifying practices and social formations. This is not our chosen agenda, the terms of debate have been set for us, but in the midst of the culture wars and the canon manoeuvres we can hardly hide behind the aprons of aporia and protest histrionically that there is nothing outside the text. Wherever I look these days I find myself staring into the eyes of a recruiting officer – sometimes he looks like Dinesh D'Souza, sometimes like Robert Hughes – who stares at me intensely and says 'Western Civ. needs you!' At the same time, a limp little voice within me also whispers, 'Critical theory needs you too!'

What is at issue today is not the essentialized or idealized Arnoldian notion of 'culture' as an architectonic assemblage of the Hebraic and the Hellenic. In the midst of the multicultural wars we are surprisingly closer to an insight from T. S. Eliot's *Notes towards the Definition of Culture*, where Eliot demonstrates a certain incommensurability, a necessary impossibility, in *thinking* culture. Faced with the fatal notion of a self-contained European culture and the absurd notion of an uncontaminated culture in a single country, he writes, 'We are therefore pressed to maintain the ideal of a world culture, while admitting it is something we cannot *imagine*. We can only conceive it as the logical term of the relations between cultures.'[1] The fatality of thinking of 'local' cultures as uncontaminated or self-contained forces us to conceive of 'global' cultures, which itself remains unimaginable. What kind of logic is this?

It seems to me significant that Eliot, at this undecidable point in his argument, turns to the problematic of colonial migration. Although writing in the main about settler colonial societies, Eliot's words have an ironic resonance with the contemporary condition of third world migration:

> The migrations of modern times . . . have transplanted themselves according to some social, religious, economic or political determination, or some peculiar mixture of these. There has therefore been something in the removements analogous in nature to religious schism. The people have taken with them only a part of the total culture. . . . The culture which develops on the new soil must therefore be bafflingly alike and different from the parent culture: it will be complicated sometimes by whatever relations are established with some native race and further by immigration from other than the original source. In this way, peculiar types of culture-sympathy and culture-clash appear.[2]

This 'part' culture, this *partial* culture, is the contaminated yet connective tissue between cultures – at once the impossibility of culture's containedness and the boundary between. It is indeed something like culture's 'in-between', bafflingly both alike and different. To en*list* in the defence of this 'unhomely', migratory, partial nature of culture we must revive that archaic meaning of 'list' as 'limit' or 'boundary'. Having done so, we introduce into the polarizations of liberals and liberationists the sense that the translation of cultures, whether assimilative or agonistic, is a complex act that generates borderline affects and identifications, 'peculiar types of culture-sympathy and culture-clash'. The peculiarity of cultures' partial, even metonymic presence lies in articulating those social divisions and unequal developments that disturb the self-recognition of the national culture, its anointed horizons of territory and tradition. The discourse of minorities, spoken for and against in the multicultural wars, proposes a social subject constituted through cultural hybridization, the overdetermination of communal or group differences, the articulation of baffling alikeness and banal divergence.

These borderline negotiations of cultural difference often violate liberalism's deep commitment to representing cultural diversity as plural choice. Liberal discourses on multiculturalism experience the fragility of their principles of 'tolerance' when they attempt to withstand the pressure of revision. In addressing the multicultural demand, they encounter the limit of their enshrined notion of 'equal respect'; and they anxiously acknowledge the attenuation in the authority of the Ideal Observer, an authority that oversees the ethical rights (and insights) of the liberal perspective from the top deck of the Clapham omnibus. In contemplating late-liberal culture's engagements with the migratory, partial culture of minorities, we need to shift our sense of the terrain on which we can best understand the disputes. Here our theoretical understanding – in its most general sense – of 'culture-as-difference' will enable us to grasp the articulation of culture's borderline, unhomely space and time.

Where might this understanding be found?

Despite his susceptibility to consensus, for which he is so widely criticized, Jürgen Habermas's work suggests something of the stressed terrain of culture in the face of social differentiation. Once we give up the universalizing sense of 'the self-referential subject-writ-large, encompassing all individual subjects', Habermas suggests, the risky search for consensus results in the kind of differentiation of the life-world of which loss of meaning, anomie and psychopathologies are the most obvious symptoms.[3] As a result, 'the causes of social pathologies that once clustered around the class subject now break into widely scattered historical contingencies'.[4] The effect of this scattering – migratory difference once more – produces the conditions for an 'ever more finely woven net of linguistically generated intersubjectivity. Rationalization of the life world means differentiation and condensation at once – a thickening of the floating web of intersubjective threads that simultaneously holds together the ever more sharply differentiated components of culture, society and person.'[5]

Multiculturalism – a portmanteau term for anything from minority discourse to postcolonial critique, from gay and lesbian studies to chicano/a fiction – has become the most charged sign for describing the scattered social contingencies that characterize contemporary *Kulturkritik*. The multicultural has itself become a 'floating signifier' whose enigma lies less in itself than in the discursive uses of it to mark social processes where differentiation and condensation seem to happen almost synchronically. To critique the terms in this widely contested, even contradictory terrain one needs to do more than demonstrate the logical inconsistencies of the liberal position when faced with racist belief. Prejudicial knowledge, racist or sexist, does not pertain to the ethical or logical 'reflectiveness' of the Cartesian subject. It is, as Bernard Williams has described it, 'a belief guarded against reflection'. It requires a 'study of irrationality in social practice . . . more detailed and substantive than the schematic considerations of philosophical theory'.[6] Multiculturalists committed to the instantiation of social and cultural differences within a democratic socius have to deal with a structure of the 'subject' constituted within the 'projective field' of political alienation.[7] As Etienne Balibar writes, the identificatory language of discrimination works in reverse: 'the racial/cultural identity of "true nationals" remains invisible but is inferred from . . . the quasi-hallucinatory visibility of the "false nationals" – Jews, "wops", immigrants, *indios*, *natives*, blacks'.[8]

Thus constructed, prejudicial knowledge is forever uncertain and in danger, for, as Balibar concludes, 'that the "false" are *too* visible will never guarantee that the "true" are visible enough'.[9] This is one reason why multiculturalists who strive to constitute non-discriminatory minority identities cannot simply do so by affirming the place they occupy, or by returning to an 'unmarked' authentic origin or pre-text: their recognition requires the negotiation of a dangerous indeterminacy, since the too-visible presence of the other underwrites the authentic national subject but can never guarantee its visibility or truth. The inscription of the minority subject *somewhere between the too visible and the not visible enough* returns us to Eliot's sense of cultural difference, and intercultural connection, as being beyond logical demonstration. And it requires that the discriminated subject, *even in the process of its reconstitution*, be located in a present moment that is temporarily disjunctive and effectively ambivalent. 'Too late. Everything is anticipated, thought out, demonstrated, made the most of. My trembling hands take hold of nothing: the vein has been mined out. Too late!' Franz Fanon, clearly, is speaking from this time lag[10] in the place of enunciation and identification, dramatizing the moment of racist recognition. The discriminated subject or community occupies a contemporary moment that is historically untimely, forever belated. 'You come too late, much too late. There will always be a world – a white world – between you and us. . . . In the face of this effective ankylosis . . . it is understandable that I could have made up my mind to utter my Negro cry. Little by little, putting out pseudopodia here and there, I secreted a race.'[11]

By contrast, the liberal dialectic of recognition is at first sight right on time. The subject of recognition stands in a synchronous space (as befits the Ideal Observer), surveying the level playing field that Charles Taylor defines as the quintessential liberal territory: 'the presumption of equal respect' for cultural diversity. History has taught us, however, to be distrustful of things that run on time, like trains. It is not that liberalism does not recognize racial or sexual discrimination – it has been in the forefront of those struggles. But there is a recurrent problem with its notion of equality: liberalism contains a non-differential concept of cultural time. At the point at which liberal discourse attempts to normalize cultural difference, to turn the presumption of equal cultural respect into the recognition of *equal cultural worth*, it does not recognize the disjunctive, 'borderline' temporalities of partial, minority cultures. The sharing of equality is genuinely intended, but only so long as we start from a historically congruent space; the recognition of difference is genuinely felt, but on terms that do not represent the historical genealogies, often postcolonial, that constitute the partial cultures of the minority. This is how Taylor puts it:

> The logic behind some of these [multicultural] demands seems to depend upon a premise that we owe equal respect to all cultures. . . . The implication seems to be that . . . true judgements of value of different works would place all cultures more or less on the same footing. Of course, the attack could come from a more radical, neo-Nietzschean standpoint which questions the very status of

judgements of worth. . . . As a presumption, the claim is that all human
cultures that have animated *whole* societies over some considerable stretch of
time have something important to say to all human beings. I have worded it in
this way to *exclude partial cultural milieux within a society as well as short phases of a
major culture.* [my emphasis][12]

Or again:

Merely on the human level, one could argue that it is reasonable to suppose that
cultures that have provided the horizon of meaning for *large numbers* of human
beings, of diverse characters and temperaments, *over a long period of time* . . . are
almost certain to have something that deserves our admiration and respect. [my
emphasis]

Obviously the dismissal of partial cultures, the emphasis on large
numbers and long periods, is out of time with the modes of recognition of
minority or marginalized cultures. Basing the presumption on 'whole
societies over some considerable stretch of time' introduces a temporal
criterion of cultural worth that elides the disjunctive and displaced
present through which minoritization interrupts and interrogates the
homogeneous, horizontal claim of the democratic liberal society. But this
notion of cultural time functions at other levels besides that of semantics
or content. Let us see how this passage locates the observer – how it
allows Taylor to turn the presumption of equality into the judgement of
worth. The partial, minority culture emphasizes the internal differentiations, the 'foreign bodies', in the midst of the nation – the interstices of
its uneven and unequal development, which give the lie to its self-
containedness. As Nicos Poulantzas brilliantly argues, the national state
homogenizes differences by mastering social time 'by means of a single,
homogeneous measure, which only reduces the multiple temporalities
. . . by encoding the distances between them'.[13] This conversion of time
into distance is observable in the way Taylor's argument produces a
spatial binary between whole and partial societies, one as the principle of
the other's negation. The double inscription of the part-in-the-whole, or
the minority position as the outside of the inside, is disavowed.

Yet something of this 'part-in-the-whole', the minority as at once the
internal liminality and the 'foreign body', registers symptomatically in
Taylor's discourse. It is best described as the desire for the 'dialogic', a
term he takes from Mikhail Bakhtin. But he deprives the 'dialogic' of its
hybridizing potential. The most telling symptom of this is that despite his
'presumption of equality' Taylor always presents the multicultural or
minority position as an imposition coming from the 'outside' and making
its demands from there. 'The challenge is to deal with *their* sense of
marginalization without compromising our basic political principles' (my
emphasis).[14] In fact the challenge is to deal not with them/us but with the
historically and temporally disjunct positions that minorities occupy
ambivalently within the nation's space. Taylor's evaluative scheme,
which locates the presumption of equality and the recognition of value
(the before and the after of liberal judgement) in the *longue durée* of major

national and nationalizing cultures, is in fact antithetical to the Bakhtinian
hybrid, which precisely undermines such claims to cultural totalization:

> The . . . hybrid is not only double-voiced and double-accented . . . but is also
> double-languaged; for in it there are not only (and not even so much) two
> individual consciousnesses, two voices, two accents, as there are [doublings of]
> socio-linguistic, consciousnesses, two epochs . . . that come together and
> consciously fight it out on the territory of the utterance. . . . It is the collision
> between differing points of view on the world that are embedded in these forms
> . . . such unconscious hybrids have been at the same time profoundly productive
> historically: they are pregnant with potential for new world views, with new
> 'internal forms' for perceiving the world in words.[15]

Indeed Bakhtin emphasizes a space of enunciation where the
negotiation of discursive doubleness by which I do not mean duality or binarism
engenders a new speech act. In my own work I have developed the concept
of hybridity to describe the construction of cultural authority within
conditions of political antagonism or inequity. Strategies of hybridization
reveal an estranging movement in the 'authoritative', even authoritarian
inscription of the cultural sign. At the point at which the precept attempts
to objectify itself as a generalized knowledge or a normalizing, hegemonic
practice, the hybrid strategy or discourse opens up a space of negotiation
where power is unequal but its articulation may be equivocal. Such
negotiation is neither assimilation nor collaboration. It makes possible the
emergence of an 'interstitial' agency that refuses the binary representation
of social antagonism. Hybrid agencies find their voice in a dialectic that
does not seek cultural supremacy or sovereignty. They deploy the partial
culture from which they emerge to construct visions of community, and
versions of historic memory, that give narrative form to the minority
positions they occupy; the outside of the inside: the part in the whole.

In Toni Morrison's novel *Beloved* (1987), cultural and communal
knowledge comes as a kind of self-love that is also the love of the 'other'. It is
an ethical love in that the 'inwardness' of the subject is inhabited by the
'radical and an-archical reference to the "other"'[16]. This knowledge is
visible in those intriguing chapters where Sethe, Beloved, and Denver
perform a ceremony of claiming and naming through intersecting and
interstitial subjectivities: 'Beloved, she my daughter', 'Beloved is my
sister', 'I am beloved and she is mine.'[17] The women speak in tongues, from
a fugal space 'in between each other' which is a communal space. They
explore an 'interpersonal' reality: a social reality that appears within the
poetic image as if it were in parenthesis aesthetically distanced, held back,
yet historically framed. It is difficult to convey the rhythm and the
improvisation of those chapters, but it is impossible not to see them in the
healing of history, a community reclaimed in the making of a name. As I
have written elsewhere.

> Who is Beloved?
>   Now we understand. She is the daughter that returns to Sethe so that her mind
> will be homeless no more.

Who is Beloved?
Now we may say: She is the sister that returns to Denver, and brings hope of
her father's return, the fugitive who died in his escape.
Who is Beloved?
Now we know: She is the daughter made of murderous love who returns to
love and hate and free herself. Her words are broken, like the lynched people
with broken necks, disembodied, like the dead children who lost their ribbons.
But there is no mistaking what her live words say as they rise from the dead
despite their lost syntax and their fragmented presence.
'My face is coming I have to have it I am looking for the join I am loving my
face so much I want to join I am loving my face so much my dark face is close to
me I want to join.'[18]

The idea that history repeats itself, commonly taken as a statement
about historical determinism, emerges frequently within liberal discourses when consensus fails, and when the consequences of cultural
incommensurability make the world a difficult place. At such moments,
the past is seen as returning, with uncanny punctuality, to render the
'event' timeless, and the narrative of its emergence transparent.

Do we best cope with the reality of 'being contemporary', its conflicts
and crises, its losses and lacerations, by endowing history with a long
memory that we then interrupt, or startle, with our own amnesia? How
did we allow ourselves to forget, we say to ourselves, that the nationalist
violence between Hindus and Muslims lies just under the skin of India's
secular modernity? Should we not have 'remembered' that the old Balkan
tribes would form again? These questions emphasize an observation that
is becoming increasingly commonplace: the rise of religious 'funda-
mentalisms', the spread of nationalist movements, the redefinitions of
claims to race and ethnicity, it is claimed, have returned us to an earlier
historical movement, a resurgence or restaging of what historians have
called the long nineteenth century. Underlying this claim is a deeper
unease, a fear that the engine of social transformation is no longer the
aspiration to a democratic common culture. We have entered an anxious
age of identity, in which the attempt to memorialize lost time, and to
reclaim lost territories, creates a culture of disparate 'interest groups' or
social movements. Here affiliation may be antagonistic and ambivalent;
solidarity may be *only* situational and strategic: commonality is often
negotiated through the 'contingency' of social interests and political
claims.

Narratives of historical reconstruction may reject such myths of social
transformation: communal memory may seek its meanings through a
sense of causality shared with psychoanalysis, that negotiates the
recurrence of the image of the past while keeping open the question of the
future. The importance of such retroaction lies in its ability to reinscribe
the past, reactivate it, relocate it, *resignify it*. More significant, it commits
our understanding of the past, and our reinterpretation of the future, to
an ethics of 'survival' that allows us to *work through the present*. And such a
working through, or working out, frees us from the determinism of

historical inevitability repetition *without a difference*. It makes it possible for us to confront that difficult borderline, the interstitial experience between what we take to be the image of the past and what is in fact involved in the passing of time and the passage of meaning.

Acknowledgements

This essay honours my seminar participants and colleagues at the School of Criticism and Theory, Dartmouth, 1993 without whose stimulation and support it would not have taken the form it has.

Notes

1 T.S. Eliot, *Notes towards the Definition of Culture*, Harcourt Brace, New York, 1949, p. 62.

2 Ibid., pp. 63–64.

3 Jürgen Habermas, 'The normative content of modernity', in *The Philosophical Discourse of Modernity*, trans. Frederick G. Lawrence, MIT Press, Cambridge, MA: 1987, p. 348.

4 Ibid.

5 Ibid., p. 346.

6 Bernard Williams, *Ethics and the Limits of Philosophy*, Harvard University Press, Cambridge, MA, 1985, p. 116.

7 Etienne Balibar, 'Paradoxes of universality,' in David Theo Goldberg (ed.), *Anatomy of Racism*, University of Minnesota Press, Minneaplis and Oxford, 1990, p. 284.

8 Ibid.

9 Ibid., p. 285.

10 See my 'Race, time, and the revision of modernity', in *The Location of Culture*, Routledge, London, 1994.

11 Franz Fanon, *Black Skin, White Masks*, trans. Charles Lamb Markmann, Grove Weidenfeld, New York, 1967, pp. 121–2.

12 Charles Taylor, *Multiculturalism and 'The Politics of Recognition'*, Princeton: University Press, Princeton, 1992, pp. 66–7.

13 Nicos Poulantzas, *State Power and Socialism*, trans. Patrick Camiller, NLB, London, 1978, p. 110.

14 Taylor, *Multiculturalism*, p. 63.

15 Mikhail Bakhtin, 'Discourse in the novel', in Michael Holquist (ed.), *The Dialogic Imagination*, trans. Caryl Emerson and Michael Holquist, University of Texas Press, Austin, 1981, p. 360.

16 See Emmanuel Lévinas, 'Reality and its shadow', in *Collected Philosophical Papers*, trans. Alphonso Lingis, Martinus Nijhoff, Dordrecht, the Netherlands, and Boston 1987, pp. 1–13.

17 Toni Morrison, *Beloved*, Plume/NAL, New York, 1987, pp. 200–17.

18 From my essay 'The home and the world', in *Social Text*, 10: 2 and 3, 1992, pp. 141–53, in which I develop this line of argument concerning Morrison's *Beloved* at greater length.

5

Interrupting Identities: Turkey/Europe

Kevin Robins

Seen from this perspective, the world today lives in the climate of a single
universal civilization, but one which has its own specificities, obvious or
hidden, that depend on the various peoples.

Adonis

. . . for amnesty and against amnesia.

Adam Michnik

In general, I am concerned with the possibilities of dynamism and
openness in cultural identities, and consequently with what inhibits and
resists such qualities, promoting in their place rigidity and closure.
Change implies the capacity to relinquish at least aspects of a given
identity. This, however, is likely to provoke feelings of anxiety and fear in
the collectivity (Shall we not suffer through our loss? What shall we be
turned into?). This is a basic fear about the mortality of the collective
institution. It is, as Cornelius Castoriadis maintains, 'the fear, which is in
fact quite justified, that everything, even meaning, will dissolve'.[1] In
defence against such a catastrophic eventuality, the collectivity will assert
the possibility of its self-perpetuation, elaborating myths and symbolic
representations concerned with a 'perennial meaning' and 'imaginary
immortality' in the culture. Following Castoriadis, we might see these in
terms of cultural repetition: repetition (in the psychoanalytical sense)
being 'the small change of death' through which an institution defends
itself against the reality of 'wholesale death'.[2] There is a kind of living
deadness in a culture that does not admit the possibility of its own
mortality.

In Castoriadis's view, it is western culture that has most effectively and
creatively resisted this logic of closure, through what he calls its 'project of
autonomy'. He argues that what has been distinctive in Graeco-Western
history 'is the rupture of this closure, and the questioning of all
signification, institutions and representations established by the tribe'.[3]
In thus acknowledging the potential mortality of every instituted
signification, it has made itself into a historical culture – the historical
culture *par excellence*. For Castoriadis, it was in the high period of
European modernity that this questioning and self-questioning spirit

reached its creative apogee in all spheres of life. Agnes Heller makes the
same point about western, and particularly modern western, culture:

> Modernity asserts and reasserts itself through negation. Only if several things
> are constantly changed, and at least certain things are continuously replaced by
> others, can modernity maintain its identity . . . Moderns do not acknowledge
> limit, they transcend it. They challenge the legitimacy of institutions, they
> criticise and reject them: they question everything.[4]

This is what she describes as 'modernity's dynamic'.

At the same time as acknowledging this achievement (in this philosophical perspective, at least), we must note as disturbingly significant
the way in which modernity defined itself against the 'pre-modern'. As
Heller argues, 'the juxtaposition to the Other (to the pre-modern) remains
the essential, albeit never the sufficient, condition of self-understanding';
the modern dynamism differentiated itself from the 'natural artifice' of
the pre-modern order.[5] The story of how this temporal contrast became
mapped on to a geographical polarization – with the dynamic West
distinguishing itself from the static and immobile Orient – is now a
familiar one. Through this dualistic imagination, the world was divided
between the enlightened and the benighted. Its Other was made to
symbolize whatever was alien to western modernity and its project of
development. Europe thereby closed itself imperiously to the reality of
these other cultures.

In this cultural context, the predicament of the 'pre-modern' world was
a painful one. Europe was closed to their realities, but they must be open
to its. It was not possible to shut out this new cultural dynamism coming
from modern Europe. Indeed, the western achievement provoked
admiration, if also trepidation. Was not this the new 'universal' culture,
the cultural future and even destiny of all the world's peoples? The
not-yet-modern cultures felt the compulsion to emulate the western
model; they too must set themselves on the course of 'development' and
'modernization'. There was an openness to change, but the experience,
we know, was rarely a felicitous one. While the social arrangements of
modernity were put into place, its dynamic element was invariably
absent: 'Regardless of whether it was a forced or voluntary transplant, the
total absence of such a dynamic, or its merely intermittent operation, has
kept the modern arrangement in an unstable state in all regions where,
compared to its model, it had a distorted character'.[6] The efforts of
imitation were rarely translated into authentic modernization. Adonis, in
the context of the Arab world, refers to 'an illusory, specious modernity',
arguing that 'the intellectual principles which gave birth to modernity are
lost to us, their substance wiped out'.[7] The exposure to modern culture
(that is to say, western culture) resulted, not in cultural creativity and
emancipation, but in conformism and dependency. This was the consequence of an excessive openness.

At the same time, there was the fearful sense that the dissolvent
principles of modernization would be fatal to the historical culture.

Westernization seemed to threaten everything, especially meaning. In consequence, there was cultural reaction, involving the reassertion of origins and traditions. There was reversion to the language of 'authenticity', which, like other forms of essentialism, postulates a cultural identity that is 'self-identical, essentially in continuity over time, and positing itself in essential distinction from other historical subjects'.[8] Adonis describes it in terms of regression towards a 'foetal relationship' to the traditionalist past.[9] But, of course, the past cannot be recovered; the cohesion and coherence of the culture – always an imaginary ideal – cannot be reconstituted. This compensating and protective retreat into the closure of tradition in fact represents 'a dependency on the past, to compensate for the lack of creative activity by remembering and reviving'. In this dependency, too, as in the technological dependency on the West, 'there is an obliteration of personality; in both cases, a borrowed mind, a borrowed life'.[10]

There is choice, it seems, between assimilation of an alien modernity and reversion to the spurious authenticity of (ethnic or religious) origins. It is a false choice, an absurd choice. It was the choice that the West imposed. Daryush Shayegan sees it as giving rise to a kind of schizoid disorder at the heart of the collective identity (a 'wounded consciousness').[11] This is an intolerable condition. But it is also a prevalent condition, and its consequences have been both damaging and destructive. It remains one of the fundamental issues to be confronted in the contemporary world. What are the possibilities for transcending this impossible choice? We must be concerned with those developments, both intellectual and political, that have potential for destabilizing and deconstructing this dualist logic.

Things are in movement. There is an increasing sense of what Castoriadis describes as the 'dilapidation' of the western project and ideals (this is surely what the debate around postmodernism must be concerned with). Empty of significations, western societies now seem incapable of exercising an emancipatory influence on the rest of the world.[12] The question is whether this will lead to cultural retrenchment and xenophobia, or whether it is possible to reconstitute the project of autonomy on a new basis. At the same time, there are developments beyond the western core which are significant in this respect and which must find full accommodation within any revised project. In these places, too, there are those who are concerned with questions of democracy, social and human emancipation, and the creative transmission of culture.[13] Here, too, can be found a concern to construct universal values, on the basis of consensus between different societies and cultures. 'If there is any sort of solidarity that can provide a basis for a truly universal aspiration,' argues Hichem Djait, 'it is surely the solidarity of cultures, including that of the West, against the enemy that denies them all: uncontrolled modernity.'[14] The imperative is for connection between those pursuing similar constructive objectives out of their different

experiences. Progress can only be achieved through cultural recep-
tiveness and reciprocity. At this point, we have to move from thinking in
terms of cultural identity to consider the significance of cultural exchange;
in Paul Ricoeur's terms, we have to be ready 'to *cross* our memories, to
exchange our memories'.[15] We have to think in terms of cultural experience, and of whether or how collectivities may be capable of learning from
experience.

These preliminary thoughts remain abstract, disengaged as they are
from the more intractable realities of actual cultural identity and encounter. How might we give them some substance? What do they amount to in
a particular context? In the following discussion, I want to consider the
question of Turkish identity and cultural experience, and to do so particularly through the relationship between Turkey and the European West (I
believe it cannot be considered outside this relation). First, we shall have
to consider the 'Turkey' of the European imagination, associated with
memories of the Ottoman threat to Christendom (the 'Eastern Question'),
fear of Islamic revival, and resentment against Turkish migration. The
projections of the European psyche have been, and remain, fundamental
impediments to cultural encounter and understanding.

In the following sections, I want to look at the reality of Turkish culture
and cultural transformation, taking into account particularly its European
orientation and context (the 'Western Question' in Turkish cultural identity). I shall consider the nature of its assimilation of western modernity,
especially in the period since the foundation of the Turkish Republic in
1923, and the discomforts and discontent that this entailed for its cultural
life. Then I shall examine recent developments, involving the resurgence
of repressed elements of the culture, and endeavours to construct an
alternative form of modernity and modern identity. Finally, I come to the
question of what the changing identity of Turkey might entail for its
relation to Europe. The question, really, is whether Europe can be open to
these developments; open to their singularity, and consequently to their
significance. Coming to terms with 'the Turk' is a crucial aspect of the
cultural reordering and re-association that must be undertaken in the
European space.

'A Turk doesn't go to the opera'

Writing in 1925, Arnold Toynbee described the emergence of the Turkish
nation in terms of the wholesale abandonment of one civilization and way
of life and the adoption of another, likening it to a 'spiritual conversion'.
This 'mental change' was motivated, says Toynbee, by the question of
status:

> The Turks, like the Jews, have been, since they first made contact with the
> West, a 'peculiar people'; and while this is an enviable position so long as you
> are 'top dog' . . . it becomes an intolerable humiliation as soon as roles are

reversed. . . . In both cases the status of 'peculiar people' has ceased to be a source of pride and has become a source of humiliation; and in both cases, therefore, a strong movement has risen to escape from it.[16]

The Turks 'sought to be admitted as full members of Western society in order to escape from the terrible position of being its pariahs'.[17] In certain respects, they have succeeded in establishing their credentials as a westernized and a modernized society (though at a psychic cost, as I shall argue later). Among Europeans, however, there has remained the sense that Turkey is not authentically of the West; the sense that it is alien, an outsider, an interloper in the European community. As Zafer Şenocak puts it, there is the belief that 'a Turk reads the Koran, he doesn't go to the opera'.[18] In European eyes, Turks remain a 'peculiar people'.

Turkey has found a certain accommodation within the western order. Its membership (since 1952) of NATO reflects its key significance in western defence and foreign policy agendas. During the Cold War era, Turkey's strategic geographical location and reach were seen as vital assets; it figured as both a 'barrier' to Soviet expansion and a 'bridge' to the Middle East.[19] Since the end of the Cold War, Turkey has demon-strated its military value during the Gulf War, and is now seen as a key player in a number of the geopolitical zones of the New World Order (the Middle East, South-East Europe, the Black Sea, the Caucasus, Central Asia).[20] Turkey must continue to be accommodated because of its significance in the changing European security environment. But this military involvement has not translated into political and cultural acceptance. Most significant, and symbolic, in this respect, of course, is Turkey's application for membership of the European Union. In this case, we can see very clearly the nature of Turkey's accommodation within the western order. As Richard Falk puts it, 'Turkey is not so much stranded at the European doorstep, but confined to the servants' quarters in the European house'.[21] Its accommodation, on those terms, is a decidedly precarious one.

The case for Turkish membership of the Union has been forcefully put by successive governments. 'We are Europeans,' says the Turkish President, Süleyman Demirel. 'We would like to stay as Europeans. We would like to live with Europe. We would like to act with Europe. We share the values of European civilisation in addition to our own values. As a member of NATO, we have defended those values.'[22] Europe is not persuaded, however. Those who are more sympathetic to the Turkish petition will put forward the argument that Turkey has not yet become sufficiently western to be accepted, or that it has not thoroughly resolved its identity crisis in favour of westernization. What is invoked is the 'uncertainty of identity' within Turkey: 'There appears to be some considerable doubt even among Turks of similar socio-economic back-ground as to the exact nature of the country and its people'.[23] In this case, it is what seems equivocal in Turkish culture that is so unsettling for Europe. Turkey is seen as 'an in-between place'.[24] In its hybridity – its particular kind of hybridity – it still does not conform to European standards. Those who outrightly oppose Turkish membership have more fundamental grounds for objection. They draw attention to Turkey's Middle-Eastern and Islamic connections. 'You have to have clarity about where the boundaries of Europe are, and the boundaries of Europe are not on the Turkish–Iran border,' argues Lord Owen.[25] More recently, attention has been drawn to Turkey's Asiatic origins. 'It was Genghis Khan's need for tough mercenaries that brought the Turks from their ancient homelands of central Asia to the shores of the Mediterranean,' writes Peter Millar in the *European*.[26] For these objectors, there is something essentially un-European about Turkish culture; there can be no question of its assimilation into the Union.

According to these perspectives, it is the Turk, uncertain or alien, who is the problematical element in the encounter – the only problematical element. What they manifest, I would argue, is a cultural arrogance in European attitudes. We can consider it as a development of what Arnold Toynbee, seventy years ago, described as the 'Western Question' confronted by Turkish society. He was referring to the indifference and contempt exhibited by the western powers towards the newly emerging republic: 'This conjunction of great effect on other people's lives with little interest in or intention with regard to them.'[27] This arrogant stance is apparent now in the insensibility shown towards Turkey's European aspirations. There is the demand that the Turks should assimilate western values and standards, alongside the conviction that, however much they try to do so it will be impossible for them to succeed. Ivaylo Ditchev sees it as a basic aspect in the relation of the European centre to its peripheries. These cultures, he argues, 'are asked to become part of the universal culture, but at the same time they are told that they will not be capable of doing so; Europe demands a sacrifice and does not accept it'.[28] The Turkish case simply shows how far it is possible to pursue this elusive universal culture, yet still be derided and rejected.

It also shows – more tragically still – how cultural arrogance can turn into cultural hatred. When it is declared that the other is marked by an insurmountable particularity, and consequently can never be assimilated (converted) into our culture, then we have the basis of racism. Turks have come to be seen in this way by many Europeans. In Germany, the so-called *Gastarbeiter* have been seen as a kind of continuation (this time by economic means) of the Ottoman (Islamic) onslaught on Europe. There is the sense of being overwhelmed by an alien culture. Describing a National-Socialist commemorative bronze in celebration of the liberation of Vienna in 1683, Claudio Magris notes the banner of the defeated Turks bore, not the Crescent, but the Star of David: 'The Turks were simply identified with the enemy, which is to say the Jews, by means of a falsification which today, in the xenophobic attitudes towards the seasonal foreign workers, runs the risk of becoming tragically true'.[29] The Turks were treated as pariahs. 'What has become a taboo in the case of the

Jews because of the Holocaust,' argues Zafer Şenocak, 'has become acceptable in the case of the Turks: the wholesale stigmatization of an entire people because of their otherness'.[30] Solingen, Mölln, Rostock, Hoyerswerda . . .

The repression of identity

I want to turn now to consider the consequences of modernization within Turkish culture and identity. Turkey made its sacrifice; it made the westward turn. From the period of the *Tanzimat* reforms, through to the movements of the Young Ottomans and Young Turks, the Ottoman Empire struggled to find some accommodation to Europe. The social 'revolution' undertaken by Mustafa Kemal (Atatürk) in the 1920s was the culmination of this long process. Turkey opened itself unconditionally to the forces of western modernization. 'We cannot close our eyes and imagine that we live apart from everything and far from the world,' Mustafa Kemal declared. 'We cannot shut ourselves in within our boundaries and ignore the outside world. We shall live as an advanced and civilised nation in the midst of contemporary civilisation'.[31] In so far as the West was equated with the very principle of 'civilization' the logic of westernization had come to seem necessary and inevitable. The Kemalist elite was attracted to the light of the universal culture, the world of science and technology, rationalism and progress. It recognized that this would require fundamental social transformation of the Turkish people; as Stéphane Yerasimos puts it, the necessity was recognized 'to civilise the people, in order to appear as the representatives of a civilised people'.[32] It was resolved to adopt the western institutions of nationalism and the nation state.[33] Westernization was the road to salvation for the Turkish people, and its adoption was to be absolute.

What has been achieved? What kind of modernization and national culture have been instituted in the Turkish Republic? Turkey's modernization has been an arid and empty affair. The arrangements of a modern society have been put in place, to use Agnes Heller's terms, but anything resembling a modern dynamic has been lacking. In this respect, the European reluctance to acknowledge Turkey as 'genuinely' modern has a certain justification (what is utterly unjustifiable, of course, is the West's encouragement – which still persists – of this particular logic of 'development' as the only possibility; its inability, that is to say, to imagine modernity on the basis of any other sense of universalism). Modern Turkish culture has been imitative and derivative in its emulation of the European model. Şerif Mardin has bemoaned 'the real impoverishment of Turkish culture that resulted from Republican reform', arguing that its symbolism 'was too shallow and lacking in aesthetic richness to "take".'[34] Cultural meaning is created only through affiliation and comparison to the western ideal: the Turkish elites have constantly measured their achievement according to their resemblance to the European model (or, rather, their image of what it is). Cultural development is consequently to be understood in terms of more effective counterfeiting or simulation of the original paradigm. But, of course, however good the simulation, it does not amount to the real thing. There has been a creative void at the heart of modern Turkish culture. The elite put the old order into question, but it was not able through this process to liberate new meaning of a creative kind. It was an ersatz modernism that supplanted Ottoman culture.

It would be possible to tell the Turkish story from the perspective of Kemalism's openness to Europe, and in terms of the vicissitudes of cultural assimilation and 'development'. Alternatively, we could interpret it as a narrative of disavowal and denial. In terms, that is to say, of what in Turkish culture and society Kemalism closed itself to. This is the line of argument that we shall pursue here. For the Kemalist elite, it seemed as if the principles of modernity could be accommodated only on the basis of the massive prohibition and interdiction of the historical and traditional culture. To make way for the new, rational worldview the culture had to be purged of its theocratic, mystified and superstitious ways of life. To become 'civilized' it must purify itself of all that was particular, and by that token pre-modern, in the local culture. What this resulted in was not only disavowal and suppression of historical memory in the collectivity, but also, and even more problematically, denial and repression of the actuality of Turkish culture and society. As much as it has been shaped by the assimilation of western culture, modern Turkish identity 'is also a product of various negations': Turkish society became 'practised in the art of repression'.[35]

The Ottoman past was disdained for its backwardness, particularly its religiosity, and the imperial culture denounced as the source of all evils. The new Turkish state initiated a series of drastic reforms, intended to erase and nullify the historical legacy. These were aimed pre-eminently at the secularization of Turkish society (abolition of the caliphate; disestablishment of the state religion; closure of holy places (shrines); dissolution of dervish orders and brotherhoods, etc.), also entailing momentous changes in the way of life (the adoption of the Gregorian calendar; the creation of a western-style penal code; the proscription of the fez and other forms of 'uncivilized' headgear; the adoption of the Latin alphabet in preference to Arabic script; the purgation of Persian and Arabic influences from the language). Mustafa Kemal maintained that 'the new Turkey has no relationship to the old. The Ottoman government has passed into history. A new Turkey is now born'.[36] What was being attempted by the Republican elite was no less than the annihilation of the past. The new nation and state were born out of this fundamental disavowal: 'The Turkish nation was born as an autonomous and independent entity, but in seeking its reference points, it could find only itself, since its past was denied.'[37] It emerged as a state without history (how this lack was compensated for, I shall come to in a moment).

What was at issue, however, was far more than a foreclosure of the past: the Republican order was also instituted through the suppression of contemporary actuality in the new society. In so far as they were – and could be nothing other than – products of the Ottoman past, the contemporary society and its popular culture were themselves problems for the Kemalist regime. The elite committed itself to efface or to eradicate the real Turkey that seemed to perpetuate the old ways and stand in the way of the new. Its endeavours were damaging in a number of respects, inhibiting the vitality and creativity necessary to sustain a democratic culture.

The Ottoman Empire had been characterized by a spirit of cosmopolitanism; by ethnic, linguistic and religious mixture and interchange.[38] The Turkish state that emerged out of its collapse was fundamentally opposed to such pluralism of identity. It resolved to build a nation without minorities, which it did first through exclusion – the Armenian massacres (1915), the exchange of populations with Greece (1923) – and subsequently through cultural assimilation and integration.[39] The enormous diversity and complexity of the population was considered to be inimical to the achievement of national community and consensus. The new government pursued the goal of cultural homogenization. As S.D. Salamone argues, it 'reacted to its own past as inherently centrifugal', seeking to restructure the culture 'by means of a countervailing principle of corporate consolidation and demographic homogenisation'; it aimed to transform Turkish natural identity 'through *uniform incorporation*, connecting the concept of citizenship with that of social-cultural-linguistic assimilation'.[40] In many cases, the new 'Turks' did not yet speak the Turkish language (Circassians, Lazes, Georgians). The Kurdish people were described as 'mountain Turks' who had forgotten their true language.[41] The monochrome vision of a Turkish culture in common was layed over the heterogeneity of lived identifications. Local and particular attachments could no longer be admitted. It was not just that these real identifications were suppressed; the point is that their very reality actually came to be disavowed.

I have already referred to the critical attitude of the new regime towards the worldview of Islam. Religious attachment was also seen as a subversive force, also posing a threat to the modernization and nationalization process in Turkey. Kemalist ideology was conceived as a national and secular alternative, conforming to the values of the 'civilized' world; a revolution in values, offering western-style identifications in place of what were regarded as the old mystifications of Muslim culture. It was an empty substitution, however. In attacking religious authority, symbolism and meaning, the new civil outlook could not put anything substantial in its place. As Richard Tapper argues, Kemalist doctrine 'was no alternative to Islam in providing identity and organising principles of life. At the public level, it was no substitute for the divine laws of Islam; at the individual level, it could not meet intellectual needs for an ethics and an eschatology, and its ideology and values were inadequate, shallow and thin'.[42] These dimensions of spirituality and belief that were so vital to the popular culture were denied as meaningful in the new modern outlook. 'Islam and its world of values and ethics having been taken out of our frame of reference,' writes Şerif Mardin of the new secular perspective, 'we had no appreciation of existential quandaries'.[43] Through this denial, civilizational values were diminished and impoverished.

So, too, were democratic values. Kemalism was an ideology imposed on the people from above. Its self-declared mission was to revolutionize the society for the good of the people. For the good of a backward and uncivilized people, however, a people whose commitment to progress and civilization could not be relied on. The consequence was that the society – the real people, that is to say – could not be trusted to take part in its own revolution. What developed was a situation in which the Kemalist elite 'sought to perpetuate its guardianship whilst limiting both political participation and the autonomy of civil society'.[44] Repression was exercised in the name of democracy in the future. Popular aspirations and initiatives had to be blocked because they went against the grain of modernizing rationalization. The new regime was essentially paternalistic and authoritarian, and, as one might expect of such an order, it constructed its image of the ideal people, the people it could imagine itself governing. It was the image of a unitary and unified people, the People-as-One, that figured in the project to create a new life in Turkey. There was no place for ethnic and religious differences in this project, but neither, too, was there room for social and political differences. As Cengiz Aktar argues, 'substantial conflict in the social order was condemned, even sacrificed, to unitary representation', and thereby 'the people [were] excluded, by definition, from the body of this nation'.[45] The conditions of diversity and pluralism necessary to democratic life were stifled from the beginning. Democratic culture is impossible so long as the real Turkey (the Turkey of adversarial values and beliefs) is disavowed.

The actuality of popular culture and popular aspirations was denied. But, more than this, as Aktar says, there was a 'hate of the people: they must be civilized in spite of themselves'. They were regarded as barbarians: 'consequently, what [was] lacking in them [could] only be made good through the perfection to be found in civilization, and not from any particular or local feature they might possess, and which did not exist anyway in the eyes of the elite'.[46] The nation – what Aktar describes as the 'ontological nation', since it was not made up of real individuals – was imagined as the embodiment of civilized values. Defined in opposition to the Islamic past, it would be a secular and rational nation. Defined in opposition to the cosmopolitanism of the Ottoman Empire, it would have a strictly national identity. A new history and new traditions were invented to compensate for the real ones that were being abandoned. The origins of the burgeoning nation were located in Sumerian and Hittite societies; principles of Turkism (and pan-Turkism) were elaborated, with all the appropriate paraphernalia and customs.[47] The real Turkey was the 'other' against which this official nation was constituting its identity. The state was endowed with the task of protecting the ideal nation against the encroachments and assertions of the barbarians within. In the last instance – as in the military coups of 1960, 1971 and 1980 – it was the military that was entrusted with the preservation of the Kemalist nation. Physical repression became the ultimate means to pursue the civilizing process.

Of course, the real people could never be banished. Since its foundation, the state has been continually confronted with popular reaction, and has had to make accommodations to democratic and cultural aspirations. In 1946, the principle of multi-party politics was finally recognized. This may be seen as a partial concession to democracy, though it was primarily about a redistribution of power between the state elite and other elites (economic and social). At the same time, and in part as a consequence of the need now to compete for votes, there was a liberalization in attitudes to religion. The revival of Islam that followed reflected 'an attempt to reinstate religion as civic ethics to fill in the ethical void created, especially among those born under the Republic, by the erosion of religious beliefs'.[48] The 1970s saw a growth in the radical Left (as in other parts of the world), posing questions of modernization and democracy with great vehemence (and often violence). It took a military coup, in 1980, to terminate this phase of Turkish political life, and again religion figured in the strategies to 'normalize' the situation. Under the National Security Council, which ruled the country for three years, the influence of Islam in Turkish polities increased dramatically. As Feroz Ahmad argues, Islam has become an instrument of social control.[49] Religion was mobilized as a means to staunch ideological confrontation and division. Whilst the generals professed to be Kemalists, they developed a new idea of national culture in which Islam played a fundamental role (it drew on the idea of a 'Turkish-Islamic synthesis', developed by the conservative elites of the "Intellectuals' Hearth" (*Aydınlar Ocağı*)). The emphasis continued to be on consensus and unification among the Turkish people, however. As Baskın Oran argues, the new compromise perpetuated the faults of Kemalism – anti-pluralism and top-down politics – but in a different way.[50]

We may identify a series of adjustments, then, through which the state has managed to reassert its hold over the people; through which it has perpetuated its authoritarian and autocratic management of society. It has continuously denied the real diversity of civil society, which it can only comprehend in terms of social fragmentation, and against which it has mobilized the idealized fantasy of the Turkish People-as-One. S.D. Salamone argues that ethnic and religious groups have been driven to see themselves as 'outsiders', suggesting that the Turkish state has created 'a social environment where even other-than-ethnic corporate groups begin to acquire the look and feel of contentious minorities in their own right'.[51] The official culture has been closed to the real Turkey.

The return of the repressed

There is still iron in the soul of the state; seemingly devoid of political imagination or nuance, it continues to pursue the uncompromising defence of its adamantine principles. In the society at large, however, there have been some significant developments since the mid-1980s, opening up new cultural and political possibilities. In the West, they tend to be seen in simplistic terms as the breakdown of modernization, the rise of Islamic fundamentalism, or the reawakening of Turkic expansionism. When considered more closely and carefully, though, it is clear that something rather more interesting is at issue. The proliferation of Islamic publications, the growing recognition of ethnic heterogeneity, the increasing references to the Ottoman past, are all about the real Turkey reasserting itself against official and state culture.

We may see these developments in terms of the return of the elements that were repressed in the Kemalist culture (religion, ethnic diversity, the imperial heritage). They reflect, as Nilüfer Göle maintains, the resurgence of civil society, a culture that is autonomous from the state, and now with its 'tongue untied'.[52] The 'other' Turkey is making its declaration of independence, making its reality felt, manifesting the complexity of its social being. This has nothing to do with cultural reversion (to tradition, religion, or whatever), as many western commentators like to believe: what are at issue are precisely questions about modern identity and values in Turkey. The Kemalist state elite is 'no longer the exclusive source of modernity in Turkey', argues Ali Kazancigil, 'and there is now a broader debate, concerning modernity and democracy, cultural identity, and a humanism open to both the world and the Islamic moral order'.[53] We should, of course, be cautious in our estimation of these developments. They are in their very early stages, and there are certainly dangers as well as potential. At the same time, however, we should be open to the possibilities they offer for greater cultural creativity and plural democracy.

First, let us consider what has propelled these transformations (which have happened in a remarkably short time). We may identify both external and internal factors. As to the former, Turkey, like most of the world's cultures, has been significantly affected by the forces of globalization. The increasing transnationalization of markets, the growth of global media and communications, the mobility of populations (tourism, migration), have all worked towards the dissolution of the old rigidities in the national culture.[54] The end of the Cold War and the putting into place of a New World Order have also had dramatic consequences for Turkey.

There is a new eastward orientation, as relations are re-established with Central Asia (Kazakhstan, Kyrgyzstan, Turkmenistan, Uzbekistan). Since 1989, Turkey's historical and strategic significance has become increasingly apparent in the Middle East, the Balkans, and the Black Sea area. The Cold War isolationism of its political culture is now ceding to a new sense of engagement and mission. The Turks 'may now come to see themselves once again at the centre of a world emerging around them rather than at the tail-end of a European world that is increasingly uncertain about whether or not it sees Turkey as part of itself'.[55]

As well as enhancing Turkish self-esteem in the world context, there have been significant implications for collective identity. Turks have become increasingly aware of their Ottoman past (though there has also been a certain reactivation of Turkism and pan-Turkism). They have also become more aware of their ethnic diversity as developments in such areas as the Balkans or the Caucasus remind them of where many Turks have their origins. The state's exhortations for national unity and consensus against 'external threat' have also lost much of their force with the collapse of the Soviet Union, making way (as in other European countries) for the expression of internal differences. The old schism between Left and Right has, to a large extent, been replaced by ethnic, cultural and religious factors of difference and disagreement. In sum, developments in the external environment have helped to loosen the rigidities of cultural and political identity, bringing the real Turkey into focus and thereby fostering the development of civil society.[56]

There were also crucial developments within Turkey, contributing to the unblocking of cultural and political life. The military coup in 1980 created a political and cultural vacuum, and, as I have already indicated, it was apparent that the Kemalist ideology was no longer capable of filling it. There was the need to find a new compromise which would not sacrifice Kemalist principles, but which could hold Turkish society together and give it a new identity in changing times. This is what the new Anavatan Partisi (ANAP; Motherland Party), which was established after the coup under the leadership of Turgut Özal, set out to achieve. The project of what has been called 'Özalism' involved the unification of the mainstream political groupings under the banner of ANAP, along with a refocusing of the cultural orientation of Turkish society. Özal spoke of a 'general reconciliation' and 'a new synthesis',[57] by which he intended a bringing together of religious conservative circles and liberal Kemalist tendencies. The new cultural orientation emphasized the significance of Islam as a unifying element in the society. The nationalism and religious ideas of the 'Turkish-Islamic synthesis' were influential within one wing of ANAP. In this respect, Özalism may be seen as a conservative project, in continuity with the earlier political culture of unity and consensus, merely giving a religious inflection to an authoritarian state.

That is one way of seeing the political reconfigurations of the 1980s. But Özal's new approach also contained other, more dynamic, elements that have to be taken into account. A crucial factor here was the new economic policy developed by ANAP, with the intention of opening up market forces and integrating Turkey into the global economy. Özal was opposed to what he called the 'deification of the state', arguing that 'development was no longer the prerogative only of the state'.[58] The objective was a new liberalized economic order, open to foreign investment and trade. Islam could play a crucial part in this transformation in so far as 'it reduces the role of the state, while inculcating a sense of freedom and responsibility in the ordinary people'.[59] Özal was looking for ways to stimulate the economy from below. He was also aspiring to a new kind of moderniz- ation. He is said to have expressed envy of the Japanese, and their ability to combine technological development with the preservation of their identity. Özal's hope was that Turkey could become 'conservative like the Japanese, but also universal and global'.[60]

These economic changes had profound cultural implications. But Özal pushed further with more directly cultural and political aspirations, trying to set in motion what he called a 'mental revolution'. His objective was to foster a more plural cultural identity, as well as recognizing and reinstating traditional aspects of the culture. Özal himself boasted of uttering the word 'Kurd', thereby paving the way for the destruction of a taboo.[61] Religious taboos were also broken. Özal explicitly criticized the secular intelligentsia. They must recognize, he argued,

> that the days of imposing one's own elitist values on the masses are over, values which have been borrowed in a wholesale manner in the guise of universalism and expressed in a foreign or at best in a hybrid idiom. . . . In no way does this approach deny the universal features of culture. It only emphasises that no people can be creative unless it draws its strength mainly from its own cultural heritage through an intensive updating and upgrading effort.[62]

Özal's aspiration was to engage the real Turkey in the modernization process. In place of top-down reform, he sought 'a change from below, in other words, the real change'.[63] In this respect, he was beginning to release political culture from its Kemalist shackles.

Özalism was a phenomenon, then, of considerable complexity in its combination of conservatism and change. It maintained stability through its emphasis on continuity (with both the Kemalist and the Islamic pasts),[64] yet at the same time it sought to release repressed and dynamic elements in the culture. Transformation was necessary if Turkey was to become 'synchronized' with a changing world, and if it was to find the real idiom of its cultural identity. Once the psychic repression had been lifted, lost identities and experiences began to be recovered. A diversity of voices made themselves heard, all demanding recognition. An energy was released.

Ethnic diversity and diversity of geographical origins have become increasingly recognized and appreciated in Turkish cultural identity. Turks are more and more conscious of the demographic heterogeneity and complexity which evolved out of the Ottoman Empire. The 'one nation' contains a whole array of molecular identities (Laz, Georgians, Abkhazians, Azeris, Kurds, Turkmen, Yoruks, Circassians, Greeks, Albanians, Bosnians, Tatars, etc.). Turks have now rediscovered 'lost homelands', 'lost worlds'.[65] This 'recovery' of identities is in line with a resurgent concern with ethnicity across Europe as a whole. What has been particularly significant in the Turkish context has been the reactivation of historical affiliations and connections through the collapse of the Cold War order and boundaries. These are identities that are shared across the borders of nation states. We may consider these developments in terms of cultural revitalization and enrichment, but there are also clear dangers. If these were to become primary identifications, the situation could become rapidly destabilized (one has the sense that certain western European observers, in the name of cultural 'authenticity', have a perverse interest in encouraging the proliferation of small national peoples in this part of the world).[66]

The dangers of ethnic confrontation are manifest in the effective war between the Turkish state and the Kurdish guerrillas in the south-east. Whilst there have been certain cultural concessions to the Kurds (since 1991 they have been free to speak their own language and practise their own customs), other more significant ones continue to be denied to them (Kurdish broadcasting, education in Kurdish). As the situation in the Kurdish area becomes more and more destructive – for one journalist, 'the term "ethnic cleansing" does not seem out of place'[67] – the need for a political solution to cultural confrontation becomes ever more urgent. It has now become possible to speak of federalism as a way forward; Özal considered a 'Basque solution' to the problem. The issue will be to find some means of decentralization without fragmentation, and not only in the case of the Kurds. Özal seems to have looked to Islam as a unifying identity over and above ethnic differences, but, of course, such an approach would not be accepted among secular Turks.

As well as ethnic differences, social and cultural divisions have become increasingly apparent in Turkish life. This has been in large part a consequence of the massive migration, during the 1980s, from the east and south-east to the large cities. The Anatolian people – village people, religious people, Kurdish people – have invaded the life-space of the secular and westernized middle classes. The return of the repressed. Feroz Ahmad describes it in terms of the arrival in the cities of an 'Ottoman-Islamic' culture, a popular culture that 'had hardly been touched by the secular culture of the republic and therefore continued to identify with the only cultural tradition they knew'.[68] The real Turkey made its presence felt. These people built their sprawling and illegal squatter settlements (*gecekondu*), constructed their mosques, and developed a culture which sustained their village customs and way of life. They wore their village clothing and headscarves. Out of the *gecekondu* come the music and culture of *arabesk*, the culture of the migrant in the city:

It portrays a world of complex and turbulent emotions peopled by lovers doomed to solitude and a violent end. It describes a decaying city in which poverty stricken migrant workers are exploited and abused, and calls on its listeners to pour another glass of *rakı*, light another cigarette, and curse the fate of the world.[69]

It is a culture that expresses the discrepancies between the official culture and real experiences of upheaval and disruption.

Those with a Kemalist orientation were scandalized by the new cultural developments under their noses. The new social contacts provoked feelings of contamination in what has come to be called 'white Turkey'. The question is whether they can be overcome and the potential of the new developments harnessed. New possibilities are being opened up for cultural revitalization, for elaborating a new cosmopolitan spirit in the culture. Istanbul has now become a global city, a melting pot in which the diverse cultures of Turkey are juxtaposed, and then mixed further with the diversity of world cultures.[70] The proliferation of new commercial television channels has become a crucial means of facilitating the encounter with the diversity of civil society. Under the old state broadcasting system (TRT), Turks only ever saw images of the official culture. The new commercial companies are eager to reach the new populations (and markets), and are consequently making programmes about the real Turkey. Ignorance, and consequently fear, may be dispelled. As Ayşe Öncü argues, commercial television has given visibility to Islam in the culture, helping to dissipate fears, making it an issue, something to be acknowledged and confronted.[71] In so far as it becomes apparent that the culture of the other Turkey is ordinary (in Raymond Williams's sense), cultural encounter and exchange become more possible.

Religion has clearly been central in the developments that have occurred over the last decade. Islam has emerged again as a dynamic element in the culture, and has increasingly been recognized as such. It has developed a strong presence in civil society, with religious foundations (*vakıfs*) providing support in education, housing and health for those who are let down by the inadequate social services of the state, and also developing a parallel Islamic market (books, cassettes, clothing, food, newspapers, television).[72] Through the Refah Partisi (Welfare Party), Islam has emerged as an important force in national politics, but also, on the basis of its grassroots activism, at the urban level, taking control of both the Istanbul and Ankara municipal administrations in the elections of March 1994. Furthermore, it has been the source of new ideas and intellectual perspectives; for the moment, at least, Muslim thinkers seem to be responding more thoughtfully and imaginatively to the structural problems and difficulties of change in Turkish society than their secular counterparts.

We should of course, acknowledge the diversity of Islamic culture (it is a question of Islams, not Islam). It is constituted of a variety of sects, movements, parties, forms of activity, and points of view. This has inevitably given rise to difference and debate, over issues ranging from the interpretation of religious principles to the dilemmas of transforming the economy and society. Radical and innovative ideas have been developed in the public sphere by the new Muslim intellectuals of the 1980s. *Zaman* newspaper was for a brief period the locus of fertile debate on questions of modernization, westernization and Islam.[73] *Zaman*, and the intellectuals associated with this current, pursued what might be called a utopian project. They developed a critique of industrialization and modernization, influenced in certain respects by Green politics, arguing that western models of science and technology are opposed to the principles of Islam.[74] Theirs was to be an Islam both open and vital, opposed to rather than supportive of the rigidities of traditionalist thinking. Ali Bulaç makes an important distinction:

> As I see it, among the Islamists there is one group which views the Islamic life in a relatively dynamic way, and there is another which views the Islamic life as one devoted to the preservation of traditional values. The one group is concerned with effecting political change through lawful means. It is also inclusive and in favour of openness and dialogue. The other group, following a traditional conservative line, is exclusive, fond of generalisations, and not in favour of dialogue.[75]

The first group is concerned with creative intervention in the issues facing the Turkish people. It is concerned with questions of democracy, and particularly with the conditions of plural democracy. Ali Bulaç has sought to develop ideas for coexistence out of the principles developed by Muhammad in the Medinan period.[76] Within this perspective, there is a serious concern with civil society, and with the constitutional reforms necessary to ensure plural democracy.

Such ideas have been widely heard, though they remain those of a minority. The dominant aspect of Islamic politics (represented by the Refah Partisi) is conservative and traditional, more committed to its vested interests. Here too, however, there are significant developments in play. Rusen Çakir observes the growth of a liberalism among these more pragmatic Muslims, as they become more and more involved in public life. This liberalism, which is something the Kemalists could never accept, 'is no guarantee of pluralism, but at least the new situation could provide the basis for constructing a pluralistic society'.[77] What is also being evolved in this milieu is a new accommodation between modernity and the particularities of Turkish culture. Nilüfer Göle refers to the emergence of a significant new social group of Muslim engineers during the 1980s. Ambitious and well integrated into the society, they aimed to counter the rationalistic and materialistic ethos of western modernity through their allegiance to religious principles and morality. 'Through this mixed behaviour,' she argues, 'the engineers are changing the paradigm of modernity.'[78] In this liberal-conservative perspective, modernity is being separated from westernization. Islamic movements are realizing that 'modernity can only be produced through local cultural identities and social structures'.[79]

The whole complex of change that I have been describing is fraught with dangers (as is any such social upheaval). There is no room for illusion or complacency. The Kurdish situation remains bitter and desperate. The potential exists for a resurgence of Turkish nationalism, in response to both ethnic separatism and the developments occurring in Turkic Central Asia.[80] In July 1993, demonstrating Muslims set fire to a hotel in the Anatolian town of Sivas, where a group of writers and intellectuals – including the outspoken secularist writer Aziz Nesin, who had translated sections of *The Satanic Verses* into Turkish – had assembled to commemorate the sixteenth-century poet, Pir Sultan Abdal.[81] Thirty-seven were slain. Religious passions are deep-seated. So, too, are secular passions. There is a profound anxiety among the secular population that Muslims will instate a system of Sharia law. Nilüfer Göle argues that modern Turkish society has evolved a 'caste-like' culture, in which Islamic people figure as the untouchables. What are at issue are not social or political disagreements, but something more elemental: 'feelings of difference and strangeness, felt through the body, unconsciously and without articulation, and shaping life-styles, identities and cultures'.[82] The fundamental issue is whether these pre-rational attitudes and emotions can be given conscious expression and modified through political rationality and negotiation.

There are dangers, but there are also possibilities. Indeed, because there are dangers, there *have* to be possibilities. 'Plural democracy is the recognition of the diversity of the principles of being both among individuals and even within each person,' argues Ahmet Insel. 'The irreducibility of these principles of being to a single one, and the refusal of all exclusion that feeds upon this diversity, are the minimum conditions for this democratic ideal.'[83] The diversity of social being is increasingly entering into the consciousness of Turkish society. What is at issue now is mutual recognition between these diverse interests, and then, beyond that, their ability to relate to each other in political ways. The Medina Project – defined against the Rafah Partisi's consensualist ideal of the 'Just Order' – constitutes one programme for acknowledging the diversity of civil society and working towards principles of coexistence (the problem with it, however, is that what it seems to envisage is precisely coexistence: the mutual tolerance of groups that remain relatively separate from each other). Another is to be found in the proposals among liberals around the idea of the 'Second Republic'. These represent a continuation of the spirit of Özalism (Özal died in April 1993), and involve opposition to the unitary state, economic liberalism, and social pluralism. What is disappointingly lacking is any programme from the social-democratic Left, which, after years of Kemalist complacency, has become intellectually moribund. This constituency now has to face the difficult task of acknowledging the mortality of Kemalism, recognizing its own particularity, and arguing for what would be socially democratic in the context of the new Turkish situation. The responsibility in all cases is to avoid regression to primary identities (whether Muslim or Kemalist), which means that all constituencies must recognize the primacy of their sociality over their particularities.

The return to history

> Then again, we can meet ourselves only at an unexpected bend in the road.
>
> Eugène Ionesco

In conclusion, I want to come back to the general issue of cultural identity and encounter, with which I began this discussion, and I want to do this by returning to the consideration of Europe and the Western Question. Turkish culture and society have been historically pulled into the sphere of European influence, shaped by it in ways that have invariably been difficult and frustrating. Now, as Turkey experiences significant transformations and confronts new difficulties of its own, the nature of the European response will be a significant issue. European acceptance of what is happening (for what it really is) could help considerably in the development of a more creative and democratic culture in Turkey. At the same time, this unexpected bend in history offers possibilities for Europeans to meet themselves. If they could but make use of them, then we might see a revitalization and remoralization of European culture too.

The point of this whole discussion has been to argue that we must think of cultural identities in the context of cultural relationships. What would an identity mean in isolation? Isn't it only through the others that we become aware of who we are and what we stand for? We must consider identities in terms of the experience of relationships: what can happen through relationships, and what happens to relationships. In this way, we can take up again the question of dynamism versus closure in identity.

Ideally, cultural relationship and interaction will be open to new experience. It will be possible to confront and modify more basic cultural emotions (fears and anxieties) and to recognize the other as a culture apart, not a projection or extension of one's own culture. On this basis, reciprocity becomes feasible, and it will be possible to display empathy, concern and responsibility in the cultural relationship. Jonah Goldstein and Jeremy Rayner evoke such an ideal when they argue for the

> possibility that collective identity in late modern society might often be strengthened through a process of continuous interaction with other collectivities – a process that requires each community to see itself from the perspective of others, and incorporate those perspectives through the prism of its own consciousness in a continuous reflexive process. Collective identity would be

recognized as selectively *chosen* (within certain parameters) rather than merely given.[84]

In such a case there will be cultural dynamism. The relationship will be appreciated because of the valuable different possibilities it offers; because of the potential for creative transformation that it contains.

That is the ideal. In reality, things can be (are likely to be) rather different, the relationship characterized more by cultural closure. Cultural relationships may easily become dominated by fears and anxieties, or by fantasies involving the projection of collective emotions on to the others. They may become restricted by cultural arrogance, denying the possibilities inherent in the others, and producing feelings of indifference or resentment towards them. Cultural relationships develop through history, through the accumulation of stories that we tell ourselves about the others; often reflecting fear or ignorance, these stories evolve into mythologies that obscure and deny the reality of the others. All of these factors may work to inhibit cultural interaction, experience and transformation. The source of cultural dynamism is then cut off; the potential space that exists between cultures is closed down.

To turn again now to the real and particular, let us consider the predicament of European culture in such terms as these. We have described Europe's relationship to Turkey precisely in terms of closure (and of course this is only one example, among very many, of such relational impoverishment). 'Turkey is not alien to Europe, as is the popular belief, but is her *alter ego*, her "complementary identity",' says Turgut Özal in his petition to the European Community. But still Europe cannot see anything but an alien presence; it can only see the Turks in terms of a 'negative identity'. 'Such an image has less to do with reality than with the pathology of those who embrace it,' Özal argues: 'The problem lies in the fact that, in order to be strong enough, the so-called self-identity of Europe needs to be exclusive and different'.[85] Towards the realities of Turkish culture there is arrogant disinterest or disdain: indifference to those in Turkey who still see Europe as a source of values and ideals; callous resentment towards the Turkish workers who have made Europe their home. These European attitudes are pernicious and destructive. In refusing to recognize the difficult realities of Turkish society – in misrecognizing them in terms of regression and threat – they work to undermine creative change. They in fact give force to those very elements that would identify with European projections, defining what they stand for in opposition to the Christian West.[86] For Turks concerned with constructive relations, the ruthlessness of the European cultural outlook is a fundamental obstacle.

In a different – and perhaps more tragic – way, it is increasingly an obstacle for Europeans too. In its cultural development, Europe came to see itself as self-identical and self-sufficient. Georges Corm writes of 'the narcissistic history of its modernity'.[87] Its identity has been instituted in continuity with the (supposedly endogenous) tradition and heritage of

Judaeo-Christian and Graeco-Roman cultures. Other influences, particularly western Islam, have been dispelled from the collective memory. The positivity of European culture was defined against the negative image of 'non-Europe'. In the period of its expansion, this self-confident culture appeared dynamic, projected across the globe as the universal culture. But such times are no more. Europe is now drawing back, trying 'to build a new identity, restricted and particular, based on specific features that distinguish it from everything which it has projected outside itself or conquered and denied'.[88] In constructing new frontiers and boundaries, it is seeking to exclude those who cannot be assimilated because of their different (alien) origins and traditions. Now it aims to protect its patrimony against whatever forces seem to threaten its dissolution or dilution. The historical dynamism has turned into 'a negative passion, a rejection, repulsion', as Jean Baudrillard puts it. 'Identity today finds itself in rejection; it hardly has a positive basis any longer'.[89] The only positivity is to be found in perpetuation of the received culture: in conservation, the impossible project. There seems to be no other resolution to the crisis of European culture. There is only repetition.

It is, says Baudrillard, 'a denial of the course of history, a kind of block or regression'.[90] There is no more history to be made, no more change. The closure of European culture may be seen in terms of the loss of historical purpose: the 'End of History' fantasy. Europe no longer sees itself in terms of creation of history. It is no longer open to the indeterminacy of the historical process. There is no longer the sense of modernity as dynamic transformation. Modernity has become Europe's tradition now, to be remembered and revered, not for revision or reinvention. There can be no way forward where there is no sense of the incompletion of history. There can be no more change when the sources of change have been disavowed.

The Western Question, which Toynbee saw as so critical, remains a fundamental problem for the whole geopolitical region of which Western Europe is a part (the Balkans, the Middle East, the Mediterranean, Eastern Europe, Turkey). Europe still casts its shadow. Where once Europe brought the disruption and upheaval of change, now it aims to block change and arrest the historical process. In a global region where history is again on the move, Europe is unable to play a constructive part. It is a fundamental problem, indeed. 'People have traditionally come for psychoanalytic conversation because the story they are telling themselves about their lives has stopped, or became too painful, or both,' Adam Phillips tells us. 'The aim of the analysis is to restore the loose ends – and the looser beginnings – to the story.'[91] But what should happen in the case of collective identities? What are cultural collectivities to do when their stories have become empty or painful? The European problem is of this order; it requires the analysis, which must be the self-analysis, of a whole culture.

One cannot be optimistic. There are no solid grounds for believing that

Europe might re-commit itself to the historical process. Is it actually capable of transforming its perceptions of the 'non-Europe' that surrounds it? In order to do so it would need to rid itself of its myths of the others, and to allow that they are real, diverse and complex peoples. It would have to dissipate these myths in order to understand the part it has played in the disruption and destruction of their cultures and in the turmoil and violence that have afflicted the region. That would mean accepting its responsibilities in the events of past history. On this basis, it would, perhaps, be possible to engage in the crossing and exchanging of memories that is necessary to achieve mutual forgiveness; as Ricoeur says, 'we cannot forgive if we have forgotten'.[92] Through reconciliation, Europe might be able to turn to the future more hopefully; overcoming its past, it might take up the loose ends of its story more creatively. Might it not then acknowledge that change, and the possibilities inherent in change, cannot be created out of itself alone? Cultural experience is always experience of the others: the others, the real others, are the indispensable transformational objects in historical change. History is created out of cultures in relation and interaction: interrupting identities. 'Non-Europe' could now play a critical role in re-historicizing European culture. It affords the possibility 'to expose the whole range of European experience, in depth, to other norms, other values, and perhaps other categories'.[93] And, in certain cases, it also affords the possibility of seeing what may be achieved on the basis of those other norms and values. This is what I have tried to bring out in the case of Turkey. Europe must become open to cultural interruption. Without this there is only the past. Through it, the opportunity of redeeming the hopes of the past.

Notes

1 Cornelius Castoriadis, 'Psychanalyse et politique', in *Le Monde morcelé*, Seuil, Paris, 1990, pp. 153–4.

2 Ibid., pp. 148–9, 153.

3 Cornelius Castoriadis, 'Le Délabrement de l'Occident', *Esprit*, December 1991, p. 38.

4 Agnes Heller, 'Modernity's pendulum', *Thesis Eleven*, 31, 1992, p. 4.

5 Ibid., pp. 2, 9.

6 Ibid., p. 4.

7 Adonis, *An Introduction to Arab Poetics*, Saqi Books, London, 1990, p. 85.

8 Aziz Al-Azmeh, *Islams and Modernities*, Verso, London, 1993, p. 42; Al-Azmeh deals with the discourse of cultural authenticity in Chapter 2.

9 Adonis, *Arab Poetics*, p. 81.

10 Ibid., p. 80.

11 Daryush Shayegan, *Le Regard mutilé*, Albin Michel, Paris, 1989.

12 Castoriadis, 'Le Délabrement', pp. 39–40; see also Cornelius Castoriadis, 'The retreat from autonomy: post-modernism as generalised conformism', *Thesis Eleven*, 31, 1992.

13 Moustapha Safouan, 'Two modes of transmission: creative and fixed', *Critical Quarterly*, 36, 2, 1994.

14 Hichem Djait, *Europe and Islam*, University of California Press, Berkeley, 1985, p. 173.

See also Abdullah An-Na'im, 'What do we mean by universal?', *Index on Censorship*, 23, 4–5, September–October 1994.

15 Paul Ricoeur, 'Universality and the power of difference', in Richard Kearney (ed.), *Visions of Europe*, Wolfhound Press, Dublin, 1992, p. 123.

16 Arnold J. Toynbee, 'The Turkish state of mind', *Atlantic Monthly*, 136, October 1925, p. 556.

17 Ibid.

18 Zafer Şenocak, *Atlas des Tropischen Deutschlands*, Babel Verlag, Berlin, 1993, p. 22.

19 Dankwart A. Rustow, *Turkey: American's Forgotten Ally*, Council on Foreign Relations, New York, 1987; see also David Barchard, *Turkey and the West*, Royal Institute of International Affairs/Routledge & Kegan Paul, London, 1985.

20 Sabri Sayari, 'Turkey: the changing European security environment and the Gulf crisis,' *Middle East Journal*, 46, 1, Winter 1992; Graham E. Fuller and Ian O. Lesser, *Turkey's New Geopolitics: From the Balkans to Western China*, Westview Press, Boulder, CO, 1993.

21 Richard Falk, 'A meditative comment on European doors', in Taciser Belge (ed.), *Where Does Europe End?*, Helsinki Citizens' Assembly-Turkey, Istanbul, 1993, p. 63.

22 Interview with Süleyman Demirel, *Financial Times*, Survey on Turkey, 7 May 1993. On the background of the Turkish application for membership of the European Union, see Ahmet Evin and Geoffrey Denton (eds), *Turkey and the European Community*, Leske & Budrich, Opladen, 1990; Heinz Kramer, 'EC–Turkish Relations: unfinished forever?', in Peter Ludlow (ed.), *Europe and the Mediterranean*, Brassey's, London, 1994.

23 Philip Robins, *Turkey and the Middle East*, Royal Institute of International Affairs/Pinter Publishers, London, 1991, p. 3.

24 Scott Sullivan, 'The Turks want in', *Newsweek*, 21 May 1991, p. 16.

25 'A Europe of sixteen', *Newsweek*, 6 August 1990, p. 54. Cf. 'Turks have, in historical terms, only recently been told that they are really a part of Europe, and not, as the former Ottoman Empire, the leader and the holy centre of the world of Islam' (Hazhir Termourian, 'Why Turkey had better look East', *New European*, 4, 4, 1991, p. 35).

26 Peter Millar, 'Turkey must look to its Mongol heritage', *The European*, 25–27 October 1991. Cf. 'The Turks are an Asiatic people who have settled but not taken root in our continent' (Sir Charles Eliot, *Turkey in Europe* [1900], Frank Cass, London, 1965, p. 1).

27 Arnold J. Toynbee, *The Western Question in Greece and Turkey*, Constable, London, 2nd edn, 1923, p. 2. See also Kevin Robins and Asu Aksoy, 'Culture and marginality in the new Europe', in Costis Hadjimichalis and David Sadler (eds), *Europe at the Margins*, Wiley, Chichester, 1995; Çaglar Keyder, 'The dilemma of cultural identity on the margin of Europe', *Review*, 16, 1, Winter 1993.

28 Ivaylo Ditchev, 'Europe tragique', *Les Temps modernes*, 565–6, August–September 1993, pp. 202, 206.

29 Claudio Magris, *Danube*, Collins Harvill, London, 1990, pp. 177–8.

30 Zafer Şenocak, *War Hitler Araber? IrreFührungen an den Rand Europas*, Babel Verlag Hund & Van Uffelen, Berlin, 1994, p. 93.

31 Speech to the teachers of Bursa, 27 October 1992. Quoted in Stéphane Yerasimos, 'The monoparty period', in Irvin C. Schick and Ertugrul Ahmet Tonak (eds), *Turkey in Transition: New Perspectives*, Oxford University Press, New York, 1987, p. 77.

32 Ibid., p. 87.

33 Toynbee describes nationalism as 'this fatal Western idea'. 'The value of this nationality principle,' he argues, 'depends on the prevalence of solid blocks of "homophone" population, a condition which is unusual in the homelands of civilisations, which are perpetually drawing into their focus fresh reinforcements of populations from all quarters. No doubt this is the reason why no known civilisation except ours has made community of language the basis of political demarcation; and in this the Near and Middle East both conform to the general rule, while we are exceptions' (Toynbee, *The Western Question*, pp. 17–18, 16).

34 Şerif Mardin, 'Religion in modern Turkey', *International Social Science Journal*, 19, 2, 1977, p. 279.

35 Şenocak, *War Hitler Araber?*, pp. 82–3. In her novella set in one of the squatter settlements (*gecekondu*), Latife Tekin uses a physical, rather than psychological image:

At the time the men of Flower Hill were struggling to find work, a shiny blue sign – 'Nato Avenue' – was hung on the wall of one of the chocolate factories up Rubbish Road. United by curiosity they marched with their sideways walk until they arrived under the street sign, but as they could not figure out what the writing on it stood for or why it had been put up, they turned back. . . . Discussions went on, and they finished up by speculating on the meaning of 'Nato'. Some said that once upon a time the papers had written about Nato, and others that the radio played folk songs from Nato. One said it meant 'Armed Force', another, 'Bombing'. The hut people were upset by this talk of arms and bombs and did not warm to the name. They came in a body to Güllü Baba's place. He listened in silence. In his own mind he attributed the deformity of the Flower Hill men to the erection of the street sign. He struck the ground with his stick again and again and asked, 'Can it possibly be that Nato has some connection with deformity?' (Latife Tekin, *Berji Kristin: Tales from the Garbage Hills*, Marion Boyars, London, 1993, pp. 36–7)

36 Quoted in Taner Timur, 'The Ottoman heritage', in Schick and Ahmet Tonak (eds), *Turkey in Transition*, p. 5.

37 Yerasimos, 'The monoparty period', p. 77. The squatters in *Berji Kristin* are curious to know about the arrival of the Romanies in Turkey, but 'to be able to imagine what it was like when the Romanies first settled in these parts, the squatters had to know about a certain "Ottoman Empire" . . . that where they now lived there had once been an empire of this name' (Tekin, *Berji Kristin*, p. 109).

38 On the creative possibilities of this spirit, and its tragic impoverishment by the spread of European nationalism, see Georges Corm, *L'Europe et l'Orient: de la Balkanisation à la Libanisation – histoire d'une modernité inaccomplie*, La Découverte, Paris, 1989, part 1, 'De L'Écroulement des empires'.

39 See Stéphane Yerasimos, 'Ethnies et minorités en Turquie: quelques réflexions sur un problème insoluble', *Les Temps Modernes*, 456–7, 1984.

40 S.D. Salamone, 'The dialectics of Turkish national identity: ethnic boundary maintenance and state ideology', part 2, *East European Quarterly*, 23, 2, June 1989, pp. 238, 227.

41 'Sooner or later this attempt [to assimilate the Kurds], which will break down as soon as the spirit of nationalism catches the Kurds in their turn, will involve the Turks in fresh misfortunes' (Toynbee, 'Turkish state of mind', p. 556).

42 Richard Tapper, 'Introduction', in Richard Tapper (ed.), *Islam in Modern Turkey: Religion, Politics and Literature in a Secular State*, I.B. Tauris, London, 1991, p. 7. İlkay Sunar and Binnaz Toprak draw attention to 'the ethical lacunae left by the secular-positivism of the republican outlook', arguing that it left the people 'wandering and deprived of an ethos grounded in a symbolism believed to be true' ('Islam in politics: the case of Turkey', *Government and Opposition*, 18, 4, 1983, p. 441).

43 Serif Mardin, 'Europe in Turkey', in Taciser Belge (ed.), *Where Does Europe End?*, Helsinki Citizens' Assembly-Turkey, Istanbul, 1993, p. 119.

44 Ali Kazancigil, 'De la modernité octroyée par l'état à la modernité engendrée par la société en Turquie', *Cahiers d'Etudes sur la Méditerranée Orientale et le Monde Turco-Iranien*, 9, 1990, p. 11.

45 O. Cengiz Aktar, *L'Occidentalisation de le Turquie: essai critique*, Editions L'Harmattan, Paris, 1985, p. 125.

46 Ibid., pp. 126, 105.

47 On the origins of Turkism in the ideas of the nationalist ideologue, Ziya Gökalp (1875–1924), see Uriel Heyd, *Foundations of Turkish Nationalism: The Life and Teachings of Ziya Gökalp*, Luzac/The Harvill Press, London, 1950. Gökalp's nationalism and Turkism are akin to those of nineteenth-century Romantic nationalisms, particularly of the German type. Whilst these perspectives are now de-emphasized in the official culture, they continue to play a crucial part in right-wing and racist nationalism in Turkey. See Ayşe Neviye Çağlar, 'The Greywolves as metaphor', in Andrew Finkel and Nükhet Sirman (eds), *Turkish State, Turkish Society*, Routledge, London, 1990.

48 Sunar and Toprak, 'Islam in politics', p. 430. Cf. 'Many feel that both for moral and for

political reasons some restoration of Islamic belief and practice is necessary for the health of the Turkish people' (Bernard Lewis, 'Islamic revival in Turkey', *International Affairs*, 28, 1, January 1952, p. 46).

49 Feroz Ahmad, 'Islamic reassertion in Turkey', *Third World Quarterly*, 10, 2, April 1988, p. 757.

50 Baskın Oran, 'Occidentalisation, nationalisme et "Synthèse Turco-Islamique"', *Cahiers d'Etudes sur la Méditerannée Orientale et le Mondce Turco-Iranien*, 10, 1990, p. 50. Binnaz Toprak sees it as 'part of a global trend towards a new type of conservatism which emphasises traditional values in reaction to the political and social radicalisation of the 1960s and 1970s' ('Religion as state ideology in a secular setting: the Turkish-Islamic synthesis', in Malcolm Wagstaff (ed.), *Aspects of Religion in Secular Turkey*, Centre for Middle Eastern and Islamic Studies, University of Durham, Occasional Paper Series, no. 40, 1990, p. 10).

51 Salamone, 'Dialectics', p. 241.

52 Nilüfer Göle, 'Liberal yanılgı', *Türkiye Günlüğü*, 24, Autumn 1993, p. 13.

53 Kazancığil, 'De la modernité', p. 12.

54 On the transformation of broadcasting through commercialization, and its dramatic significance for Turkish cultural life, see Haluk Şahin and Asu Aksoy, 'Global media and cultural identity in Turkey', *Journal of Communication*, 43, 2, Spring 1993.

55 Fuller and Lesser, *Turkey's New Geopolitics*, p. 48. On Turkey's new geopolitical role, see, *inter alia*, Robins, *Turkey and the Middle East*; William Hale, 'Turkey, the Middle East and the Gulf crisis', *International Affairs*, 68, 4, 1992; Philip Robins, 'Between sentiment and self-interest: Turkey's policy towards Azerbaijan and the Central Asian States', *Middle East Journal*, 47, 4, Autumn 1993; Ömer Faruk Gençkaya, 'The Black Sea economic co-operation project: a regional challenge to European integration', *International Social Science Journal*, 138, November 1993.

56 Augustus Richard Norton argues that these global developments are promoting the development of civil society throughout the Middle East (in which he includes Turkey). They are leading, he argues, to increasing challenges to state legitimacy: 'The new language of politics in the Middle East speaks of participation, cultural authenticity, freedom, and even democracy.' Whilst the state is not disappearing, 'no understanding of the contemporary Middle East will be complete unless it takes into account the status of civil society in the region' ('The future of civil society in the Middle East', *Middle East Journal*, 47, 2, Spring 1993, pp. 206, 209).

57 Turgut Özal, *Turkey in Europe and Europe in Turkey*, K. Rustem & Brother, Nicosia, 1991, p. 305.

58 Ibid., pp. 296, 311.

59 Ibid., p. 296.

60 Vehbi Dinçerler, 'Özal, İttihat-Terraki çizgisini asmak istedi', *İzlenim*, 23 April 1994, p. 25.

61 Mustafa Çalık, 'Özal: "Türkiye'nin önünde hacet kapıları açılmıştır!"', *Türkiye Günlüğü*, 19, Summer 1992, p. 12.

62 Özal, *Turkey in Europe*, p. 310.

63 Ibid.

64 The idea of 'neo-Ottomanism', which was current in certain circles, emphasized that the constituent elements of Turkish identity sprang from both the Ottoman heritage and the Republican one. See Nur Vergin, 'Yeniden yapılanma Türkiye'nin tekamülü olacaktır', *Yeni Zemin*, 1, January 1993, p. 66.

65 Étienne Copeaux and Stéphane Yerasimos, 'La Bosnie vue du Bosphore', *Hérodote*, 67, October–December 1992, p. 152.

66 Neil Ascherson writes about a certain Wolfgang Feuerstein, a German intellectual working in a village in the Black Forest to rescue the Laz people from 'assimilation'. He has given the Laz an alphabet and schoolbooks, and is working on a dictionary and a sourcebook of Laz history. The Laz are to be reinvented as a *Volk* with their own cultural mission. 'Journey to the end of an alphabet', *Independent on Sunday*, 7 November 1993.

67 Jonathan Rugman, 'Turkey's secret war against Kurds', *Observer*, 13 February 1994.

68 Ahmad, 'Islamic reassertion', p. 758.

69 Martin Stokes, *The Arabesk Debate: Music and Musicians in Turkey*, Clarendon Press, Oxford, 1992, p. 1. See also Martin Stokes, 'Islam, the Turkish state and arabesk', *Popular Music*, 11, 2, 1992; Gilles Andrieux, 'Musique: alaturka ou alafranka', *Autrement*, Série monde, 29, March 1988.

70 See Asu Aksoy and Kevin Robins, 'Istanbul between civilisation and discontent', *New Perspectives on Turkey*, 10, Spring 1994.

71 Ayşe Öncü, 'Packaging Islam: cultural politics on the landscape of Turkish commercial television', *New Perspectives on Turkey*, 10, Spring, 1994.

72 Rusen Çakır, 'La Mobilisation islamique en Turquie', *Esprit*, August 1992. On religious foundations, see also Faruk Bilici, 'Sociabilité et expression politique islamistes en Turquie: les nouveaux *vakifs*', *Revue Française de Science Politique*, 43, 3, June 1993.

73 See Fulya Atacan, *Radical Islamic Thought in Turkey: Zaman newspaper, 3 November 1986–30 May 1987*, Current Turkish Thought, no. 64, Redhouse Press, Istanbul, 1991.

74 See Michael E. Meeker, 'The new Muslim intellectuals in the Republic of Turkey', in Tapper, *Islam in Modern Turkey*; Binnaz Toprak, 'Islamist intellectuals: revolt against industry and technology', in Metin Heper, Ayşe Öncü and Heinz Kramer (eds), *Turkey and the West: Changing Political and Cultural Identities*, I.B. Tauris, London, 1993.

75 Quoted in Atacan, *Radical Islamic Thought*, p. 8.

76 Ali Bulaç, 'Medine vesikası hakkında genel bilgiler', *Birikim*, 38–9, 1992; 'Sözleşme temelinde toplumsal proje', *Birikim*, 40, 1992. On the significance of the Medinan regime in Islamic utopianism, see Al-Azmeh, *Islams*, pp. 97–8.

77 Rusen Çakır, 'Islami bir liberalizm doğacak', *Aydınlık*, 15 July 1993.

78 Nilüfer Göle, 'Ingénieurs islamistes et étudiantes volées en Turquie: entre le totalitarisme et l'individualisme', in Gilles Kepel and Yann Richard (eds), *Intellectuels et militants de l'islam contemporain*, Editions du Seuil, Paris, 1990, p. 181.

79 Nilüfer Göle, 'Islami dokunulmazlar, laikler ve radikal demokratlar', *Türkiye Günlüğü*, 27 March–April 1994, p. 17.

80 On the dangers of right-wing nationalism, see Étienne Copeaux, 'Le rêve du Loup Gris: les aspirations turques en Asie Centrale', *Hérodote*, 64, 1992.

81 Pir Sultan Abdal was an Alevi Muslim. The Alevis are in the Shi'ite tradition, and constitute a large minority in the Turkish population (somewhere between ten and fifteen million). Historically they have aligned themselves with Kemalism, as a defence against hostility from Turkey's majority Sunnis. The Sivas massacre also highlights the tensions, then, between Sunni and Alevi Muslims. On the Alevis, see Altan Gökalp, 'La question réligieuse en Turquie', *Projet*, 231, Autumn 1991.

82 Göle, 'Islami dokunulmazlar', p. 14.

83 Ahmet Insel, 'On unachieved democracy', *Thesis Eleven*, 33, 1992, p. 89.

84 Jonah Goldstein and Jeremy Rayner, 'The politics of identity in late modern society', *Theory & Society*, 23, 1994, pp. 381–2.

85 Özal, *Turkey in Europe*, pp. 304, 302, 317.

86 On the anti-western sentiments of the extreme Right, see Copeaux, 'Le rêve'. On the way in which such sentiments have been intensified by western attitudes to Bosnia, see Copeaux and Yérasimos, 'La Bosnie'. With regard to the potential for anti-western and anti-European attitudes among Muslims, see Rusen Çakır, 'Les mouvements Islamistes Turcs et l'Europe', *Cahiers d'Etudes sur la Méditerrannée Orientale et le Monde Turco-Iranien*, 14, 1990.

87 Corm, *L'Europe et l'Orient*, p. 372.

88 Djait, *Europe and Islam*, p. 1.

89 François Ewald, 'Jean Baudrillard: "une ultime réaction vitale"', *Magazine Littéraire*, 323, July–August 1994, p. 22.

90 Ibid.

91 Adam Phillips, *On Kissing, Tickling and Being Bored*, Faber & Faber, London, 1993, p. xx.

92 Ricoeur, 'Universality', p. 123.

93 Djait, *Europe and Islam*, p. 6.

6

Identity and Cultural Studies: Is That All There Is?

Lawrence Grossberg

There are many surprising aspects of the current success of cultural studies. I want here to focus on one of the most puzzling: namely, that even as the space of cultural studies seems to encompass an expanding range of theoretical positions, disciplinary matrices and geographical traditions, cultural studies itself seems to be identified with a shrinking set of theoretical and political issues. There is a noticeable tendency to equate cultural studies with the theory and politics of identity and difference, especially as a result of the influence of so-called postcolonial theory and critical race theory. I do not mean to deny the importance of such work in cultural studies, or for contemporary political struggles. But I do want to question some of its theoretical underpinnings and political consequences. Of course, a concern with the politics of identity is not limited to cultural studies, and broader currents of feminist, anti-racist and anti-colonialist investigation have produced important and influential work. Certainly, the assumption that contemporary politics is and should be organized around struggles over identity is not limited to contemporary academic movements. The model of identity and difference, as the dominant model of political organization, is in fact very recent. What constitutes such a politics is the assumption of a self-defined constituency acting in the interests (for the politics) of that definition. Within such constituencies, every individual is a representative of the totality. But in fact, such constituencies do not and need not exist, except as the work of power – or of articulation. My argument is not with the fact that identity has been – and may still be – the site around which people are struggling, nor even with the significant advances that such struggles enabled over the past decades. Rather, it is a question of whether this is a fruitful path to continue following. Appropriating a statement from Bailey and Hall (1992: 15).

> It is perfectly possible that what is politically progressive and opens up new discursive opportunities in the 1970s and 1980s can become a form of closure – and have a repressive value – by the time it is installed as the dominant genre. . . . It will run out of steam; it will become a style; people will use it not

because it opens up anything but because they are being spoken by it, and at that point, you need another shift.

Again, I do not mean to reject the concept of identity or its political importance in certain struggles. I do however want to challenge a number of elements of contemporary work: the subsumption of identity into a particular set of modernist logics and the assumption that such structures of identity necessarily define the appropriate models and sites of political struggle. That is, I want at least to raise the question of whether every struggle over power can and should be organized around and understood in terms of issues of identity, and to suggest that it may be necessary to rearticulate the category of identity and its place in cultural studies as well as in cultural politics. Thus, my project is not to escape the discourse of identity but to relocate it, to rearticulate it by placing it within the larger context of modern formations of power. I want to propose that cultural studies needs to move beyond models of oppression, both the 'colonial model' of the oppressor and oppressed, and the 'transgression model' of oppression and resistance. Cultural studies needs to move towards a model of articulation as 'transformative practice', as a singular becoming of a community. Both models of oppression are not only inappropriate to contemporary relations of power, they are also incapable of creating alliances; they cannot tell us how to interpellate various fractions of the population in different relations to power into the struggle for change. For example, how can we involve fractions of the empowered in something other than a masochistic, guilt-ridden way? My feeling is that an answer depends upon rearticulating the question of identity into a question about the possibility of constructing historical agency, and giving up notions of resistance that assume a subject standing entirely outside of and against a well established structure of power.

For example, discussions of multiculturalism too quickly assume a necessary relation between identity and culture. But in what sense does a culture 'belong' to a group? If it is historical, then we are likely to be pulled into strongly conservative positions (for example American culture is European) and certainly, in that case, the ideology of progress will reinscribe structures of racism, imperialism and ethnocentrism. If it is ethnic, then the US – in fact, every society – is, and probably always has been, multicultural. If it is spatial, then the problems of contemporary mobility appear insurmountable. I would suggest that the question of a multicultural society is a normative ethical one: to what extent can a society continue to exist without a common, albeit constantly rearticulated and negotiated, culture? What are the conditions through which people can belong to a common collective without becoming representatives of a single definition? After all, one cannot deny that the US is and has been a multi-ethnic society with a wide range of cultural practices. What is it that is changing? What are the questions that need to be addressed? What are possible new models of political communities and alliances?

It is by now common to assert that the centrality of the concept of identity in both theoretical and political discourses is a 'modern' development. If identity as a central problematic is modern, there are at least three aspects or logics that constitute the terrain within which that relationship is constituted: a logic of difference; a logic of individuality; and a logic of temporality. I want to contest the current direction of cultural studies by locating its theoretical foundations in each of these logics, and offering three corresponding alternatives: a logic of otherness; a logic of productivity; and a logic of spatiality. If identity is somehow constituted by and constitutive of modernity, then the current discourses of identity fail to challenge their own location within, and implication with, the formations of modern power. Obviously, I can only hope to provide the barest outlines of my argument here.[1]

Identity and difference in cultural studies

Within cultural studies, investigations of the constitution and politics of identity are often predicated on a distinction, nicely articulated by Hall (1990), between two forms of struggle over – two models of the production of – identities. It is important to recognize that Hall offers this, not as a theoretical distinction, although it certainly can be mapped on to the dispute between essentialists and anti-essentialists, but as a historical and strategic distinction. The first model assumes that there is some intrinsic and essential content to any identity which is defined by either a common origin or a common structure of experience or both. Struggling against existing constructions of a particular identity takes the form of contesting negative images with positive ones, and of trying to discover the 'authentic' and 'original' content of the identity. Basically, the struggle over representations of identity here takes the form of offering one fully constituted, separate and distinct identity in place of another.

The second model emphasizes the impossibility of such fully constituted, separate and distinct identities. It denies the existence of authentic and originary identities based in a universally shared origin or experience. Identities are always relational and incomplete, in process. Any identity depends upon its difference from, its negation of, some other term, even as the identity of the latter term depends upon its difference from, its negation of, the former. As Hall (1991: 21) puts it: 'Identity is a structured representation which only achieves its positive through the narrow eye of the negative. It has to go through the eye of the needle of the other before it can construct itself.' Identity is always a temporary and unstable effect of relations which define identities by marking differences. Thus the emphasis here is on the multiplicity of identities and differences rather than on a singular identity and on the connections or articulations between the fragments or differences. The fact of multiple identities gives rise to the necessity of what Kobena Mercer has called 'the mantra of race, class and gender (1992b: 34). 'The challenge is to be able to theorize more than one difference at once.' This suggests a much more difficult politics, because the sides are not given in advance, nor in neat divisions. As Michele Wallace (1994: 185) says, echoing June Jordan, 'the thing that needed to be said – women are not to be trusted just because they're women, anymore than blacks are to be trusted because they're black, or gays because they're gay and so on.' Here struggles over identity no longer involve questions of adequacy or distortion, but of the politics of representation itself. That is, politics involves questioning how identities are produced and taken up through practices of representation. Obviously influenced by Derrida, such a position sees identity as an entirely cultural, even an entirely linguistic, construction.[2] While this model certainly suggests that the identity of one term cannot be explored or challenged without a simultaneous investigation of the second term, this is rarely the case in practice. Most work in cultural studies is concerned with investigating and challenging the construction of subaltern, marginalized or dominated identities, although some recent work has begun to explore dominant identities as social constructions. Rarely, however, are the two ever studied together, as the theory would seem to dictate, as mutually constitutive.

It is obviously this second model which defines work around identity in cultural studies, but I do not mean to suggest that this model defines a singular theoretical position or vocabulary. On the contrary, there are a number of different, overlapping, intersecting and sometimes even competing figures which, taken together, define the space within which cultural studies has theorized the problem of identity. Often, they function together to define specific theories. Interestingly, these figures construct a continuum of images of spatiality, although, as I will suggest, they are, for the most part, structures of temporality. I will describe these figures as: *différance*, fragmentation, hybridity, border and diaspora.

The figure of *différance* describes a particular constitutive relation of negativity in which the subordinate term (the marginalized other or subaltern) is a necessary and internal force of destabilization existing within the identity of the dominant term. The subaltern here is itself constitutive of, and necessary for, the dominant term. The instability of any dominant identity – since it must always and already incorporate its negation – is the result of the very nature of language and signification. The subaltern represents an inherent ambiguity or instability at the centre of any formation of language (or identity) which constantly undermines language's power to define a unified stable identity. We can identify two variants of this figure: notions of the 'supplement' locate the other outside of the field of subjectivity as it were, as pure excess; notions of 'negativity' locate the other within the field of subjectivity as a constitutive exotic other. In the former, the subaltern constitutes the boundaries of the very possibility of subjectivity; in the latter, the subaltern may be granted an incomprehensible subjectivity. There are numerous examples of these two variants of the figure of *différance* in contemporary theories of identity. For example, Lyotard (1990) sees 'the Jews' as that which European culture cannot identify because its exclusion, its unnameability, is itself constitutive of European identity. Similarly, Bhabha's (1994) notion of mimicry as an intentional misappropriation of the dominant discourse locates the power of the subaltern in a kind of textual insurrection in which the subaltern is defined only by its internal negation of the colonizer. De Certeau's (1984) attempt to define subordinate populations only by their lack of a place which would entitle them to their own practices or strategies similarly ends up defining the subaltern as pure *différance*. Finally, there is a common reading of Said's *Orientalism* (1978) in which the dominant power necessarily constructs its other as a repressed and desired difference.

The figure of *fragmentation* emphasizes the multiplicity of identities and of positions within any apparent identity. It thus sees a particular concrete or lived identity as 'a kind of disassembled and reassembled unity' (Haraway, 1991: 174). Identities are thus always contradictory, made up out of partial fragments. Theories of fragmentation can focus on the fragmentation of either individual identities or of the social categories (of difference) within which individuals are placed, or some combination of the two. Further, such fragmentations can be seen as either historical or constitutive. This is perhaps the most powerful image, certainly in British cultural studies, with echoes in Hebdige's notion of 'cut "n" mix' and Gilroy's notion of syncretism. Donna Haraway (1991: 174) also seems to offer such a figure in the image of a cyborg as 'a potent subjectivity synthesized from the fusion of outsider identities'. Or, from David Bailey and Stuart Hall (1992: 21): 'Identities can, therefore, be contradictory and are always situational. . . . In short, we are all involved in a series of political games around fractured or decentered identities . . . since black signifies a range of experiences, the act of representation becomes not just about decentering the subject but actually exploring the kaleidoscopic conditions of blackness.'

The figure of *hybridity* is more difficult to characterize for it is often used synonymously with a number of other figures. Nevertheless, I will use it to describe three different images of *border* existences, of subaltern identities as existing between two competing identities. Images of a *'third space'* (as in Bhabha) see subaltern identities as unique third terms literally defining an 'in-between' place inhabited by the subaltern. Images of *liminality* collapse the geography of the third space into the border itself; the subaltern lives, as it were, on the border. In both of these variants of hybridity, the subaltern is neither one nor the other but is defined by its location in a unique spatial condition which constitutes it as different from either alternative. Neither colonizer nor precolonial subject, the postcolonial subject exists as a unique hybrid which may, by definition, constitute the other two as well. Closely related to these two figures of hybridity is that of the *'border-crossing'*, marking an image of between-ness which does not construct a place or condition of its own other than the mobility, uncertainty and multiplicity of the fact of the constant border-crossing itself. Often, these three versions of hybridity are conflated in various ways, as in Gloria Anzaldua's (1987: 37) description of the *Atzlan*: 'A borderland is a vague and undetermined place created by the emotional residue of an unnatural boundary. . . . People who inhabit both realities . . . are forced to live in the interface between the two.'

Finally, the figure of *diaspora* is closely related to that of border-crossing, but it is often given a more diachronic inflection. This figure has become increasingly visible, through the work of anthropologists such as James Clifford and Smadar Lavie, cultural critics such as Paul Gilroy, and various postcolonial theorists. As Jim Clifford describes it (1994: 308), 'the term "diaspora" is a signifier not simply of transnationality and movement, but of political struggles to define the local – I would prefer to call it place – as a distinctive community, in historical contexts of displacement'. That is, diaspora emphasizes the historically spatial fluidity and intentionality of identity, its articulation to structures of historical movements (whether forced or chosen, necessary or desired). Diaspora links identity to spatial location and identifications, to 'histories of alternative cosmopolitanisms and diasporic networks' (Clifford, in press). While this figure offers significantly new possibilities for a cultural politics that avoids many of the logics of the modern – by rooting identity in structures of affiliations and ways of belonging, it is, too often, drawn back into the modern. Identity is ultimately returned to history, and the subaltern's place is subsumed within a history of movements and an experience of oppression which privileges particular exemplars as the 'proper' figures of identity.

Such theories – built on the range of diverse figures described above – have recently come under attack (e.g. Parry, 1987; O'Hanlon, 1988): for ignoring the fragmentary and conflictual nature of the discourses of power (different at different places and spaces of course); for ignoring the heterogeneity of power and apparently reducing it to discourses of representation and ignoring its material realities; for ignoring the positivity of the subaltern – as the possessor of other knowledges and traditions; as having their own history in which there are power relations defined within the ranks of the subordinated. And one might add yet another problem concerning the status of the marginal or subordinate in these figures. On what grounds do we assume that a privileged or even different structure of subjectivity belongs to the subaltern? And if, as Hall suggests, the marginal has become central, is it not descriptive of the contemporary subject? The other side of the question is, can one form of subordination become the model of all structural domination? In so far as we have now created a figure of the subaltern, have we not developed another universalizing theory, providing answers to any local struggle before we have even begun, since we know we will always find the production of the other as different?

Cultural identity and the logic of difference

But, as I have said, I want to contest such theories of identity on broader grounds: namely, that they have failed to open up a space of anti- or even counter-modernity. In other words, they are ultimately unable to contest the formations of modern power at their deepest levels because they remain within the strategic forms of modern logic: difference, individuality, and temporality. I will begin by considering the nature of the logic of difference which offers a particular interpretation of the relation between identity and modernity, an interpretation which, by its very logic, denies the possibility of any alternative which might escape its logic (the logic of the modern). Since the modern constitutes its own identity by differentiating itself from an-other (usually tradition as a temporal other or spatial others transformed into temporal others), identity is always constituted out of difference. The modern makes identities into social constructions. And thus a counter-modern politics has to contest the particular relations of identity and difference that have been constructed by, offered and taken up in the modern. Here, we have no choice but to start with questions of difference, and to explore the nature of difference and its relation to identity. This is certainly the dominant response in cultural studies, but the real question is, to what end? If difference is irrevocable, then modernity is inescapable. It may seem somewhat ironic that just as we discover that not only particular identities but identity itself is socially constructed, we organize political struggle within the category of identity, around particular socially constructed identities.

But there is, of course, an alternative understanding of the relation of the modern and identity which suggests that the modern transforms all relations of identity into relations of difference. Thus, the modern constitutes not identity out of difference but difference out of identity. The modern never constitutes itself as an identity (different from others) but as a difference (always different from itself – across time and space). In this sense, the fundamental structures of modernity are always productions of difference. Here the problem is to avoid starting with questions of difference; a counter-modern politics has to elude the logic of difference, and to (re-)capture the possibility of a politics of otherness. If the first interpretation condemns itself (and every possible counter-strategy) to remaining within the modern, the second attempts to escape the determining boundaries of the modern by seeing the first interpretation as itself an historical product of modern power.

Let me attempt to clarify the relation between theories of difference and what I will call theories of otherness. The former are certainly dominant in contemporary theories and are built upon a very strong notion of difference, derived largely from structuralist and post-structuralist theory: that the identity or meaning of a term depends entirely (except perhaps for a necessary but indeterminate excess) on its relation to, its difference from, other terms. In fact, theories of difference take difference itself as given, as the economy out of which identities are produced. Theories of otherness, on the other hand, assume that difference is itself an historically produced economy, imposed in modern structures of power, on the real. Difference as much as identity is an effect of power. While such theories obviously accept a weak notion of difference (a is not b or c or d), they do not see such differences as fundamentally constitutive. Rather, they begin with a strong sense of otherness which recognizes that the other exists, in its own place, as what it is, independently of any *specific* relations. But what it is need not be defined in transcendental or essential terms; what it is can be defined by its particular (contextual) power to affect and be affected. That is, such views of otherness grant to each term an unspecified, but specifiable, positivity. After all, modern thought is not just binary but a particular kind of binary-producing machine, where binaries become constitutive differences in which the other is defined by its negativity. As Deleuze and Guattari put it (1987: 42):

> How to think about fragments whose sole relationship is sheer difference – fragments that are related to one another only in that each of them is different – without having recourse to any sort of original totality (not even one that has been lost), or to a subsequent totality that may not yet have come about.

In more philosophical terms, these alternatives can be located within the argument between Derrida and Foucault: for example, around their differing readings of Descartes (Derrida, 1978; Foucault, 1979). Derrida argues that Descartes's exclusion of madness from reason itself constituted the possibility and identity of reason. The relation between reason and madness is, then, an originary structure of difference in the sense that, once again, difference always exists at the centre of identity. And in that sense, for Derrida, Descartes is still alive since any conception of reason must produce and negate madness. For Foucault, on the other hand, Descartes's exclusion of madness was a philosophical representation of a real historical event; the exclusion was material and spatial as much as discursive. While this exclusion was necessary to establish the status of reason and to naturalize the identification of reason and subjectivity, it is not itself constitutive, either of reason or of madness. Each of these terms has its own positivity or exteriority which can and does affect the other. In that sense, for Foucault, Descartes is irrelevant today. It is not coincidental, of course, that Derrida argues that philosophy can never escape the logocentrism which, I would argue, is constitutive of modernity. Foucault often writes as if he had already done so.

Much of the contemporary work on identity can be seen as a struggle taking place in the space between Derrida and Foucault. Thus, for example, Laclau and Mouffe's (1985) influential work, which has contributed significantly to the theoretical frameworks within which cultural studies has approached questions of identitiy, can be seen as an attempt to bring Foucault and Derrida together (with the aid of Gramsci). But what has really happened is that Laclau and Mouffe have reread Foucault as if he were Derrida. Foucault's notion of the regularity of dispersion becomes an ensemble of differential positions; the rarity of discourse becomes exteriority as an excess found in the surplus of meaning. And Foucault's concern with subjectivization becomes the centrality of the production of subjects as the basis of the chain of discourse which produces both temporary fixity and the excess which destabilizes it.

Similarly, Edward Said claims to have based much of his work in *Orientalism* (1978) on Foucault. As numerous commentators have pointed out, however, the notion of 'Orientalism' is intentionally ambiguous in a way that makes it quite difficult to actually pin down Said's theoretical position. At times, Said seems to suggest that Orientalism is a mode of representation by which we distinguish ourselves from others, but again, as numerous critics have pointed out, this is insufficient for it would seem to condemn any attempt to represent the other. At another point, Said describes Orientalism as 'a style of thought based on an ontological and epistemological distinction', but he fails to consider the political history of the relationship between epistemology and ontology. Is it that any ontological distinction is an act of power, or is it that when such ontological distinctions are defined by and placed in the service of knowledge – that is, when epistemology is equated with or supersedes ontology – Orientalism emerges? Of course, Said actually does begin to sound like Foucault when he connects specific discourses and their distribution to the institutions of colonialism itself. Here we can see the crucial ambiguity in Said's thesis, an ambiguity which has itself defined the field of identity theories. To put it rather too simply, the question is, does 'the Oriental exist' apart from Orientalism? While many interpreters have responded in the negative, they have failed to distinguish a number of possible explanations. One possible interpretation of the existence of the Orient is tautological: since the Orient and the Oriental are constructions of colonial discourses, they cannot exist outside of those discourses. The Orient as an object of knowledge is the product of colonial relations of power. But is it so simple because, as numerous critics have pointed out, if this is the case, then all knowledge – and the construction of any object of knowledge – must itself be condemned as appropriative and oppressive. Is it not the articulation of knowledge into particular geo-economic and political relations that reconfigures curiosity into power?

There are at least three different positions on the existence of the Oriental which can be laid out along a continuum: the first sees it as pure excess or supplement, as the negativity at the heart of the Occident's own self-understanding. On this view, if it weren't the Orient that the West created, it would have had to have been somewhere else (and obviously, it was other places as well). The second position places the Orient and the Occident in an unequal relation of constitutive difference; each is necessary to the self-definition of the other. Each defines itself by marking itself as different from the other. But like any theory of constitution, there is a necessary uncertainty at the centre, for the fact is that each must exist independently of the relationship in order to be appropriated into the relation, and each must therefore, in some sense, have its own positivity. But this positivity is itself never specified for it is always deferred, always irrelevant to the constitutive relation itself. The third position would seem to have been Said's – that Orientalism involves actual material processes of colonization, travel, exploitation and domination. That is, people travelled to places and cultures that already existed. The Oriental, as it were, existed independently of the Orientalist. The act of power comes not in creating something from nothing, but in reducing something to nothing (to pure semantic and differential terms), in negating the positivity of the Arab world with all of its diversity, for example, to nothing but a singular constitutive other, to the different. Thus, it is precisely the articulation of difference on top of otherness that becomes the material site of discursive power and which is, I would argue, a fundamental logic of formations of modern power.

Starting from the last position, Said has, in his more recent work, explicitly attempted to define a practice that both inscribes and tran-scends cultural identity. As Benita Parry (1992) and others have pointed out, such a project opens up a series of potentially significant materialist questions: about the interdependence of metropolitan and colonial histories and cultures; about the changing modes of western capitalist penetration into other worlds; about the possibilities of (morally) representing others; about the relations between power and distinctions; about the specificity of western structures of power; about the relations between the cultures of imperialism and colonialism, and imperialism's non-discursive or non-cultural dynamics; and about the geopolitical configurations of power and power relations within cultural processes. But instead, the dominant deployment of Said has been to establish a simple chain from colonialism to the construction of cultural identities to the production of subjects (and sometimes, the 'discovery' of resistance). Thus a very different range of questions is raised: about how colonialism produces a particular subjectivity of the colonized or how it closes off the possibility of subjectivity, or some combination of the two. As Parry describes it, this involves theorizing 'the specificities of a (polymorphic) (post) colonial condition', understood almost entirely in terms of identity and subjectivity, whether it is assumed to be 'authentic' or not.[3] This use of Said also raises questions about how (post)colonial subjects (via cultural production and practices) subvert western colonial authority (usually as it is embodied in cultural forms themselves).[4] Or finally, it can be used to raise questions about the very politics of subjectivity and the search for a subject-position for the colonial subject, because subjectivity is only possible in the places constructed by the colonizer.[5] In fact, Spivak (1988) seems to argue that subjectivity is itself a western category and that, in the colonial relation, the West seeks to construct a subject as its other, what Parry refers to as the subject as the 'space of the Imperialist's self-consolidating other'. What all of these questions leave unanswered is the relationship between subjects, identities and agents, even though each is ultimately interested in the complex intersection of these questions. Instead, they seem content to study 'the continual struggle of the colonized to resolve the paradoxes which this displacement and dehumanization of indigenous processes of identification sets up in [his] daily existence' (O'Hanlon, 1988: 204–5).

I have already suggested that the modern itself is constituted by the logic of difference through which the modern is constructed as an 'adversarial space' living in 'an anxiety of contamination by its other' (Huyssen, 1986: vii). As Nietzsche pointed out, this logic of difference, in which the other is defined by its negativity, can only give rise to a politics of resentment. Increasingly, this logic of difference has come under attack: 'There is nothing remotely groovy about difference and diversity as political problems. . . . The management of diversity and difference through the bureaucratic mantra of race, class and gender encouraged the divisive rhetoric of being more marginal, more oppressed' (Mercer, 1992b: 33). And despite the intentions of anti-modernist critics, celebrations of difference do not give up a totalizing speaking situation of the modern; instead, 'it becomes the master of differing, offering a unified theory of difference' (Wark, 1992: 436). The alternative is to begin to construct a theory of otherness which is not essentialist, a theory of positivity based on notions of effectivity, belonging and, as Paul Gilroy (1993) describes it, 'the changing same'.

Cultural identity and the logic of individuality

Renato Rosaldo (1989: 201) has argued that we need to move away from the tacit assumption 'that conflates the notion of culture with the idea of difference' and towards an alternative notion of culture as productive. Deleuze and Guattari (1987: 210) suggest such a notion: 'the question . . . is not whether the status of women, or those on the bottom, is better or worse, but the type of organization from which that status results'. But I do not believe that the failure to articulate such a theory of culture is the product of the logic of difference; instead, what has prevented the development of a view of culture as production is a particular (modern) logic of individuality which has equated the various processes of individuation and thus collapsed the various planes of effectivity through which individuality is constituted into a single and simple structure.

In political terms, this is the modern invention of what O'Hanlon (1988) calls 'the virile figure of the subject-agent', that is, the modern 'humanistic individual' which is predicated on the identification of three different planes (and hence, three different issues): (1) the subject as a position defining the possibility and the source of experience and, by extension, of knowledge; (2) the agent as a position of activity; and (3) the self as the mark of a social identity. This equation of different 'maps of identification and belonging' – maps which define and produce where and how individuals fit into the world – inevitably gave rise to a paradox, especially when anti-essentialist arguments were mounted against any claims to the unity of both the subject and the self (again, often conflated in these arguments) and when critical arguments were mounted to demonstrate the social construction of both the subject and the self. The paradox is, quite simply, how can the individual be both cause and effect (an old question), both subject and subjected? Or in other words, how and where does one locate agency? This problem has animated the large body of contemporary political and theoretical work on the production of subordinate identities and the possibilities of resistance, whether in the name of the subaltern, feminism, anti-racism or postcolonialism. But the paradox may in fact be a disguise for the operation of modern power, if we see these three aspects of individuality as three distinct individuating productions. In this case, the task is to locate the 'machinery' by which each of these planes of identification and belonging is produced and subsequently articulated into structures of individuality (including bodies). Such machines describe the nature of human subjectivity, identity and agency as technologically produced relations which impose a particular organization and a particular conduct on the specific multiplicities operating on different planes of effects.

The question of the subject is an epistemological one, in the broadest sense of the term. The subject describes a position within a field of subjectivity or within a phenomenological field, produced by a particular subjectivating machine (since not all subjectivations are subjectifications). In so far as everyone experiences the world, subjectivity in some form must be a universal value (which in fact may be available to more than just the human). Everyone has some form of subjectivity and thus, in at least one sense, exists as a subject, although further research would have to specify the different forms of the existence of the subject. Everyone exists at the centre of a phenomenological field and thus has some access to experience, to some knowledge about themselves and their world. Of course, it may be that subjectivity as a value necessary for life is also unequally distributed, that some individuals may have the possibility of occupying more than one such position, that some positions may offer specific perspectives on reality that are different from others, that some positions come to be more valued than others. We can specify something about the modern form of subjectivity by drawing upon – and rereading – Althusser's (1971) argument: modern subjectivity must function, to some extent, to 'authorize' experience itself, even though, again, some positions may be better able to articulate and defend their 'authority'. In this sense, subjectivity[6] is not an ontological question but a contextually produced epistemological value. In Deleuzean terms, it is the product of a stratifying machine which produces the real as a relation of content (bodies) and expression (subjectivity as value).

Of course, subjectivity in this sense is abstract. And within human societies at least, it is always inscribed or distributed within cultural codes of differences that organize subjects by defining social identities. Such codes differentially value particular positions within the field of subjectivity. In other words, although everyone exists within the strata of subjectivity, they are also located at particular positions, each of which enables and constrains the possibilities of experience, of representing those experiences and of legitimizing those representations. Thus, the question of identity is one of social power and its articulation to, its anchorage in, the body of the population itself. In that sense, the self as the material embodiment of identities, the material points at which codes of difference and distinction are inscribed upon the socius, exists only after the inscription of historical differences. Hall (1992: 16), for example, describes the work of racism as being 'directed to secure us "over here" and them "over there", to fix each in its appointed species place'. In Deleuzean terms, the self is a product of a differentiating machine.

While it is clear that structures of subjectivity and self may influence and be articulated to questions of power and the possibilities of agency, there is no reason to assume that they are the same or equivalent. In fact, the question of agency is a matter of action and the nature of change. In its most common form, it is Wittgenstein's question: what is the difference between my raising my arm and my arm rising? It raises questions of intentionality but without assuming a mentalist or voluntarist answer. Obviously, within cultural studies, the question of agency involves more than a simple question of whether or how people control their own actions through some act of will. In classical modern terms, the issue of agency raises questions of the freedom of the will, or of how people can be responsible for their determined actions. But in broader cultural terms, questions of agency involve the possibilities of action as interventions into the processes by which reality is continually being transformed and power enacted. That is, in Marx's terms, the problem of agency is the problem of understanding how people make history in conditions not of their own making. Who gets to make history?

As O'Hanlon (1988: 207, 221) has argued, when the issue shifts to questions of agency and the possibilities of action, 'the subaltern is not a social category but a statement of power'. She continues:

> the subaltern is rendered marginal . . . in part through his inability, in his poverty, his lack of leisure, and his inarticulacy, to participate to any significant degree in the public institutions of civil society, with all the particular kinds of power which they confer, but most of all, through his consequently weaker ability to articulate civil society's self-sustaining myth.

That is, agency involves relations of participation and access, the possibilities of moving into particular sites of activity and power, and of belonging to them in such a way as to be able to enact their powers. In that sense, marginalization is not a spatial position but a vector defining access, mobility and the possibilities of investment. The question of agency is, then, how access and investment or participation (as a structure of belonging) are distributed within particular structured terrains. At the very least, this suggests that agency as a political problem cannot be conflated with issues of cultural identity or of epistemological possibilities. In other words, agency is not so much the 'mark of a subject, but the constituting mark of an abode'.[7] In Deleuzean terms, agency is the product of a territorializing machine.[8]

Cultural identity and the logic of temporality

But the modern is not merely defined by the logics of difference and individuality; it is also built upon a logic of temporality. That is, the modern embodies a specific temporalizing logic and a specific temporality. But the relationship goes deeper, for at the heart of modern thought and power lie two assumptions: that space and time are separable, and that time is more fundamental than space. This bifurcation and privileging of time over space is, I would argue, the crucial founding moment of modern philosophy. While many would locate the beginning of modern philosophy in the Cartesian problematic of the relation between the individual and reality (or truth) which was 'solved' by postulating the existence of a self-reflecting consciousness, it is, I believe, the Kantian solution which opened up the space of modern thought. Kant identified this consciousness with the mediating position of experience (giving rise to both phenomenological and structural theories of culture and knowledge). This privileging of consciousness (or in Romanticism, of imagination) as the space of the mediation of opposition depended upon two identifications: of opposition with difference and of subjectivity with temporality. Only thus was consciousness capable of appropriating the other in order to totalize and transcend chaos. The unity of the subject depended upon the unity of time. When this is filtered through the post-structuralist notion of textuality, the result is the assumed temporal discontinuity of discourse or what Bhabha (1992: 58) calls the 'temporal non-synchronicity of discourse'. The result is not only that identity is entirely an *historical* construction but that each of the three planes of individuation is constructed temporally: subjectivity as internal time consciousness; identity as the temporal construction of difference; and agency as the temporal displacement of difference. However, rather than developing this critique, I would like to briefly elaborate how the three planes of individuation might be understood within a spatial logic.[9]

Subjectivity as spatial is perhaps the clearest, for it involves taking literally the statement that people experience the world from a particular position – recognizing that such positions are in space rather than (or at least as much as in) time. In fact, much of the contemporary writing on diaspora points in this direction in so far as diaspora is understood as 'a whole range of phenomena that encourage multi-locale attachments, dwelling and travelling' (Clifford, in press). According to Gilroy (1992), such identifications or affiliations, rather than identities, are ways of belonging. They are the positions which define us spatially in relation to others, as entangled and separated. Similarly, Eric Michaels (1994) argued that people's access to knowledge is determined in part by the places – of conception, birth, death and residence – from and by which they speak, for one is always speaking for and from a specific geography of such places.[10] That is, subjectivity describes the points of attachment from which one experiences the world.

The self, or identity more narrowly understood, can be reconceptualized in spatial terms as different modes or vectors of spatial existence. Thus, if we wanted to describe the complex politics of identity in contemporary American urban society, we could contrast four such vectors: first, a population largely demobilized, with little or no ability to move out of predefined and enclosed spaces; second, a population with highly constrained but extensive lives of mobility; third, a highly mobile population which is nevertheless excluded from certain key places; and finally, a population living in a voluntarily imposed, increasingly fortress-like space but which, from within that space, as the result of a variety of technologies, is granted an extraordinary degree of mobility. These rather abstract descriptions can be made more concrete if we apply them to the antagonisms which erupted not long ago in Los Angeles. At the time of the event, the antagonisms seem to have been defined in largely essentialist terms. The only apparent alternative, based on the social construction of identity, seemed to preclude effective alliance as much as the antagonism itself. But it may be possible to displace the antagonisms from questions of identity *per se* to the more potentially sympathetic relations among different maps of spatial existence. Los Angeles would be seen then, not merely as a 'dual city', but as a complex system of competing and overlapping mobilities (which of course, would have to be located within national, regional and global spaces as well). The various populations of Los Angeles would not be defined simply in ethnic or racial or class terms but in terms of the ways these identities are articulated by the different maps of spatial existence available in contemporary urban America with the groups identified by the press as, respectively, 'Black', 'Latino', 'Korean' and 'White' replaced by the above spatial vectors (since the ethnic identifications were often mistaken in their simplicity).

Finally, agency, like identity, is not simply a matter of places, but is more a matter of the spatial relations of places and spaces and the distribution of people within them. As Meaghan Morris (1988) points out, such places do not pre-exist as origins; they are the products of efforts to organize a limited space. It is a matter of the structured mobility by which people are given access to particular kinds of places, and to the paths that allow one to move to and from such places. If such 'ways of belonging', operating on the plane of subjectivity, define kinds of persons in relation to the kinds of experience they have available, then 'ways of belonging' constitutive of agency define a distribution of acts. If subjectivity constitutes 'homes' as places of attachment, temporary addresses for people, agency constitutes strategic installations; these are the specific places and spaces that define particular forms of agency and empower particular populations. In this sense, we can enquire into the conditions of possibility of agency, for agency – the ability to make history, as it were – is not intrinsic either to subjects or to selves. Agency is the product of diagrams of mobility and placement which define or map the possibilities of where and how specific vectors of influence can stop and be placed. (I am deliberately avoiding a language which would make it sound simply like people who stop and place themselves.) Such places are temporary points of belonging and identification, of orientation and installation, creating sites of strategic historical possibilities and activities, and as such they are always contextually defined. They define the forms of empowerment or agency which are available to particular groups as ways of going on and of going out. Around such places, maps of subjectivity and identity, meaning and pleasure, desire and force, can be articulated. A territorializing machine attempts to map the sorts of places that can be occupied and how they can be occupied; it maps how much room there is to move and where and how movement is possible. It produces lines of specific vectors, intensities and densities that differentially enable and enact specific forms of mobility and stability, specific lines of investment, anchoring and freedom. It maps the ways mobility is both enabled by and limited within a field of force. Agency as a human problem is defined by the articulations of subject positions and identities into specific places and spaces – fields of activity, in O'Hanlon's terms – on socially constructed territories. Agency is the empowerment enabled at particular sites, along particular vectors. At the very least, this analysis, however sketchy, suggests that cultural and political identities which do not themselves correspond exactly to self and agency, while always articulated together in any instance, are, nevertheless, neither equivalent nor reducible to each other. And neither is equivalent to or reducible to epistemological positions of subjectivity.

Culture and the politics of singularity

Recently, a number of authors have challenged the particular confluence of logics which have defined modern theories of identity. Ahmad (1992), for example, argues that there is often a rather easy slide from an 'absence of belonging' to an 'excess of belonging' predicated on the assumption of migrancy as an ontological and epistemological condition. Similarly, Dhareshwar (1989: 142–3) warns against the desire for 'an identity that fully coheres with the narrative force of theory', which takes the figures of a theoretical system as the 'storyline' for narrative identity: 'for example, "decentered subjectivity" as postmodern reality, dissemination as "immigritude" (my word for the whole narrative of displacement which has become a normative experience in metropolitan politics of cultural description)'. I would argue that, in so far as the various theories of identity remain grounded in modern logics of difference, individuality and temporality, the radical implications of the increasingly spatial language of such theories remains unrealized and unrealizable. With Dhareshwar (1989: 146), I wonder whether we need to raise 'the possibility and necessity of an entirely different theoretical practice'.

I am interested in the implications of the alternative logics of otherness, production and spatiality for a theory of human agency and historical change. In particular, for the moment, I am interested in the possibilities of political identities and alliances. My discussion of agency – and its difference from either subjectivity or 'identity' (self) – would seem to suggest the need for a radical rethinking of political identity (and the possibilities of collective agency). It seems to suggest the concept of a belonging without identity, a notion of what might be called *singularity* as the basis for an alternative politics, a politics based on what Giorgio Agamben (1993) has called 'the coming community'. This project is political at its core, for as Young (1990: 11) says, this quest for the singular can 'be related to the project of constructing a form of knowledge that respects the other without absorbing it into the same', or, I might add, the different. As Dhareshwar (1990: 235) points out, 'the fetishization and relentless celebration of "difference" and "otherness" [used here to describe a post-structuralist appropriation of Said's thesis] has displaced any discussion of political identity'.

Agamben describes singularity as a mode of existence which is neither universal (i.e. conceptual) nor particular (i.e. individual). He takes as an example of such a mode of existence, the existence of the example *qua* example itself, for the example exists both inside and outside of the class it exemplifies. The example exists 'by the indifference of the common and the proper, of the genus and the species, of the essential and the accidental. [It] is the thing with all its properties none of which, however, constitutes difference. Indifference with respect to properties is what individuates and disseminates singularities' (1993: 19). Moreover, the status of the example is not accomplished once and for all; it is a line of becoming, 'a shuttling between the common and the singular' (ibid.: 20). In other words, the example is defined, not by an appeal to a common universal property – an identity – but by its appropriation of belonging (to the class, in this instance) itself. The example belongs to the set which exists alongside of it, and hence it is defined by its substitutability, since it always already belongs in the place of the other. This is 'an unconditioned substitutability, without either representation or possible description' (ibid.: 24–5), an absolutely unrepresentable community. This community

– that on which the example borders – is an empty and indeterminate totality, an external space of possibilities. Thus, a singularity can be defined as 'a being whose community is mediated not by any condition of belonging . . . nor by the simple absence of conditions . . . but by belonging itself' (ibid.: 85). To put this all in simpler terms, Agamben is arguing that the example functions as an example not by virtue of some common property which it shares with all the other possible members of the set, but rather by virtue of its metonymical (understood both literally and spatially) relation to the set itself. Any term can become an example of the set because what is at stake is the very claim of belonging to the set.

Agamben turns this to politics by considering the events – the alliance – of Tiananmen Square:

> Because if instead of continuing to search for a proper identity in the already improper and senseless form of individuality, humans were to succeed in belonging to this impropriety as such, in making of the proper being – thus not an identity and an individual property but a singularity without identity, a common and absolutely exposed singularity . . . then they would for the first time enter into a community without presuppositions and without subjects. (ibid.: 65)

Consider, how one would describe the common identity of those who gathered in Tiananmen Square and, whether intentionally or not, came to define and embody a community of opposition, not only to the Chinese state, but to the state machine itself. In fact, there is no common identity, no property that defines them apart from the fact that they were there, together, in that place. It was the fact of belonging that constituted their belonging together. Such a singularity operates as a 'transport machine' following a logic of involvement, a logic of the next (rather than of the proper). It refuses to take any instance as a synecdochal image of the whole. It is only at the intersection of the various lines at the concrete place of belonging that we can identify the different processes of 'individuation carried out through groups and people', new modes of individuation and even subjectivation with no identity. Such a community would be based only on the exteriority, the exposure, of the singularity of belonging.

In this sense, we might also reconsider the civil rights movement as a machine of mobilization whose product was a singular belonging rather than a structure of membership. A politics of singularity would need to define places people can belong to or, even more fundamentally, places people can find their way to. Hall and Held (cited in Giroux, 1994: 31) describe this as the problem of citizenship: 'the diverse communities to which we belong, the complex interplay of identity and identification and the differentiated ways in which people participate in social life'. Similarly, Mercer (1992b: 33) describes 'what was important' about the politics of race of the 1980s as the result of the fact 'that we actively constructed an elective community of belonging through a variety of practices'. Perhaps Hall and Mercer would assent to the argument that, in specific contexts, identity can become a marker of people's abiding in such a singular community, where the community defines an abode marking people's ways of belonging within the structured mobilities of contemporary life. That would be an identity worth struggling to create.

Notes

1 For a fuller elaboration of some of the arguments here, see Grossberg (1993). I would also like to thank Stuart Hall, Cameron McCarthy, John Clarke and Henry Giroux for their encouragement and comments. I am aware of the potential charge that, as a white middle class man, I am attempting to undermine a concept which has proved to be empowering for various subaltern populations. I can only plead that I am not trying to undermine political empowerment and struggle, but to find more powerful theoretical tools which may open up more effective forms and sites of struggle.

2 This points to another 'modern' logic which I will not discuss here: what might be called the semanticization of reality or, in other words, the reduction of the real to meaning. It is only on this basis that the modern can assert its most fundamental proposition: that reality is socially constructed.

3 Here one might consider the work of, for example, Trinh Minh-ha.

4 The work of Homi Bhabha would be an obvious example.

5 One might consider the work of Rey Chow here.

6 In Deleuzean terms, subjectivity is the content of the body as expression, produced as a folding of the outside upon itself to create a stratum of the inside.

7 It is here that we can understand Foucault's distinction between different machines of power – societies of sovereignty and disciplinary societies – as different ways in which agency is itself constituted. In the former, agency is constructed on the materiality of the body; in the latter, through vision (surveillance) and structure (normalization). In disciplinary societies, the individual is placed into a mass space and monitored. Life is organized through enclosed environments (and capitalism is defined by processes of concentration and production). I might add a third category here – societies of disciplined mobilization – in which agency is organized through the control of mobility (and capitalism is defined by dispersion and futures/services).

8 For a more adequate description of these three machines, see the discussion in Grossberg (1993).

9 I am using the notion of a logic of space as an anti-modern alternative, rather than a more conciliatory notion of space-time, for two reasons. First, without a lot of work on other issues, such a 'synthetic' notion is likely to appear as a dialectical resolution of the antitheses of the modern. Second, like any other repressed term, it will probably continue to be repressed in such new compromise formations. We might start with space-time but it will quickly fall back into modern formulations and assumptions.

10 We must be careful not to assume that the notion of 'geography' is either universal or politically neutral.

References

Agamben, Giorgio (1993) *The Coming Community*, Minneapolis: University of Minnesota Press.

Ahmad, Aijaz (1992) *In Theory: Classes, Nations, Literatures*, London: Verso.

Althusser, Louis (1971) 'Ideology and ideological state apparatuses', in *Lenin and Philosophy and Other Essays*, trans. B. Brewster, New York: Monthly Review Press.

Anzaldua, Gloria (1987) *Borderlands/La Frontera: The New Mestiza*, San Francisco: Spinsters/Aunt Lute.

Bailey, David and Hall, Stuart (eds) (1992) 'The vertigo of displacement: shifts within black documentary practices', in *Critical Decade: Black British Photography in the 80s, Ten–8*, 3: 15–23.

Bhabha, Homi (1992) 'Postcolonial authority and postmodern guilt' in Lawrence Grossberg et al., (eds) *Cultural Studies*, New York and London: Routledge (56–66).

Bhabha, Homi (1994) *The Location of Culture*, London: Routledge.

Clifford, James (1994) 'Diasporas', *Cultural Anthropology*, 9: 302–38.

De Certeau, Michel (1984) *The Practice of Everyday Life*, trans. S.S. Rendall, Berkeley: University of California Press.

Deleuze, Gilles and Guattari, Felix (1987) *A Thousand Plateaus: Capitalism and Schizophrenia*, trans. B. Massumi, Minneapolis: University of Minnesota Press.

Derrida, Jacques (1978) *Writing and Difference*, trans. A. Bass, London: Routledge.

Dhareshwar, Vivek (1989) 'Toward a narrative epistemology of the postcolonial predicament', *Inscriptions*, 5.

Dhareshwar, Vivek (1990) 'The predicament of theory', in M. Kreisworth and M.A. Cheetham (eds.), *Theory between the Disciplines*, Ann Arbor: University of Michigan Press.

Foucault, Michel (1979) 'My body, this paper, this fire', *Oxford Literary Review*, 4: 9–28.

Gilroy, Paul (1992) 'Cultural studies and ethnic absolutism' in Lawrence Grossberg et al., (eds), *Cultural Studies*, New York and London: Routledge (187–97).

Gilroy, Paul (1993) *The Black Atlantic: Modernity and Double Consciousness*, Cambridge, MA: Harvard University Press.

Giroux, Henry (1994) 'Living dangerously: identity politics and the new cultural racism', in Henry Giroux and Peter McLaren (eds), *Between Borders: Pedagogy and the Politics of Cultural Studies*, New York: Routledge (29–55).

Grossberg, Lawrence (1992) *We Gotta Get Out Of This Place: Popular Conservatism and Postmodern Culture*, New York and London: Routledge.

Grossberg, Lawrence (1993) 'Cultural studies and new worlds', in C. McCarthy and W. Crichlow (eds), *Race, Identity and Representation*, New York: Routledge.

Grossberg, Lawrence (in press) 'Space and globalization in cultural studies', in I. Chambers and L. Curti (eds), *The Question of Post-colonialism*, London: Routledge.

Grossberg, Lawrence, Nelson, Cary and Treichler, Paula (1992) *Cultural Studies*, New York and London: Routledge.

Hall, Stuart (1990) 'Cultural identity and diaspora', in J. Rutherford (ed.), *Identity: Community, Culture, Difference*, London: Lawrence & Wishart (222–37).

Hall, Stuart (1991) 'The local and the global: globalization and ethnicity' in A. King (ed.), *Culture, Globalization and the World-System*, London: Macmillan (19–39).

Hall, Stuart (1992) 'Race, culture and communications: looking backward and forward at cultural studies', *Rethinking Marxism*, 5: 10–18.

Haraway, Donna (1991) *Simians, Cyborgs and Women: The Reinvention of Nature*, New York: Routledge.

Huyssen, Andrea (1986) *After the Great Divide: Modernism, Mass Culture, Postmodernism*, Bloomington: Indiana University Press.

Laclau, Ernesto and Mouffe, Chantal (1985) *Hegemony and Socialist Strategy*, London: Verso.

Lyotard, Jean-François (1990) *Heidegger and 'the Jews'*, trans. A. Michel and R. Roberts, Minneapolis: University of Minnesota Press.

Mercer, Kobena (1992a) '"1968": periodizing postmodern politics and identity', in Lawrence Grossberg et al., *Cultural Studies*, New York and London: Routledge (424–38).

Mercer, Kobena (1992b) 'Back to my routes: a postscript to the 80s', in David Bailey and Stuart Hall (eds), *Critical Decade: Black British Photography in the 80s, Ten-8*, 3 (32–9).

Michaels, Eric (1994) *Bad Aboriginal Art: Traditional, Media and Technological Horizons*, Minneapolis: University of Minnesota Press.

Morris, Meaghan (1988) 'At Henry Parkes Motel', *Cultural Studies*, 2: 1–47.

O'Hanlon, Rosalind (1988) 'Recovering the subject: subaltern studies and histories of resistance in colonial South Asia', *Modern Asian Studies*, 22: 189–224.

Parry, Benita (1987) 'Problems in current theories of colonial discourse', *Oxford Literary Review*, 9: 27–58.

Parry, Benita (1992) 'Overlapping territories and intertwined histories: Edward Said's postcolonial cosmopolitanism', in M. Sprinker (ed.), *Edward Said: A Critical Reader*, Oxford: Basil Blackwell.

Rosaldo, Renato (1989) *Culture and Truth: The Remaking of Social Analysis*, Boston: Beacon Press.

Said, Edward (1978) *Orientalism*, New York: Vintage.

Spivak, Gayatri Chakravorty (1988) 'Can the subaltern speak?', in C. Nelson and L. Grossberg (eds), *Marxism and the Interpretation of Culture*, Urbana: University of Illinois Press (272–313).

Wallace, Michele (1994) 'Multiculturalism and oppositionality', in Henry Giroux and Peter McLaren (eds), *Between Borders: Pedagogy and the Politics of Cultural Studies*, New York: Routledge (180–91).

Wark, McKenzie (1992) 'Speaking trajectories: Meaghan Morris, antipodean theory and Australian cultural studies', *Cultural Studies*, 6.

Young, Robert (1990) *White Mythologies: Writing History and the West*, London: Routledge.

7

Music and Identity

Simon Frith

Henry Rollins once said that music exists to put furniture in your mind, 'because life is so cruel and TV is so mean.'

Gina Arnold[1]

Becoming what one is is a creative act comparable with creating a work of art.

Anthony Storr[2]

It is not easy, however, to be evil when music is playing.

John Miller Chernoff[3]

The academic study of popular music has been limited by the assumption that the sounds must somehow 'reflect' or 'represent' the people. The analytic problem has been to trace the connections back, from the work (the score, the song, the beat) to the social groups who produce and consume it. What's been at issue is homology, some sort of *structural* relationship between material and musical forms.

The search for homology is most commonly associated these days with subculture theory, with accounts of punk or heavy metal, for example;[4] but the supposed fit (or lack of it) between aesthetic and social values has a much longer history in the study of popular culture. This is T.S. Eliot on Marie Lloyd:

> It was her understanding of the people and sympathy with them, and the people's recognition of the fact that she embodied the virtues which they genuinely most respected in private life, that raised her to the position she occupied at her death . . . I have called her the expressive figure of the lower classes.[5]

More recently the rise of identity politics has meant new assertions of cultural essentialism, more forceful arguments than ever that, for example, only African-Americans can appreciate African-American music, that there is a basic difference between male and female composition, that the 'globalization' of a local sound is a form of cultural 'genocide'.[6]

The assumptions in such arguments about the necessary flow from social identity (whether defined in terms of race or sexuality or age or nation) to musical expression (and appreciation) seem straightforward enough in the abstract (who could possibly deny that African-American music is music made by African-Americans; that the difference between male and female experience will be embedded in male and female music; that Phil Collins is an imposition on the soundscape of the Australian outback?). But they are less convincing in the everyday practice of music making and listening· how do we make sense of the obvious *love* of European listeners and players for the music of the African diaspora? Who is expressing what when, say, Ella Fitzgerald sings Cole Porter? When Yothi Yindi *rocks*?[7]

The problem here is not just the familiar postmodern point that we live in an age of plunder in which musics made in one place for one reason can be immediately appropriated in another place for quite another reason, but also that while music may be *shaped* by the people who first make and use it, as experience it has a life of its own. Marx remarks somewhere that it is easy enough to move analytically from the cultural to the material, easy enough, that is, to *interpret* culture, to read it ideologically, to assign it social conditions. The difficult trick is to do the analysis the other way round, to show how the base produced *this* superstructure, to explain why an idea or experience takes on *this* artistic or aesthetic form, and not another, equally 'reflective' or 'representative' of its conditions of production.[8] After the cultural event, as a historian might agree, we can say why expression had to happen this way; before it there is no creative necessity at all. And if art is therefore, so to speak, originally accidental, then there is no particular reason to accept its makers' special claims on it. The interesting question, rather, is how art comes to make its own claims, in other circumstances, for itself.

In examining the aesthetics of popular music, then, I want to reverse the usual academic and critical argument: the issue is not how a particular piece of music or a performance reflects the people, but how it produces them, how it creates and constructs an experience – a musical experience, an aesthetic experience – that we can only make sense of by *taking on* both a subjective and a collective identity. The aesthetic, to put this another way, describes the quality of an experience (not the quality of an object); it means experiencing *ourselves* (not just the world) in a different way. My argument here, in short, rests on two premises: first, that identity is *mobile*, a process not a thing, a becoming not a being; second, that our experience of music – of music making and music listening – is best understood as an experience of this *self-in-process*. Music, like identity, is both performance and story, describes the social in the individual and the individual in the social, the mind in the body and the body in the mind; identity, like music, is a matter of both ethics and aesthetics. In exploring these themes I will, among other things, touch critically on their treatment under the label of 'postmodernism', but my main concern is to suggest that if music is a metaphor for identity, then, to echo Marx, the self is always an imagined self but can only be imagined as a particular organization of social, physical and material forces.

The mobile self

What's at stake has become clear in the debate about postmodernism and the unstable or 'decentred' subject, a debate which has been dominated by the problems of signification and structure. Postmodernism, that is to say, is taken to describe a 'crisis' of signification systems: how can we now tell the difference between the 'real' and the 'simulated'? The postmodern problem is the threat to our sense of place – hence the mapping metaphors, the use of terms like depth and surface. What is underplayed in such discussions is the problem of process – not the positioning of the subject as such, but our experience of the movement between positions. This is where music becomes an important area for study: what happens to our assumptions about postmodern identity when we examine a form in which sound is more important than sight, and time more important than space; when the 'text' is a performance, a movement, a flux; when nothing is 'represented'?[9]

The broad argument that I want to make here, in short, is that in talking about identity we are talking about a particular kind of experience, or a way of dealing with a particular kind of experience. Identity is not a thing but a process – an experiential process which is most vividly grasped *as music*. Music seems to be a key to identity because it offers, so intensely, a sense of both self and others, of the subjective in the collective. As Mark Slobin puts it,

> Music seems to have an odd quality that even passionate activities like gardening or dog-raising lack: the simultaneous projecting and dissolving of the self in *performance*. Individual, family, gender, age, supercultural givens, and other factors hover around the musical space but can penetrate only very partially the moment of enactment of musical fellowship. Visible to the observer, these constraints remain unseen by the musicians, who are instead working out a shared vision that involves both the assertion of pride, even ambition, and the simultaneous disappearance of the ego.[10]

The experience of identity describes both a social process, a form of interaction, and an aesthetic process; as Slobin argues, it is the 'aesthetic rather than organizational/contextual aspects of performance' that 'betray a continuity between the social, the group, and the individual'.[11] It is in deciding – playing and hearing what sounds *right* (I would extend this account of music from performing to listening, to listening as a way of performing) – that we both express ourselves, our own sense of rightness, and suborn ourselves, lose ourselves, in an act of participation.[12]

The implication of this argument is that we need to rethink the usual sociological approach to aesthetic expression. My point is not that a social group has beliefs which it then articulates in its music, but that music, an aesthetic practice, articulates *in itself* an understanding of both group relations and individuality, on the basis of which ethical codes and social ideologies are understood.[13]

What I want to suggest, in other words, is not that social groups agree on values which are then expressed in their cultural activities (the assumption of the homology models) but that they only get to know themselves *as groups* (as a particular organization of individual and social interests, of sameness and difference) *through* cultural activity, through aesthetic judgement. Making music isn't a way of expressing ideas; it is a way of living them. As John Miller Chernoff concluded from his study of drumming in Ghana,

> African music is a cultural activity which reveals a group of people organizing and involving themselves with their own communal relationships – a partici-pant-observer's comment, so to speak, on the processes of living together. The aesthetic point of the exercise is not to reflect a reality which *stands behind it* but to ritualize a reality that is *within* it.[14]

And this is not just a characteristic of African music, Philip V. Bohlman concludes his study of the role of chamber music in the lives of the *Yekkes*, the German-speaking Jews in Israel, as follows:

> But this essay is not really about an ethnic group. Nor is it about the music per se of that group [though] I am here concerned with the music history resulting from the response of a group with a shared value system to a musical repertory that articulated those values. Such groups have long populated the history of Western music. Sometimes we call them ethnic groups or communities, sometimes national cultures, and sometimes we label by coupling place with abstraction, for example in 'Viennese classicism'. All these acts of labelling suggest the process of standing outside a group and looking in to see what sort of music is to be found. Suppose the group is really the product of its musical activities and the cultural values bound to them? What if excessive concern with the musical text deflects one from seeing the formation of diverse groups and music histories. What if one looked at the Yekkes, with their devotion to chamber music, as just another justification for the conditions of absolute music?[15]

Bohlman's target here is musicology. As an ethnomusicologist he is arguing that the meaning of classical music, as an experience, is not to be found in the text, but in the performance of the text, in the process in which it is realized. The Yekke chamber music groups don't have an abstract belief in 'absolute' (or transcendent) music; rather the concept of 'absolute music' is dependent on a particular way of being – playing – together.

Bohlman's argument is particularly interesting because it is applied to 'high' music making. His suggestion, with which I strongly agree, is that in terms of aesthetic process there is no real difference between high and low music. As he notes, from his perspective, 'Western art music functions not unlike styles and repertories most commonly accepted as the ethnomusicologist's field, namely folk and non-Western music.' And I would add, from my perspective, not unlike commercial popular music either. In short, different sorts of musical activity may produce different sorts of musical identity, but *how* the musics work to form identities is the same. The distinction between high and low culture, in other words, describes not something caused by different (class-bound) tastes, but is an effect of different (class-bound?) social activities.[16]

Let me make the point in a different way, by quoting two music critics, one low and one high, and then considering the difference between them. First the low critic, Frank Kogan, writing about Spoonie Gee in a fanzine in the mid-1980s.

> 'Spoonin Rap' and ' Love Rap' by Spoonie Gee are my favourite American-made records of the last ten years. They came out about five years ago, 'Spoonin Rap' in late '79 and 'Love Rap' in '80. I've never read a review of either.
>
> On the basis of his voice alone, the way it balances coolness with angry passion while keeping a dance beat, Spoonie is a major artist; in addition, he's a writer. His lyrics are as intense as his singing, and embody the same tensions. Example: both 'Spoonin Rap' and 'Love Rap' start with detailed and explicit bragging – about how cool and sexy he is, about how girls go for him, how they're impressed with his rapping and his car. He puts on his eight-track. He makes love to the girl in his car. In his Mercedes. The seat's so soft, just like a bed. At the moment of sexual triumph the lyrics make a jarring change, as if there's a second song hidden behind the first, as if the bragging were a set-up for something else. . . . And then it's like the first part of the song, but turned inside out – the guys and girls are drawn to his flashy clothes and car only so they can rip him off and leave him in the gutter. The girls are gonna play him for a fool. . . . Then it shifts back to what a great lover he is, nice descriptions of his girl friends. 'Spoonin Rap' shifts around in the same way. It's about how cool he is, about how sexy women are; then it's about don't do dope, don't steal, you'll go to jail and they'll fuck you in the ass. Then it's about jumping the turnstile and the cop pulls a gun but he doesn't shoot.
>
> There's a lot of precedent in black lyrics for jarring emotional juxtapositions – in the blues particularly, also in Smokey Robinson's deliberate paradoxes. But the nearest emotional equivalent isn't in black music, it's in punk – early Stones, Kinks, Velvets, Stooges, Dolls – where a song will seem to be one thing, then be another. The ranting part of 'Love Rap' could be Lou Reed in one of his bad moods – except that, unlike a Jagger or a Reed, Spoonie hasn't calculated – may not even be aware of – his juxtapositions. Which adds to his power. The feelings have great impact because they come from an unexpected source. If Spoonie were in punk or rock his alienation and rage would fill an expectation of the genre. In disco, they seem truer. . . .
>
> Spoonie Gee has made some great records and an equal number of mediocre ones. I think he's a genius, but I don't think he knows what he's doing. He's drawn to a vision of the world as a fake and treacherous place. Maybe something's bugging him. Maybe unconsciously he feels that it's not only the world that's fake, or women that are fake – it's himself.
>
> Spoonie's not one of us. He has nothing to do with punk culture or post-punk culture. I don't know if I could carry on an interesting conversation with him, if we could find any cultural or moral common ground. But there is a common ground, that part of the intellect called the 'emotions', where I do my deepest analysis of life. However much I admire current heroes like Mark E. Smith and Ian Mackaye, people I identify with, I know they don't make music as strong as this. Listening to Spoonie is like hearing my own feelings, and I have to confront my own fear. This means maybe that I'm not really unlike him. Maybe I'm more like him that I am like you.[17]

I've quoted this at length because this is how the piece works as criticism – in the steady move from description to emotion to identity, via questions of voice and genre, text and performance, knowledge, truth and feeling, all here focused on one artist, on a couple of tracks.

Now compare high criticism: Gregory Sandow on Milton Babbitt:

Like any Babbitt piece, *Dual* is a labyrinth of closely packed information: every detail means something, or – which to me is the awe and almost the horror if it – could mean something. The F sharp, E flat, and B natural isolated in the highest register of the piano in the first two measures return in measure six as the first three notes of a melodic phrase, accompanied by the B flat, G natural, and C natural that were the next notes heard in the highest register at the end of measure two and the start of measure three – and these are just the most obvious connections that could be made between two parts of the piece chosen almost at random. Babbitt likes to say that moments in his music can be memories of what came before, and presentiments of what is to come. Serial technique produces ever-new associations of familiar elements giving every-thing that happens the power of an omen. Following a Babbitt piece in close detail is like reading entrails or tea leaves: every rearrangement in every bar might mean something. So many rearrangements are possible that you never know what the omens really mean; new developments seem, if not arbitrary, then at least wilful. This is a sort of higher-order zaniness, something unpredictable and even wild that transcends Babbitt's logic, and finds its way into something I haven't mentioned yet, which I'll call Babbitt's mode of musical speech. . . .

For in the end I do find Babbitt eccentric. He's a superb musical craftsman, and, I think, an authentically great composer, though in some ways hard to take, but he's also zany, wild, and – I say this again with admiration – more than a little bit mad. His music, and the whole school he represents, are products of the 1950s, as much the symptoms of the eruption of tumultuous subterranean forces into above ground life as monster movies, rock and roll, the beat generation, and abstract expressionism. But in Babbitt's case the eruption is controlled, disguised, and unmentioned, the secret nobody will acknowledge or even name. In a videotaped interview with Ann Swartz of Baruch College, Babbitt calls himself 'a man of the university', whose music 'reflects the life of the academy, in the best sense of the word'. That's partly true, of course, but there's much more there. There's no point in thinking that Babbitt should do or think anything but what he does. . . . But I can't help thinking that he's sold himself short by trying both to extend the boundaries of his art and to remain academically respectable, and by acknowledging only the verifiable (and therefore trivial) aspects of his amazing work. If – like Joyce, Jackson Pollock, or John Cage – so passionate a man had chosen to define himself as an artist and not as an academic, what might he have achieved?[18]

The descriptive terms here are different (the language of notational rather than lyrical analysis), the genre distinction draws attention to a different context (the academy rather than the market), but the overall shape of the review is the same – the move from describing the music to describing the listener's response to the music to considering the relationship of feeling, truth and identity. And Kogan's and Sandow's judgements are, in fact, much the same: both Spoonie Gee and Milton Babbitt show flawed genius; in both cases the critics seem to know better than the artists what they are – or should be – doing.

What links these responses, in other words, is the assumption that music, the experience of music for composer/performer and listener alike, gives us a way of being in the world, a way of making sense of it. And if both critics begin by stressing their distance from the musicians – both Spoonie Gee and Milton Babbitt are set up as decidedly odd; both critics also end up in a sort of collusion with them: musical appreciation is, by its very nature, a process of musical identification, and the aesthetic response is, implicitly, an ethical agreement.

Postmodernism and performance

The blurring of the high/low cultural boundary (here between critics) is, of course, a sign of the postmodern, and in bringing Kogan and Sandow together I need to distinguish my position from the one usually adopted. The confusion of the high and low is conventionally indicated by quotation (or appropriation) across the divide: the pop recycling of classical music and the art re-use of pop are taken to mark an underlying shift of aesthetic sensibility. In practice, as Andrew Goodwin has pointed out, such arguments mostly concern a relationship between the artistic avant-garde and certain pop forms (pop art remains the model): the most cited postmodern musicians are people such as Laurie Anderson, David Byrne and Brian Eno, who are clearly 'artists' rather than 'pop stars'. The institutional boundary between high and mass art seems intact – there remains a clear difference between a Philip Glass and a Madonna in terms of packaging, marketing, performance space, recording sound, and so forth; just as we can continue to distinguish between the pop Eno (producer of U2 and James) and the art Eno (producer of ambient video). The *frisson* of blurring of the art/mass boundary depends on the boundary still being clearly drawn.[19]

And if we go back to eighteenth-century debates about musical meaning, and to the origins of the Romantic view of art that underpins high cultural arguments (the view which was duly appropriated by would-be artist rock musicians in the 1960s), it becomes apparent that the high/low distinction doesn't really concern the nature of the art object, or how it is produced, but refers to different modes of *perception*. The crucial high/low distinction is that between contemplation and 'wallowing', between intellectual and sensual appreciation, between hard and easy listening (which is why a comparison of high and low critics becomes interesting).

To add low cultural goods to lists of 'art' objects available for intellectual (or 'serious') appreciation (which is what postmodern theorists tend to do) is not, then, to get rid of the traditional boundaries between the high and the low, and the much more interesting issue is whether we can really continue to sustain the implicit separation of emotion and feeling, sense and sensuality, body and mind. (This is the issue raised, for example, by the ambient house music of groups like Future Sound of London and the Aphex Twin, music which draws simultaneously on rave culture and minimalism.) The question, in fact, is whether musical experience has ever really been mapped by the high/low, mind/body distinction. The nineteenth century ideologues of absolute music may have worked hard to make musical appreciation a purely mental experience, but this was hard work precisely because most listeners didn't listen to music this way, however much they wanted to. Even high music making and listening remained a physical as well as a 'spiritual' activity, a sensual as well as a cognitive experience; to enjoy music of all sorts is to feel it.

At the same time, musical pleasure is never just a matter of feeling; it is also a matter of judgement. Take the postmodern reading of contemporary pop in terms of pastiche. Digital technology has certainly speeded up the process in which composition means quotation, but what we need to consider here are not so much the specific texts that result, as the way our attention is drawn to the *performance* of quotation. On rap tracks, for instance, far from musical authority being dissipated into fragments and second-hand sounds it is enhanced by the attention drawn to the quoting act itself. As Paul Gilroy suggests, 'the aesthetic rules that govern it are premised on a dialect of rescuing appropriation and recombination that creates special pleasures'. Pleasures in which 'aesthetic stress is laid upon the sheer social and cultural distance that formerly separated the diverse elements now dislocated into novel meanings by their provocative aural juxtaposition', and in which the continuing importance of performance is 'emphasised by [tracks'] radically unfinished forms'.[20]

Hip-hop, in other words, with its cut-ups, its scratches, breaks and samples, is best understood as producing not new texts but new ways of performing texts, new ways of performing *the making of meaning*. The pleasure of montage comes from the act of juxtaposition rather than from the labour of interpretation – and for the listener and dancer too, the fun lies in the process not the result. Not for nothing is rap a voice-based form with an exceptionally strong sense of presence. The aesthetic question about this postmodern music, at least, concerns not meanings and their interpretation – identity translated into discursive forms which have to be decoded – but *mutual enactment*, identity produced *in* performance.

Space, time and stories

It is conventional, nowadays, in the academy at least, to divide the arts into separate categories such that the performing arts (theatre, dance and music) are differentiated from the fine arts (literature, painting, sculpture) and, on the whole, the performing arts are taken to be inferior to the fine arts, incapable of providing such rich aesthetic experience or social commentary. This is a relatively recent hierarchy, an effect of nineteenth-century conventions, the impact of Romanticism, the simultaneous emphases on art as individual expression and as private property. 'High' art was thus institutionalized by the bourgeoisie as a transcendent, asocial, experience (in the contemplative bank-like setting of the gallery and the concert hall, the museum and the library).

In the eighteenth century, with its concern for rhetoric and oratory, the distinction between the performing and the fine arts was not so clear and there were ways in which the former were clearly superior to the latter. One way of thinking about the contrast here is to see the fine arts as being organized around the use of space, and the performing arts as organized around the use of time. In spatial arts value is embodied in an object, a text; the analytic emphasis is on structure – a detached, 'objective' reading is possible, and artistic meaning can be extricated from the work's formal qualities. In temporal arts the value of the work is experienced as something momentary, and the analytical emphasis is on process; 'subjective' reading is necessary – a reading taking account of one's own immediate response – and the work's artistic meaning lies in that response, the work's rhetorical qualities.

The first point to make about such distinctions is that they do not, in fact, describe different art forms so much as different approaches to art forms, different ways of framing 'the aesthetic experience', different assumptions about what is artistically valuable or meaningful. The nineteenth century argument that art was 'timeless' meant, then, an attempt to objectify all art, the performing arts too; one effect was to redefine music as a musical object, to put the analytic emphasis on the work, the score, rather than on its performance. And, given that to be 'music' the score had to be performed, the performance itself was also objectified, made the object of repeated performance, such that the tradition, the history of performance could be claimed as defining music's meaning, rather than the immediate effect, which was, by its nature, inevitably distorted by social, historical and material exigencies.

This process of objectification was also a process of academicization (hence, eventually, Milton Babbitt), as art became an object of study, and scholars became guardians of its traditional meaning, as they had always been in matters of religion and law. Here too the emphasis was, by necessity (the necessity of what can be stored and taught), on the qualities of a work in space, structural qualities, rather than on the qualities of a work in time, the qualities of immediacy, emotion, sweat – suspect terms in both the library and the classroom.

It should be stressed too, though, that what I'm describing here is a discursive process, an idealistic attempt to grasp an experience through a particular evaluative framework which was not, and perhaps could not be, entirely successful. In the end, how people (or, rather, critics and scholars) talked about music became detached from how people (musicians and listeners) felt about it. There was always an excess in musical experience, something unreasonable, something that *got away*. And if it is relatively easy to illustrate the problems of treating temporal arts in spatial terms (analysing a score or a playscript is not, in the end, to treat the experience of music or drama), it is just as important to note that the 'spatial' arts also have temporal elements. We do, after all, experience books in time; poems too have a beginning, a middle and an end. Reading is a process, and an emotional process at that; oratory is an aspect of the fine art experience too.[21]

The linking concept here is narrative – structured time, temporal space: if narrative gives the fine arts their dynamism, it gives the performing arts their structure. Musical pleasure is also a narrative pleasure, even when the music is at its most abstract – compare Greg Sandow's response to Milton Babbitt cited earlier to Greg Tate's appreciation of Cecil Taylor:

> Someone once said that while Coleman Hawkins gave the jazz saxophone a voice, Lester Young taught it how to tell a story. That is, the art of personal confession is one jazz musicians must master before they can do justice by their tradition. I couldn't relate to Cecil's music until I learned to hear the story he was shaping out of both black tradition and his complex 'life as an American Negro'.[22]

For Tate, as for other jazz writers, the 'story' in music describes an entanglement of aesthetics and ethics; such a narrative is necessary to any claim that art has something to do with life. A good jazz performance, that is to say (like any good musical performance), depends on rhetorical truth, on the musicians' ability to convince and persuade the listener that what they are saying matters. This is not a matter of representation or 'imitation' or ideology but draws, rather, on the African-American tradition of 'signifying'; it puts into play an emotional effect, a collusion between the performer and an audience which is engaged rather than detached, knowing rather than knowledgeable.

This is the reason why popular music (and I don't believe the argument is confined to African-derived forms, though it does help to explain their remarkable global impact) must be understood not to represent values but to embody them. The point is well made in Christopher Waterman's study of *jùjú:*

> Jùjú history suggests that the role of musical style in the enactment of identity makes it not merely a reflexive but also a potentially *constitutive* factor in the patterning of cultural values and social interaction. Yoruba musicians, responding creatively to changes in the Nigerian political economy, fashioned a mode of expression that enacted, in music, language, and behaviour, a syncretic metaphoric image of an ideal social order, cosmopolitan yet firmly rooted in autochthonous tradition. This dynamic style configuration, consonant with Yoruba ideologies of the 'open hierarchy' as an ideal pattern of aesthetic and social organization, allowed jùjú performance to play a role in the stereotypic reproduction of 'deep' Yoruba values during a period of pervasive economic and political change.[23]

This echoes Paul Gilroy's comments on the ways in which in the history of black culture, 'the politics of trans-figuration strives in pursuit of the sublime, struggling to repeat the unrepeatable, to present the unpresentable'. If the politics of fulfilment, in pursuit of rational western politics, seeks to 'assimilate the semiotic, verbal and textual', the politics of transfiguration 'pushes towards the mimetic, dramatic and performative'. Hence 'the traditions of performance that continue to characterize the production and reception of African diaspora musics'.[24] Gilroy notes that

> The power of music in developing our struggles by communicating information, organising consciousness and testing out, deploying, or amplifying the forms of subjectivity which are required by political agency, individual and collective, defensive and transformational, demands attention to both the formal attributes of this tradition of expression and its distinctive *moral* basis. . . . In the simplest possible terms, by posing the world as it is against the world as the racially subordinated would like it to be, this musical culture supplies a great deal of the courage required to go on living in the present.[25]

Gilroy thus suggests that 'the history of black music enables us to trace something of the means through which the unity of ethics and politics has been reproduced as a form of folk knowledge', and if music thus may 'conjure up and enact the new modes of friendship, happiness and solidarity that are consequent on the overcoming of the racial oppression on which modernity and the duality of rational western progress as excessive barbarity relied', it also conjures up and enacts dialogue, argument, call and response: 'lines between self and other are blurred and special forms of pleasure are created as a result'. Gilroy quotes Ralph Ellison on jazz:

> There is in this a cruel contradiction implicit in the art form itself. For true jazz is an art of individual assertion within and against the group. Each true jazz moment . . . springs from a contest in which the artist challenges all the rest; each solo flight, or improvisation, represents (like the canvases of a painter) a definition of his identity; as individual, as member of the collectivity and as a link in the chain of tradition. Thus because jazz finds its very life in improvisation upon traditional materials, the jazz man must lose his identity even as he finds it.[26]

But while music is thus particularly important in the complex history of black identities, this use of music, as that aesthetic process through which we discover ourselves by forging our relations to others, is not confined to black cultures. In Britain, for example, white listeners have long been engaged in their own enactments of black musical values. Take Brian Jackson's 1960s description of the importance of the Huddersfield Jazz Club to its displaced working-class grammar school girls and boys:

> If the life of New Orleans was an exaggerated image of working-class life, the stimulating generalized emotions of jazz were a hazy image of what the world of art could offer.

Jackson notes the importance of the jazz 'solo' for these self-conscious individualists as they struggled to make music for themselves (solos in which no one else in the club even feigned interest), but he also notes how jazz was used in Huddersfield as a musical practice in which to stage an understanding of collectivity:

> It didn't lead to social promotion or to high art – there was no 'transfer' at all from jazz to classical music. Its function was to hold together and sustain a steady stream of post–1944 Act pupils. As a floating community, it became admirably and intricately designed for that purpose – and the feeling of how to do *this*, was the real inheritance from working-class Huddersfield.[27]

To turn to a different world altogether, Philip Bohlman explores the role of chamber music – another form of small-scale making-music-together – in shaping German Jewish identity in Israel, in both articulating cultural values and enacting collective commitment to them (from the audience as much as from the performers). In this context the scored basis of 'absolute music' was as ethically binding as the improvised basis of jazz:

> Viewed from a performative perspective, the absence of specific meaning within the text allows meaning to accrue only upon performance, thus empowering any group – for example, an ethnic community – to shape what it will from absolute music. A gap therefore forms between the content of chamber-music repertoires and the style of performance situations. It is within the mutability allowed by style that differences in meaning and function of music arise, thereby transforming chamber music into a genre that can follow numerous historical paths. These paths may be as different as, say, the ethnic associations in Israel and the practices of amateur music making found in many American academic communities. Clearly, such cases reflect different attitudes towards both the repertoires of chamber music and the communities that lend the music its distinctive functions and form its different histories.[28]

From aesthetics to ethics

Underlying all the other distinctions critics continue to draw between 'serious' (European-derived) and 'popular' (African-derived) music is an assumption about the sources of musical value. Serious music, it seems, matters because it transcends social forces; popular music is aesthetically uninteresting because it is determined by them (because it is 'functional' or 'utilitarian'). The sociological approach to musical value has thus meant uncovering the social forces concealed in the talk of 'transcendent' values; the populist reversal of the high/low hierarchy has meant praising the 'functional' at the expense of the 'aesthetic'.

My concern is the opposite: to take seriously the aesthetic value (the aesthetic function, as one might say) of all musics, popular music too. The sociologist of contemporary popular music is faced with a body of songs, records, stars and styles which exist because of a series of decisions, made by both producers and consumers, about what is 'good'. Musicians write tunes and play solos and program computers; producers choose from different mixes; record companies and radio and television programmers decide what will be released and played; consumers buy one record rather than another and concentrate their attention on particular genres. The result of all these apparently individual decisions is certainly a pattern of success, taste and style which can be explained sociologically, but it is also a pattern that is rooted in individual judgement.

We can, as I suggested earlier, trace such judgements back to material conditions easily enough, by way, for example, of Pierre Bourdieu's concept of taste. We can point to the cultural capital embedded in technique and technology: people produce and consume the music they are capable of producing and consuming; different social groups possess different sorts of knowledge and skill, share different cultural histories, and so make music differently. Musical tastes do correlate with class cultures and subcultures; musical styles are linked to specific age groups; we can take for granted the connections of ethnicity and sound. This is the sociological common sense of rock criticism and the idea of authenticity:

> There is not a British rocker on earth who could ever turn Jack Scott's chorus-line,
>
> > Lonesome Mary's cuttin' out
> > Hate to be around when Johnnie finds this out
>
> into anything approximating a convincing statement.[29]

But while we can thus describe (or assume) general patterns of musical taste and use, the precise fit (or homology) between sounds and social groups remains unclear, which is why commonsense sociology has had to deploy its second set of arguments, about the match of music's *formal* and social functions. This approach is most sophisticated in ethnomusicology, in anthropological studies of traditional and folk musics which are explained musically (in terms of their formal and sonic qualities) by reference to their use – in dance, in rituals, for political mobilization, to solemnize events. Similar points are made about contemporary popular music, though its most important social function is assumed to be commercial – the starting analytical assumption is that the music is made to sell; research focuses on who makes marketing decisions and why, on the construction of taste and 'taste publics'. The appeal of the music itself, the reason why people like it, and what, more importantly, 'liking it' means, is buried under an analysis of sales strategies, demographics, the anthropology of consumption.

From the 'consumers' perspective, though, it is obvious that people play the music they do because it 'sounds good', and even if musical tastes are, inevitably, an effect of social conditioning and commercial manipulation, people still explain them to themselves in terms of something special. Everyone in the pop world is aware of the social forces that determine 'normal' pop music and 'normal' pop tastes, but a good record or song or sound is precisely one that transcends those forces.

From this perspective, pop music becomes the more valuable aesthetically the more independent it is of the social forces that organize it, and one way of reading this is to suggest that pop value is thus dependent on something outside pop, is rooted in the person, the *auteur*, the community or the subculture that lies behind it. Critical judgement means measuring performers' 'truth' to the experience or feelings they are describing or expressing. The problem is that it is, in practice, very difficult to say who or what it is that pop music expresses or how we recognize, independently of their music, the 'authentically' creative performers. Musical 'truth' is precisely that which is *created* by 'good music'; we hear the music as authentic (or rather, we describe the musical experience we value in terms of authenticity) and such a response is then read back, spuriously, on to the music-making (or listening) process. An aesthetic judgement of effect is translated into a sociological description of cause: good music must be music made and appreciated by good people. But the question we should be asking is not what does popular music reveal about the people who play and use it but how does it create them as a people, as a web of identities? If we start from the assumption that pop is expressive, then we get bogged down in the search for the 'real' artist or emotion or belief lying behind it. But popular music is popular not because it reflects something or authentically articulates some sort of popular taste or experience, but because it creates our understanding of what 'popularity' is, because it places us in the social world in a particular way. What we should be examining, in other words, is not how true a piece of music is to something else, but how it sets up the idea of 'truth' in the first place – successful pop music is music which defines its own aesthetic standard.

The imagined self

The experience of pop music is an experience of identity: in responding to a song, we are drawn, haphazardly, into emotional alliances with the performers and with the performers' other fans. Because of its qualities of abstractness, music is, by nature, an individualizing form. We absorb songs into our own lives and rhythm into our own bodies; they have a looseness of reference that makes them immediately accessible. At the same time, and equally significantly, music is obviously collective. We hear things as music because their sounds obey a more or less familiar cultural logic, and for most music listeners (who are not themselves music makers) this logic is out of our control. There is a mystery to our own musical tastes. Some records and performers work for us, others do not – we know this without being able to explain it. Somebody else has set up the conventions; they are clearly social and clearly apart from us. Music, whether teenybop for young female fans or jazz or rap for African-Americans or nineteenth century chamber music for German Jews in Israel, stands for, symbolizes *and* offers the immediate experience of collective identity.

If narrative is the basis of music pleasure, to put this another way, it is also central to our sense of identity. Identity, that is to say, comes from the outside not the inside; it is something we put or try on, not something we reveal or discover. As Jonathan Ree puts it,

> The problem of personal identity, one may say, arises from play-acting and the adoption of artificial voices; the origins of distinct personalities, in acts of personation and impersonation.[30]

And Ree goes on to argue that personal identity is therefore 'the accomplishment of a storyteller, rather than the attribute of a character'. He draws on Sartre and Ricoeur in suggesting that narrative is 'the unity of a life', not something achieved through some essential continuity but rather through a 'recurring *belief*' in personal coherence, a belief necessarily 'renewed in the telling of tales'.

> The concept of narrative, in other words, is not so much a justification of the idea of personal identity, as an elucidation of its structure as an inescapable piece of make-believe.[31]

This argument has two immediate implications. First, identities are, inevitably, shaped according to narrative forms. As Kwame Anthony Appiah points out,

> Invented histories, invented biologies, invented cultural affinities come with every identity; each is a kind of role that has to be scripted, structured by conventions of narrative to which the world never quite manages to conform.[32]

But if identity is always somehow constrained by imaginative forms, it is also freed by them: the personal is the cultural, and, as Mark Slobin suggests, we are not necessarily restricted in terms of such cultural imagination by social circumstances: 'We all grow up with *something*, but we can choose just about *anything* by way of expressive culture.'[33]

In broad terms we may be able to relate social and cultural identities, to finger social and cultural 'theft'. 'The blackface performer,' writes Eric Lott, 'is in effect a perfect metaphor for one culture's ventriloquial self-expression through the art forms of someone else's.'[34] But at an individual level, biology, demography and sociology seem less determining. As I have argued elsewhere, with reference to literary forms and social identities (black writing, women's writing, gay writing, etc.), the question is not 'simply whether such writing can be mapped back onto the reader (reading as a woman, a man, a black) but whether literary transformation – the process of writing *and* reading – doesn't subvert all sociological assumptions about cultural position and cultural feeling'.[35]

And this seems an even more obvious question about popular music, of which the dominant forms in all contemporary societies have originated at the social margins – among the poor, the migrant, the rootless, the 'queer'.[36] Anti-essentialism is a necessary part of musical experience, a necessary consequence of music's failure to register the separations of body and mind on which such 'essential' differences (between black and white, female and male, gay and straight, nation and nation) depend. Hence Paul Gilroy's scepticism about rap nationalism: 'How does a form which flaunts and glories in its own malleability as well as its trans-national character become interpreted as an expression of some authentic Afro-American essence?'[37]

If Gilroy remembers that growing up he was 'provided by black music with a means to gain proximity to the sources of feeling from which our local conceptions of blackness were assembled', he also realizes that 'the most important lesson music still has to teach us is that its inner secrets and its ethnic rules can be taught and learned'.[38] And as a child and young man I also learned something of myself – took my identity – from black music (just as I did later, in the disco, from gay music). What secrets was I being taught?

First, that an identity is always already an ideal, what we would like to be, not what we are. And in taking pleasure from black or gay or female music I don't thus identify as black or gay or female (I don't actually experience these sounds as 'black music' or 'gay music' or 'women's voices') but, rather, participate in imagined forms of democracy and desire. The aesthetic, as Colin Campbell has argued, these days describes a quality of experience rather than a state of being, and the popular aesthetic experience is an effect of 'modern autonomous imaginative hedonism':

> The pleasures which self-illusory hedonism supplies are largely aesthetic and emotional, the scenes created in imagination having the characteristics of both works of art and drama.[39]

In his classic account of *The Presentation of Self in Everyday Life*, Erving Goffman thus emphasizes Simone de Beauvoir's point that in dressing and making up, a woman

> does not present *herself* to observation; she is, like the picture or the statue, or the actor on stage, an agent through whom is suggested someone not there – that is, the character she represents, but is not. It is this identification with something unreal, fixed, perfect as the hero of a novel, as a portrait or a bust, that gratifies her; she strives to identify herself with this figure and thus to seem to herself to be stabilized, justified in her splendour.[40]

But if musical identity is, then, always fantastic, idealizing not just oneself but also the social world one inhabits, it is, secondly, always also real, enacted in musical activities. Music making and music listening, that is to say, are bodily matters, involve what one might call *social movements*. In this respect, musical pleasure is not derived *from* fantasy – it is not *mediated* by daydreams – but is experienced directly: music gives us a real experience of what the ideal could be. In his discussion of black identity, Paul Gilroy thus argues that it is neither 'simply a social and political category' nor 'a vague and utterly contingent construction' but 'remains the outcome of practical activity: language, gesture, bodily significations, desires'.

> These significations are condensed in musical performance, although it does not, of course, monopolise them. In this context, they produce the imaginary

effect of an internal racial core or essence by acting on the body through the specific mechanisms of identification and recognition that are produced in the intimate interaction of performer and crowd. This reciprocal relationship serves as a strategy and an ideal communicative situation even when the original makers of the music and its eventual consumers are separated in space and time or divided by the technologies of sound production and the commodity form which their art has sought to resist.[41]

And once we start looking at different musical genres we can begin to document the different ways in which music works *materially* to give people different identities, to place them in different social groups. Whether we're talking about Finnish dance halls in Sweden, Irish pubs in London, or Indian film music in Trinidad, we're dealing not just with nostalgia for 'traditional sounds', not just with a commitment to 'different' songs, but also with experience of alternative modes of social interaction. Communal values can only thus be grasped, as musical aesthetics *in action*.[42] Helen Myers, for example, quotes Channu, a village singer in Felicity, Trinidad:

> Indian music sounds much sweeter. Whatever the Indian sing and whatever music they play, they don't do it of a joke. It's serious thing for whoever understand it. It brings such serious feelings to you. Calypso they only sing. You might hear calypso. You will just feel happy to jump up. But if you hear a real technical piece of Indian music, you might sit down stiff and still, and you might be contrasting so much that you mightn't know when it start or when it finish.[43]

For these Trinidadians, 'Indianized pieces, borrowed from a twentieth-century urban Hindi culture' are therefore heard as 'more authentic than the local Westernized repertory, a reflection of their New World heritage'. Authenticity in this context is a quality not of the music as such (how it is actually made), but of the story it's heard to tell, the narrative of musical interaction in which the listeners place themselves.[44]

Conclusion

Music constructs our sense of identity through the direct experiences it offers of the body, time and sociability, experiences which enable us to place ourselves in imaginative cultural narratives. Such a fusion of imaginative fantasy and bodily practice marks also the integration of aesthetics and ethics. John Miller Chernoff has thus eloquently demonstrated how among African musicians an aesthetic judgement (this sounds good) is necessarily also an ethical judgement (this is good), The issue is 'balance': 'the quality of rhythmic relationships' describes a quality of social life. 'In this sense, style is another word for the perception of relationships.'

> Without balance and coolness, the African musician loses aesthetic command, and the music abdicates its social authority, becoming hot, intense, limited, pretentious, overly personal, boring, irrelevant, and ultimately alienating.

And

> As the dance gives visible form to the music, so too does the dance give full and visible articulation to the ethical qualities which work through the music, balance in the disciplined expression of power in relationship.[45]

Identity is thus necessarily a matter of ritual, it describes one's place in a dramatized pattern of relationships – one can never really express oneself 'autonomously'. Self-identity *is* cultural identity; claims to individual difference depend on audience appreciation, on shared performing and narrative rules. As Appiah puts it:

> The problem of who I really am is raised by the facts of what I appear to be: and though it is essential to the mythology of authenticity that this fact should be obscured by its prophets, what I appear to be is fundamentally how I appear to others and only derivatively how I appear to myself.[46]

In her study of music making in (the very white) Milton Keynes, *The Hidden Musicians*, Ruth Finnegan persuasively argues that these days people's voluntary, leisure activities are more likely to provide their 'pathways' through life than their paid employment. It was in their musical activities that her city dwellers found their most convincing narratives; it was in their aesthetic judgements that they expressed their most deep-seated ethical views.[47]

This is, perhaps ironically, to come back to music via a spatial metaphor. But what makes music special – what makes it special for identity – is that it defines a space without boundaries (a game without frontiers). Music is thus the cultural form best able both to cross borders – sounds carry across fences and walls and oceans, across classes, races and nations – and to define places; in clubs, scenes, and raves, listening on headphones, radio and in the concert hall, we are only where the music takes us.

Notes

1 Gina Arnold, *Route 666. On the Road to Nirvana*, St Martin's Press, New York, 1993, p. 228

2 Anthony Storr, *Music and the Mind*, Harper Collins, London and New York, 1992, p. 153.

3 John Miller Chernoff, *African Rhythm and African Sensibility*, Chicago University Press, Chicago, 1979, p. 167.

4 Although the best version of the argument remains the earliest, Paul Willis's *Profane Culture*, Routledge & Kegan Paul, London, 1978.

5 Quoted in Eric Lott, *Love and Theft. Blackface Minstrelsy and the American Working Class*, Oxford University Press, New York and Oxford, 1993, p. 91.

6 For the debate about race and rap see, for example, Greg Tate, *Flyboy in the Buttermilk. Essays on Contemporary America*, Simon & Schuster, New York, 1992. For the debate about gender and music see Susan McClary, *Feminine Endings. Music, Gender and Sexuality*, University of Minnesota Press, Minneapolis, 1991. For discussion of national musical identities see Deanna Robinson, Elizabeth Buck and Marlene Cuthbert, *Music at the Margins*, Sage, London, 1991.

7 For an interesting answer to the last question see Tony Mitchell, 'World music and the popular music industry: an Australian view', *Ethnomusicology*, 37, 3, 1993, pp. 309–38.

8 Or, as Charles Rosen put it more recently (and with reference to sexuality rather than class): "I presume – or I should like to presume – that a rapist and a foot fetishist would write very different kinds of music, but I am not sure how we would go about confirming this". ('Music à la mode', *New York Review of Books*, 23 June 1994, p. 60).

9 For an interesting answer to these questions, see Richard Shusterman, *Pragmatic Aesthetics*, Basil Blackwell, Oxford, 1992, Chapter 8. Shusterman, like many commentators, takes rap to be the postmodern articulation of popular music. He argues (p. 202) that rap is 'postmodern' in its appropriation, recycling and eclectic mixing of previously existing sounds and styles; in its enthusiastic embrace of technology and mass culture; in its emphasis on the localized and temporal rather than the universal and eternal. By this definition, though, other pop forms besides rap could be suitably labelled postmodern, and Shusterman's most interesting argument about rap does not really raise the spectre of postmodernism at all! Rap, he suggests (pp. 212–13) is unusual in uniting the aesthetic and the cognitive, the political-functional and the artistic-expressive; rap is dynamic culturally (p. 235) because of the *formal* tension it expresses between innovation and coherence.

10 Mark Slobin, *Subculture Sounds. Micromusic of the West*, Wesleyan University Press, Hanover and London, 1993, p. 41.

11 Ibid., p. 42.

12 I develop this argument at much greater length in my *Performing Rites*, Harvard University Press, Cambridge, MA, forthcoming.

13 For an influential and pioneering approach to music in this way see Steven Feld, *Sound and Sentiment: Birds, Weeping, Poetics and Song in Kaluli Expression*, University of Pennsylvania Press, Philadelphia, 1982.

14 Chernoff, *African Rhythm and African Sensibility*, p. 36. (original emphasis).

15 Philip V. Bohlman, 'Of *Yekkes* and chamber music in Israel: ethnomusicological meaning in western music history', in Stephen Blum, Philip V. Bohlman and Daniel M. Neuman (eds), *Ethnomusicology and Modern Music History*, University of Illinois Press, Urbana and Chicago, 1991, pp. 266–7.

16 See ibid., p. 255.

17 Frank Kogan, 'Spoonie Gee', *Reasons for Living*, 2, June 1986.

18 Gregory Sandow, 'A fine madness', *Village Voice*, 16 March 1982, pp. 76, 93.

19 For an excellent discussion of the issues here see Andrew Goodwin, 'Popular music and postmodern theory', *Cultural Studies*, 5, 2, 1990, pp. 174–90.

20 See Paul Gilroy, 'Sounds authentic: black music, ethnicity, and the challenge of a *changing* same', *Black Music Research Journal*, 10, 2, 1990, pp. 128–31.

21 This is most obvious in poetry, but for an interesting argument about painting picking up on some of the points raised here see Mieke Bal, *Reading Rembrandt*, Cambridge: Cambridge University Press, 1991 and the useful review by Sandra Kemp in *Journal of Literature and Theology*, 7, 3, 1993, pp. 302–5.

22 Tate, *Flyboy in the Buttermilk*, p. 25.

23 Christopher A. Waterman, '*Jùjú history: toward a theory of sociomusical practice*', in Blum et al. (eds), *Ethnomusicology*, pp. 66–7.

24 Gilroy, 'Sounds authentic', p.113. Gilroy suggests that the concepts of 'dramaturgy, enunciation and gesture' ('the Pre- and anti-discursive constituents of black metacommunications') thus need to be added to concerns for textuality and narrative in black cultural history.

25 Paul Gilroy, 'It ain't where you're from, it's where you're at . . .', *Third Text*, 13, 1990–1, pp. 10, 12.

26 Quoted ibid., pp. 13–14. And see Chernoff, *African Rhythm and African Sensibility*, Chapter 2, for an extensive discussion of what he calls 'the conversational mode' of African music.

27 Brian Jackson, *Working Class Community*, Routledge & Kegan Paul, London, 1968, pp. 129, 131.

28 Bohlman, 'Of *Yekkes* and chamber music', pp. 259–60. For the practices of amateur music making in American academic communities, see Robert A. Stebbins, 'Music among friends: the social networks of amateur musicians', *International Review of Sociology*, 12, 1976.

29 Timothy D'Arch Smith, *Peepin' in a Seafood Store. Some Pleasures of Rock Music*, Michael Russell (Publishing), Wilby, Norwich, 1992, p. 23.

30 Jonathan Ree, 'Funny voices: stories, "punctuation" and personal identity', *New Literary History*, 21, 1990, p. 1055.

31 Ibid., p. 1058.

32 Kwame Anthony Appiah, *In My Father's House*, Methuen, London, 1992, p. 283.

33 Slobin, *Subculture Sounds*, p. 55.

34 Lott, *Love and Theft*, p. 92.

35 Simon Frith, *Literary Studies as Cultural Studies. Whose Literature? Whose Culture?*, University of Strathclyde, Glasgow, 1991, p. 21.

36 I take this point from Veronica Doubleday's review of Martin Stokes's *The Arabesk Debate* in *Popular Music*, 13, 2, 1994, pp. 231–3.

37 Gilroy, 'It ain't', p. 6.

38 Gilroy, 'Sounds authentic', p. 134.

39 Colin Campbell, *The Romantic Ethic and the Spirit of Modern Consumerism*, Basil Blackwell, Oxford, 1987, p. 246.

40 Quoted (from *The Second Sex*) in Erving Goffman, *The Presentation of Self in Everyday Life*, Allen Lane, London, 1969 [1959], p. 65.

41 Gilroy, 'Sounds authentic', p. 127.

42 This point is emerging in interesting ways from Sara Cohen's current research on ethnic musical communities in Liverpool. See, for example, Sara Cohen, 'Localizing sound: music, place and social mobility', in Will Staw (ed.), *Popular Music: Style and Identity*, Centre for Research in Canadian Cultural Industries and Institutions, Montreal, 1995, pp. 61–7.

43 Myers, 'Indian music in Felicity', in Blum et al. *Ethnomusicology*, p. 236.

44 Ibid., p. 240.

45 Chernoff, *African Rhythm and African Sensibility*, pp. 125, 140, 144.

46 Appiah, *In My Father's House*, p. 121.

47 Ruth Finnegan, *The Hidden Musicians*, Cambridge University Press, Cambridge, 1989. And cf. Robert A. Stebbins, *Amateurs. On the Margin between Work and Leisure*, Sage, Beverly Hills and London, 1979.

8

Identity, Genealogy, History

Nikolas Rose

> To breed an animal with the right to make promises. How much all this presupposes! A man who wishes to dispose of his future in this manner must first have learned to separate necessary from accidental acts; to think causally; to see distant things as though they were near at hand; to distinguish means from ends. In short, he must have become not only calculating but himself calculable, regular even to his own perception, if he is to stand pledge for his own future.
>
> F.W. Nietzsche, *The Genealogy of Morals* (Second Essay: 'On the origins and genesis of human responsibility')

How should we do the history of the person?[1] What might be the relationship between such an historical endeavour and current concerns in social and political theory with such issues as identity, self, body, desire? More significantly, perhaps, what light might historical investigations cast upon current ethical preoccupations with human beings as subjects of autonomy and freedom, or alternatively, as bound to a national, ethnic, cultural or territorial identity, and the political programmes, strategies and techniques to which they are linked?

I would like to suggest a particular approach to this issue, an approach which I term 'the genealogy of subjectification'.[2] The phrasing is awkward but, I think, important. Its importance lies, in part, in indicating what such an undertaking is *not*. On the one hand, it is not an attempt to write the history of changing ideas of the person, as they have figured within philosophy, literature, culture, etc. Historians, philosophers and anthropologists have long engaged in the writing of such narratives, and no doubt they are significant and instructive (e.g. Taylor, 1989 and cf. the very different approach advocated in Tully, 1993). But it is unwise to assume that one can derive, from an account of notions of the human being in cosmology, philosophy, aesthetics or literature, evidence about the organization of the mundane everyday practices and presuppositions that shape the conduct of human beings in particular sites and practices (Dean, 1994). A genealogy of subjectification is, therefore, not a history of ideas: its domain of investigation is that of practices and techniques, of thought as it seeks to make itself *technical*.

Equally my approach needs to be distinguished from attempts to write the history of the person or self as a psychological entity, to see how different ages produce humans with different psychological character- istics, different emotions, beliefs, pathologies. Such a project for a history of the self is certainly imaginable and something like this aspiration shapes a number of recent studies, some of which I discuss below. But such analyses presuppose a way of thinking that is itself an outcome of history, one that emerges only in the nineteenth century. For it is only at this historical moment, and in a limited and localized geographical space, that a way of thinking emerges in which human being is understood in terms of persons each equipped with an inner domain, a 'psychology', which is structured by the interaction of biographical experience with certain laws or processes characteristic of human psychology.

A genealogy of subjectification takes this individualized, interiorized, totalized and psychologized understanding of what it is to be human as delineating the site of a historical problem, not providing the grounds for a historical narrative. Such a genealogy works towards an account of the ways in which this modern 'regime of the self' emerges, not as the outcome of any gradual process of enlightenment, in which humans, aided by the endeavours of science, come at last to recognize their true nature, but out of a number of contingent and altogether less refined and dignified practices and processes. To write such a genealogy is to seek to unpick the ways in which 'the self' that functions as a regulatory ideal in so many aspects of our contemporary forms of life – not merely in our passional relations with one another, but in our projects of life planning, our ways of managing industrial and other organizations, our systems of consumption, many of our genres of literature and aesthetic production – is a kind of 'irreal' plan of projection, put together somewhat contingently and haphazardly at the intersection of a range of distinct histories – of forms of thought, techniques of regulation, problems of organization and so forth.

Dimensions of our 'relation to ourselves'

A genealogy of subjectification is a genealogy of what one might term, following Michel Foucault, 'our relation to ourselves'.[3] Its field of investigation comprises the kinds of attention that humans have directed towards themselves and others in different places, spaces and times. To put this rather more grandly, one might say that this was a genealogy of 'being's relation to itself' and the technical forms that this has assumed. The human being, that is to say, is that kind of creature whose ontology is historical. And the history of human being, therefore, requires an investigation of the intellectual and practical techniques that have comprised the instruments through which being has historically consti- tuted itself: it is a matter of analysing 'the problematizations through which being offers itself to be, necessarily, thought – and the practices on the basis of which these problematizations are formed' (Foucault, 1986a: 11; Jambet, 1992). The focus of such a genealogy, therefore, is not 'the historical construction of the self' but the history of *the relations* which human beings have established with themselves. These relations are constructed and historical, but they are not to be understood by locating them in some amorphous domain of culture. On the contrary, they are addressed from the perspective of 'government' (Foucault, 1991; cf. Burchell et al., 1991). Our relation with ourselves, that is to say, has assumed the form it has because it has been the object of a whole variety of more or less rationalized schemes, which have sought to shape our ways of understanding and enacting our existence as human beings in the name of certain objectives – manliness, femininity, honour, modesty, propriety, civility, discipline, distinction, efficiency, harmony, fulfilment, virtue, pleasure – the list is as diverse and heterogeneous as it is interminable.

One of the reasons for stressing this point is to distinguish my approach from a number of recent analyses that have, explicitly or implicitly, viewed changing forms of subjectivity or identity as consequences of wider social and cultural transformations – modernity, late modernity, the risk society (Bauman, 1991; Beck, 1992; Giddens, 1991; Lash and Friedman, 1992). Of course, this work continues a long tradition of narratives, stretching back at least to Jacob Burckhardt, that have written histories of the rise of the individual as a consequence of a general social transformation from tradition to modernity, feudalism to capitalism, *Gemeinschaft* to *Gesellschaft*, mechanical to organic solidarity and so forth (Burckhardt, 1990). These kinds of analysis regard changes in the ways in which human beings understand and act upon themselves as the outcome of 'more fundamental' historical events located elsewhere – in production regimes, in technological change, in alterations in demography or family forms, in 'culture'. No doubt events in each of these areas have significance in relation to the problem of subjectification. But however significant they may be, it is important to insist that such changes do not transform ways of being human by virtue of some 'experience' that they produce. Changing relations of subjectification, I want to argue, cannot be established by derivation or interpretation of other cultural or social forms. To explicitly or implicitly assume that they can is to presume the *continuity* of human beings as the subjects of history, essentially equipped with the capacity for endowing meaning (Dean, 1994). But the ways in which humans 'give meaning to experience' have their own history. Devices of 'meaning production' – grids of visualization, vocabularies, norms and systems of judgement – *produce* experience; they are not themselves *produced by* experience (Joyce, 1994). These intellectual techniques do not come ready made, they have to be invented, refined and stabilized, they have to be disseminated and implanted in different ways in different practices – schools, families, streets, workplaces, courtrooms. If we use the term 'subjectification' to designate all those heterogeneous processes and practices by means of which human beings come to relate to themselves and others as subjects of a certain type, then subjectification has its own history. And the history of subjectification is more practical, more technical and less unified than sociological accounts allow.

Thus a genealogy of subjectification would focus directly upon the *practices* within which human beings have been located in particular 'regimes of the person'. This would not be a continuous history of the self, but rather an account of the diversity of languages of 'personhood' that have taken shape – character, personality, identity, reputation, honour, citizen, individual, normal, lunatic, patient, client, husband, mother, daughter. . . –and the norms, techniques and relations of authority within which these have circulated in legal, domestic, industrial and other practices for acting upon the conduct of persons. Such an investigation might proceed along a number of linked pathways:

Problematizations

Where, how and by whom are aspects of the human being rendered problematic, according to what systems of judgement and in relation to what concerns? To take some pertinent examples, one might consider the ways in which the language of constitution and character comes to operate within the themes of urban decline and degeneracy articulated by psychiatrists, urban reformers and politicians in the last decades of the nineteenth century, or the ways in which the vocabulary of adjustment and maladjustment comes to be used to problematize conduct in sites as diverse as the workplace, the courtroom and the school in the 1920s and 1930s. To pose the matter in this way is to stress the primacy of the pathological over the normal in the genealogy of subjectification – our vocabularies and techniques of the person, by and large, have not emerged in a field of reflection on the normal individual, the normal character, the normal personality, the normal intelligence, but rather, the very notion of normality has emerged out of a concern with types of conduct, thought, expression deemed troublesome or dangerous (Rose, 1985). This is a methodological as much as an epistemological point – in the genealogy of subjectification, pride of place is not occupied by the philosophers reflecting in their studies on the nature of the person, the will, the conscience, morality and the like, but in the mundane practices where conduct has become problematic to others or the self, and in the mundane texts and programmes – on asylum management, medical treatment of women, advisable regimes of child-rearing, new ideas in workplace management, improving one's self-esteem – seeking to render these problems intelligible and, at the same time, manageable.[4]

Technologies

What means have been invented to govern the human being, to shape or fashion conduct in desired directions, and how have programmes sought to embody these in certain technical forms? The notion of technology may seem antithetical to the domain of human being, such that claims about the inappropriate technologization of humanity form the basis of many a critique. However, our very experience of ourselves as certain sorts of persons – creatures of freedom, of liberty, of personal powers, of self-realization – is the outcome of a range of human technologies, technologies that take modes of being human as their object.[5] Technology, here, refers to any assembly structured by a practical rationality governed by a more or less conscious goal. Human technologies are hybrid assemblages of knowledges, instruments, persons, systems of judgement, buildings and spaces, underpinned at the programmatic level by certain presuppositions about, and objectives for, human beings. One can regard the school, the prison, the asylum as examples of one species of such technologies, those which Foucault termed disciplinary and which operate in terms of a detailed structuring of space, time and relations amongst individuals, through procedures of hierarchical observation and normalizing judgement, through attempts to enfold these judgements into the procedures and judgements which the individual utilizes in order to conduct their own conduct (Foucault, 1977; cf. Markus, 1993 for an examination of the spatial form of such assemblies). A second example of a mobile and multivalent technology is that of the pastoral relation, a relation of spiritual guidance between an authority and each member of their flock, embodying techniques such as confession and self-disclosure, exemplarity and discipleship, enfolded into the person through a variety of schemas of self-inspection, self-suspicion, self-disclosure, self-decipherment and self-nurturing. Like discipline, this pastoral technology is capable of articulation in a range of different forms, in the relation of priest and parishioner, therapist and patient, social worker and client and in the relation of the 'educated' subject to itself. We should not see the disciplinary and pastoral relations of subjectification as opposed historically or ethically – the regimes enacted in schools, asylums and prisons embody both. Perhaps the insistence upon an analytic of human technologies is one of the most distinctive features of the approach I am advocating, an analysis which does not start from the view that the technologizing of human conduct is malign, but rather examines the ways in which human beings have been simultaneously capacitated and governed by their organization within a technological field.

Authorities

Who is accorded or claims the capacity to speak truthfully about humans, their nature and their problems, and what characterizes the truths about persons that are accorded such authority? Through which apparatuses are such authorities authorized – universities, the legal apparatus, churches, politics? To what extent does the authority of authority depend upon a claim to a positive knowledge, to wisdom and virtue, to experience and practical judgement, to the capacity to resolve conflicts? How are authorities themselves governed – by legal codes, by the market, by the protocols of bureaucracy, by professional ethics? And what then is the relation between authorities and those who are subject to them – priest/parishioner; doctor/patient, manager/employee, therapist/patient . . . ? This focus upon authorities (rather than 'power'), upon all the diverse persons, things, devices, associations, modes of thought, types of judgement that seek, claim, acquire or are accorded authority, and upon the diversity of ways in which authority is authorized again seems to me to be a distinctive feature of this kind of investigation.

Teleologies

What forms of life are the aims, ideals or exemplars for these different practices for working upon persons: the professional persona exercising a vocation with wisdom and dispassion; the manly warrior pursuing a life of honour through a calculated risking of the body; the responsible father living a life of prudence and moderation; the labourer accepting his or her lot with a docility grounded in a belief in the inviolability of authority or a reward in a life to come; the good wife fulfilling her domestic duties with quiet efficiency and self-effacement; the entrepreneurial individual striving after secular improvements in 'quality of life'; the passionate lover skilled in the arts of pleasure . . . ? What codes of knowledge support these ideals, and to what ethical valorization are they tied? Against those who suggest that a single model of the person comes to prominence in any specific culture, it is important to stress the heterogeneity and specificity of the ideals or models of personhood deployed in different practices, and the ways in which they are articulated in relation to specific problems and solutions concerning human conduct. It is only from this perspective, I think, that one can identify the peculiarity of those programmatic attempts to install a single model of the individual as the ethical ideal across a range of different sites and practices. For example, the Puritan sects discussed by Weber were unusual in their attempts to ensure that the mode of individual comportment in terms of sobriety, duty, modesty, self and so forth applied to practices as diverse as the enjoyment of popular entertainment, labour and comportment within the home. In our own times, both economics, in the form of a model of economic rationality, and psychology, in the form of a model of the psychological individual, have provided the basis for similar attempts at the unification of life conduct around a single model of appropriate subjectivity. But unification of subjectification has to be seen as an objective of particular programmes, or a presupposition of particular styles of thinking, not a feature of human cultures.

Strategies

How are these procedures for regulating the capacities of persons linked into wider moral, social or political objectives concerning the undesirable and desirable features of populations, workforce, family, society, etc.? Of particular significance here are the divisions and relations established between modalities for the government of conduct accorded the status of 'political', and those enacted through forms of authority and apparatus deemed non-political – whether these be the technical knowledge of experts, the judicial knowledge of the courts, the organizational knowledge of managers or the 'natural' knowledges of the family and the mother. Typical of those rationalities of government that consider themselves 'liberal' is the simultaneous delimitation of the sphere of the political by reference to the right of other domains – the market, civil society and the family being the three most commonly deployed – and the invention of a range of techniques that would try to act on events in these domains without breaching their autonomy. It is for this reason that knowledges and forms of expertise concerning the internal characteristics of the domains to be governed assume particular importance in liberal strategies and programmes of rule, for these domains are not to be 'dominated' by rule, but must be known, understood and related to in such a way that events within them – productivity and conditions of trade, the activities of civil associations, ways of rearing children and organizing conjugal relations and financial support within household – support, and do not oppose, political objectives.[6] In the case that we are discussing here, the characteristics of persons, as those 'free individuals' upon whom liberalism depends for its political legitimacy and functionality, assume a particular significance. Perhaps one could say that the general strategic field of all those programmes of government that regard themselves as liberal has been defined by the problem of how free individuals can be governed such that they enact their freedom appropriately.

The government of others and the government of oneself

Each of these directions for investigation is inspired, in large measure, by the writings of Michel Foucault. In particular, of course, they arise from Foucault's suggestions concerning a genealogy of the arts of government – where government is conceived of, most generally, as encompassing all those more or less rationalized programmes and strategies for 'the conduct of conduct' – and his conception of governmentality – which refers to the emergence of political rationalities, or mentalities of rule, where rule becomes a matter of the calculated management of the affairs of each and of all in order to achieve certain desirable objectives (Foucault, 1991; see the discussion of the notion of government in Gordon, 1991). Government, here, does not indicate a theory, but rather a certain perspective from which one might make intelligible the diversity of attempts by authorities of different sorts to act upon the actions of others in relation to objectives of national prosperity, harmony, virtue, productivity, social order, discipline, emancipation, self-realization and so forth. And this perspective is significant also because it directs our attention to the ways in which strategies for the conduct of conduct so frequently operate through trying to shape what Foucault also termed 'technologies of the self' – 'self-steering mechanisms', or the ways in which individuals experience, understand, judge and conduct themselves (Foucault, 1986a, 1986b, 1988). Technologies of the self take the form of the elaboration of certain techniques for the conduct of one's relation with oneself, for example requiring one to relate to oneself epistemologically (know yourself), despotically (master yourself) or in other ways (care for yourself). They are embodied in particular technical practices (confession, diary writing, group discussion, the twelve-steps programme of Alcoholics Anonymous). And they are always practised under the actual or imagined authority of some system of truth and of some authoritative individual, whether these be theological and priestly, psychological and therapeutic or disciplinary and tutelary.

A number of issues arise from these considerations.

The first concerns the issue of ethics itself. In his later writings, Foucault utilized the notion of 'ethics' as a general designation for his investigations into the genealogy of our present forms of 'concern' for the self (Foucault, 1979, 1986a, 1986b; cf. Minson, 1993). Ethical practices, for Foucault, were distinguished from the domain of morality, in that moral systems are, by and large, systems of injunction and interdiction – thou shalt do this or thou shalt not do that – and are most frequently articulated in relation to some relatively formalized code. Ethics, on the other hand, refers to the domain of practical advice as to how one should concern oneself with oneself, make oneself the subject of solicitude and attention, conduct oneself in the world of one's everyday existence. Different cultural periods, Foucault argued, differed in the respective weight that their practices for the regulation of conduct placed upon codified moral injunctions and the practical repertoires of ethical advice. However, one might undertake a genealogy of our contemporary ethical regime which, Foucault suggested, encouraged human beings to relate to themselves as the subject of a 'sexuality', and were enjoined to 'know themselves' through a hermeneutics of the self, to explore, discover, reveal and live in the light of the desires that comprised one's truth. Such a genealogy would disturb the appearance of enlightenment which clothed such a regime, by exploring the way in which certain forms of spiritual practice which could be found in Greek, Roman and early Christian ethics had become incorporated into priestly power, and later into the practices of the educational, medical and psychological type (Foucault, 1986a: 11).

Clearly the approach I have outlined above has derived much from Foucault's arguments on these issues. However, I would wish to develop this argument in a number of respects. First, as has been pointed out elsewhere, the notion of 'techniques of the self' can be somewhat misleading. The self does not form the transhistorical object of techniques for being human but only one way in which humans have been enjoined to understand and relate to themselves (Hadot, 1992). In different practices, these relations are cast in terms of individuality, character, constitution, reputation, personality and the like which are neither merely *different versions* of a self, nor do they *sum into* a self. Further, the extent to which our contemporary relation to ourselves – inwardness, self-exploration, self-fulfilment and the like – does indeed take the issue of sexuality and desire as its fulcrum must remain an open question for historical investigation. Elsewhere I have suggested that the self, itself, has become the object of valorization, a regime of subjectification in which desire has become freed from its dependence upon the law of an inner sexuality and been transformed into a variety of passions to discover and realize the identity of the self itself (Rose, 1989).

Further, I would suggest, one needs to extend an analysis of the relations between government and subjectification beyond the field of ethics, if by that one means all those styles of relating to oneself that are structured by the divisions of truth and falsity, the permitted and the forbidden. One needs to examine, also, the government of this relation along some other axes.

One of these axes concerns the attempt to inculcate a certain relation to oneself through transformations in 'mentalities' or what one might term 'intellectual techniques' – reading, memory, writing, numeracy and so forth (see, for some powerful examples, Eisenstein, 1979 and Goody and Watt, 1963). For example, especially over the course of the nineteenth century in Europe and the United States, one sees the development of a host of projects for the transformation of the intellect in the service of particular objectives, each of which seeks to enjoin a particular relation to the self through the implantation of certain capacities of reading, writing and calculating. One example here would be the way in which, in the latter decades of the nineteenth century, Republican educators in the United States promoted numeracy, in particular the numerical capacities that they argued would be facilitated by decimalization, in order to generate a particular kind of relation to themselves and their world in those so equipped. A numerate self would be a calculating self, who would establish a prudent relation to the future, to budgeting, to trade, to politics and to life conduct in general (Cline-Cohen, 1982: 148–9).

A second axis would concern corporealities or body techniques. Of course, anthropologists and others have remarked upon the cultural shaping of bodies – comportment, expression of emotion and the like as they differ from culture to culture, and within cultures between genders, ages, status groups and the like. Marcel Mauss provides the classic account of the ways in which the body, as a technical instrument, is organized differently in different cultures – different ways of walking, sitting, digging, marching and so forth (Mauss, 1979; cf. Bourdieu, 1977).

However, a genealogy of subjectification is not concerned with the general problem of the cultural relativity of bodily capacities, but with the ways in which different corporeal regimes have been devised and implanted in rationalized attempts to enjoin a particular relation to the self and to others. Norbert Elias has given many powerful examples of the ways in which explicit codes of bodily conduct – manners, etiquette and the self-monitoring of bodily functions and actions – were enjoined upon individuals in different positions within the apparatus of the court (Elias, 1983; cf. Elias, 1978; Osborne, 1996). Foucault's own studies of the asylum and the prison explore programmes in which the disciplining of the body of the pathological individual not only involved the catching up of that body within an external regime of hierarchical surveillance and normalizing judgement, and the imbrication of the body in a molecular regime governing movement in time and space, but also sought to enjoin an internal relation between the pathological individual and his or her body, in which bodily comportment would both manifest and maintain a certain disciplined mastery exercised by the person over themselves (Foucault, 1967, 1977; see also Smith, 1992 for a history of the notion of 'inhibition' and its relation to the manifestation of steadfastness and self-mastery through the exercise of control over the body). An analogous, though substantively very different, relation to the body was a key element in the self-sculpting of a certain aesthetic persona in nineteenth century Europe, embodied in certain styles of dress but also in the cultivation of certain body techniques such as swimming that would produce and display a particular relation to the natural (Sprawson, 1992). Historians of gender have begun to analyse the ways in which the appropriate performance of sexual identity has historically been linked to the inculcation of certain regimes of the body (Butler, 1990). Certain ways of holding oneself, walking, running, holding the head and positioning the limbs, are not merely culturally relative or acquired through gender socialization, but are regimes of the body which seek to subjectify in terms of a certain truth of gender, inscribing a particular relation to oneself in a corporeal regime: prescribed, rationalized and taught in manuals of advice, etiquette and manners, and enjoined by sanctions as well as seductions.

These comments should indicate something of the heterogeneity of the links between the government of others and the government of the self. It is important to stress two further aspects of this heterogeneity. The first concerns the diversity of modes in which a certain relation to oneself is enjoined. There is a temptation to stress the elements of self-mastery and restrictions over one's desires and instincts that are entailed in many regimes of subjectification – the injunction to control or civilize an inner nature that is excessive. Certainly one can see this theme in many nineteenth-century debates on ethics and character for both the ruling order and in the respectable labouring classes – a paradoxical 'despotism of the self' at the heart of liberal doctrines of liberty of the subject (I derive this formulation from Valverde, 1996). But there are many other modes in which this relation to oneself can be established and, even within the exercise of mastery, a variety of configurations through which one can be encouraged to master oneself. To master one's will in the service of character by the inculcation of habits and rituals of self-denial, prudence and foresight, for example, is different from mastering one's desire by bringing its roots to awareness through a reflexive hermeneutics in order to free oneself from the self-destructive consequences of repression, projection and identification.

Further, the very form of the relation can vary. It can be one of knowledge, as in the injunction to know oneself, which Foucault traces back to the Christian confession and forward to the techniques of psychotherapeutics: here the codes of knowledge are inevitably supplied not by pure introspection but by rendering one's introspection in a particular vocabulary of feelings, beliefs, passions, desires, values or whatever and according to a particular explanatory code derived from some source of authority. Or it can be one of concern and solicitude, as in contemporary projects for the care of the self in which the self is to be nurtured, protected, safeguarded by regimes of diet, stress minimization and self-esteem. Equally, the relation to authority can vary. Consider, for example, some of the changing authority configurations in the government of madness and mental health: the relation of mastery that was exercised between asylum doctor and mad person in late eighteenth century moral medicine; the relation of discipline and institutional authority that obtained between the nineteenth century asylum doctor and the inmate; the relation of pedagogy that obtained between the mental hygienists of the first half of the twentieth century and the children and parents, pupils and teachers, workers and managers, generals and soldiers upon whom they sought to act; the relation of seduction, conversion and exemplarity that obtains between the psychotherapist and the client today.

As will be evident from the above discussion, whilst the relations to oneself enjoined at any one historical moment may resemble one another in various ways – for example the Victorian notion of character was widely dispersed across many different practices – the extent to which this is the case is a matter for empirical investigation. It is not a matter, therefore, of narrating a general history of the idea of the person or self, but of tracing the technical forms accorded to the relation to oneself in various practices – legal, military, industrial, familial, economic. And even within any practice, heterogeneity must be assumed to be more common than homogeneity – consider, for example, the very different configurations of personhood in the legal apparatus at any one moment – the difference between the notion of status and reputation as it functioned in civil proceedings in the nineteenth century and the simultaneous elaboration of a new relation to the law-breaker as a pathological personality in the criminal courts and the prison system (Pasquino, 1991).

If our own present is marked by a certain levelling of these differences, such that presuppositions concerning human beings in diverse practices share a certain family resemblance – humans as subjects of autonomy, equipped with a psychology aspiring to self-fulfilment and actually or potentially running their lives as a kind of enterprise of themselves – then this is precisely the point of departure for a genealogical investigation. In what ways was this regime of the self put together, under what conditions and in relation to what demands and forms of authority? We have certainly seen a proliferation of expertises of human conduct over the last hundred years: economists, managers, accountants, lawyers, counsellors, therapists, medics, anthropologists, political scientists, social policy experts and the like. But I would argue that the 'unification' of regimes of subjectification has much to do with the rise of one particular form of positive expertise of human being - that of the psy disciplines – and their 'generosity'. By their 'generosity' I mean that, contrary to conventional views of the exclusivity of professional knowledge, psy has been happy, indeed eager, to 'give itself away' – to lend its vocabularies, explanations and types of judgement to other professional groups and to implant them within its clients (Rose, 1992b). The psy disciplines, partly as a consequence of their heterogeneity and lack of a single paradigm, have acquired a peculiar penetrative capacity in relation to practices for the conduct of conduct. They have been able to supply a whole variety of models of selfhood and recipes for action in relation to the government of persons by professionals in different locales. Their potency has been increased by their ability to supplement these practicable qualities with a legitimacy deriving from their claims to tell the truth about human beings. They have disseminated themselves further through their ready translatability into programmes for reshaping the self-steering mechanisms of individuals. It is, of course, true that the psy disciplines are not held publicly in particularly high esteem, and their practitioners are often figures of fun. But one should not be misled by this – it has become impossible to conceive of personhood, to experience one's own or another's personhood, or to govern oneself or others without 'psy'.

Let me return to the issue of the diversity of regimes of subjectification. A further dimension of heterogeneity arises from the fact that ways of governing others are linked not only to the subjectification of the governed, but also to the subjectification of those who would govern conduct. Thus Foucault argues that the problematization of sex between men for the Greeks was linked to the demand that one who would exercise authority over others should first be able to exercise dominion over his own passions and appetites – for only if one was not a slave to oneself was one competent to exercise authority over others (Foucault, 1988: 6–7; cf. Minson, 1993: 20–1). Peter Brown points to the work required of a young man of the privileged classes in the Roman Empire of the second century, who was advised to remove from himself all aspects of 'softness' and 'womanishness' – in his gait, in his rhythms of speech, in his self-control – in order to manifest himself as capable of exercising authority over others (Brown, 1989: 11). Gerhard Oestreich suggests that the revival of Stoic ethics in seventeenth- and eighteenth-century Europe was a response to the criticism of authority as ossified and corrupt: the virtues of love, trust, reputation, gentleness, spiritual powers, respect for justice and the like were to become the means for authorities to renew themselves (Oestreich, 1982: 87). Stephan Collini has described the novel ways in which the Victorian intellectual classes problematized themselves in terms of such qualities as steadfastness and altruism: they interrogated themselves in terms of a constant anxiety about and infirmity of the will, and found, in certain forms of social and philanthropic work, an antidote to self-doubt (Collini, 1991, discussed in Osborne, 1996). Whilst these same Victorian intellectuals were problematizing all sorts of aspects of social life in terms of moral character, threats to character, weakness of character and the need to promote good character, and arguing that the virtues of character – self-reliance, sobriety, independence, self-restraint, respectability, self-improvement – should be inculcated in others through positive actions of the state and the statesman, they were making themselves the subject of a related, but rather different, ethical work (Collini, 1979: 29ff.). Similarly, throughout the nineteenth century, one sees the emergence of quite novel programmes for the reform of secular authority within the civil service, the apparatus of colonial rule and the organizations of industry and politics, in which the persona of the civil servant, the bureaucrat, the colonial governor will become the target of a whole new ethical regime of disinterest, justice, respect for rules, distinction between the performance of one's office and one's private passions and much more (Weber, 1978: cf. Hunter, 1993a, b, c; Minson, 1993; du Gay, 1994; Osborne, 1994). And, of course, many of those who were subject to the government of these authorities – indigenous officials in the colonies, housewives of the respectable classes, parents, schoolteachers, working men, governesses – were themselves called upon to play their part in the making up of others and to inculcate in them a certain relation to themselves.

From this perspective, it is no longer surprising that human beings often find themselves resisting the forms of personhood that they are enjoined to adopt. 'Resistance' – if by that one means opposition to a particular regime for the conduct of one's conduct – requires no theory of agency. It needs no account of the inherent forces within each human being that love liberty, seek to enhance their own powers or capacities, or strive for emancipation, that are prior to and in conflict with the demands of civilization and discipline. One no more needs a theory of agency to account for resistance than one needs an epistemology to account for the production of truth effects. Human beings are not the unified subjects of some coherent regime of domination that produces persons in the form in which it dreams. On the contrary, they live their lives in a constant movement across different practices that address them in different ways. Within these different practices, persons are addressed as different sorts of human being, presupposed to be different sorts of human being, acted upon as if they were different sorts of human being. Techniques of relating to oneself as a subject of unique capacities worthy of respect run up against practices or relating to oneself as the target of discipline, duty and docility. The humanist demand that one decipher oneself in terms of the authenticity of one's actions runs up against the political or institutional demand that one abides by the collective responsibility of organizational decision-making even when one is personally opposed to it. The ethical demand to suffer one's sorrows in silence and find a way of 'going on' is deemed problematic from the perspective of a passional ethic that obliges the person to disclose themselves in terms of a particular vocabulary of emotions and feelings.

Thus the existence of contestation, conflict and opposition in practices which conduct the conduct of persons is no surprise and requires no appeal to the particular qualities of human agency – except in the minimal sense that human being, like all else, exceeds all attempts to think it, simply because, whilst it is necessarily thought it does not exist in the form of thought.[7] Thus, in any one site or locale, humans turn programmes intended for one end to the service of others. One way of relating to oneself comes into conflict with others. For example, psychologists, management reformers, unions and workers have turned the vocabulary of humanistic psychology to account in a criticism of practices of management based upon a psycho-physiological or disciplinary understanding of persons. Reformers of the practices of welfare and medicine have, over the last two decades, turned the notion that human beings are subjects of rights against practices that presuppose human beings as the subjects of care. Out of this complex and contested field of oppositions, alliances and disparities of regimes of subjectification come accusations of inhumanity, criticisms, demands for reform, alternative programmes and the invention of new regimes of subjectification.

To designate some dimensions of these conflicts 'resistance' is itself perspectival: it can only ever be a matter of judgement. It is fruitless to complain, here, that such a perspective gives one no place to stand in the making of ethical critique and in the evaluation of ethical positions – the history of all those attempts to ground ethics that do appeal to some transcendental guarantor is plain enough – they cannot close conflicts over regimes of the person, but simply occupy one more position within the field of contestation (MacIntyre, 1981).

Folds in the soul

But the question may be asked: are not the kinds of phenomena that I have been discussing of interest precisely *because* they produce us as human beings with a certain kind of subjectivity? This is certainly the path followed by many who have investigated these issues, from Norbert Elias to contemporary feminist theorists who rely upon psychoanalysis to ground an account of the ways in which certain practices of the self become inscribed within the body and soul of the gendered subject (e.g. Butler, 1993; Probyn, 1993). For some, this path is advocated unproblematically. Elias, for example, did not doubt that human beings were the type of creatures inhabited by a psychoanalytic psychodynamics, and that this would provide the material basis for the inscription of civility into the soul of the social subject (Elias, 1978). I have already suggested that such a view is paradoxical, for it requires us to adopt a particular way of understanding the human being – that carved out at the end of the nineteenth century – as the basis for an investigation of the historicity of being human. For many others, this pathway is required if one is to avoid representing the human being as merely the passive and interminably malleable object of historical processes, if one is to have an account of agency and of resistance, and if one is to be able to find a place to stand in order to evaluate one regime of personhood over and above another (for one example of this argument, see Fraser, 1989). I have suggested that no such theory is required to account for conflict and contestation, and the stable ethical ground apparently provided by any given theory of the nature of human beings is illusory – one has no choice but to enter into a debate which cannot be closed by appeal to the nature of the human being as a subject of rights, of freedom, of autonomy or whatever. Is it possible, then, that one might write a genealogy of subjectification without a metapsychology? I think it is.

Such a genealogy, I suggest, requires only a minimal, weak or thin conception of the human material on which history writes (Patton, 1994). We are not concerned here with the social or historical construction of 'the person' or with the narration of the birth of modern 'self-identity'. Our concern is with the diversity of strategies and tactics of subjectification that have taken place and been deployed in diverse practices at different moments and in relation to different classifications and differentiations of persons. The human being, here, is not an entity with a history, but the target of a multiplicity of types of work, more like a latitude or a longitude at which different vectors of different speeds intersect. The 'interiority' which so many feel compelled to diagnose is not that of a psychological system, but of a discontinuous surface, a kind of infolding of exteriority.

I draw this notion of folding loosely from the work of Gilles Deleuze (1988, 1990, 1992; cf. Probyn, 1993: 128ff.). The concept of the fold or the pleat suggests a way in which we might think of human being without postulating any essential interiority, and thus without binding ourselves to a particular version of the law of this interiority whose history we are seeking to disturb and diagnose. The fold indicates a relation without an essential interior, one in which what is 'inside' is merely an infolding of an exterior. We are familiar with the idea that aspects of the body which we commonly think of as part of its interiority – the digestive tract, the lungs – are no more than the invagination of an outside. This does not prevent them from being valorized in terms of an apparently immutable body image taken as the norm for our perception of the contours and limits of our corporeality. Perhaps, then, we might think of the grasp that modes of subjectification have upon human beings in terms of such an infolding. Folds incorporate without totalizing, internalize without unifying, collect together discontinuously in the form of pleats making surfaces, spaces, flows and relations.

Within a genealogy of subjectification, that which would be infolded would be anything that can acquire authority: injunctions, advice, techniques, little habits of thought and emotion, an array of routines and norms of being human – the instruments through which being constitutes itself in different practices and relations. These infoldings are partially stabilized to the extent that human beings have come to imagine themselves as the subjects of a biography, to utilize certain 'arts of memory' in order to render this biography stable, to employ certain vocabularies and explanations to make this intelligible to themselves. However, this exposes the limits of the metaphor of the fold. For the lines of these folds do not run through a domain coterminous with the fleshly bounds of the human individual. Human being is emplaced, enacted through a regime of devices, gazes, techniques which extend beyond the limits of the flesh into spaces and assemblies. Memory of one's biography is not a simple psychological capacity, but is organized through rituals of storytelling, supported by artefacts such as photograph albums and so forth. The regimes of bureaucracy are not merely ethical procedures infolded into the soul, but occupy a matrix of offices, files, typewriters, habits of time-keeping, conversational repertoires, techniques of no-tation. The regimes of passion are not merely affective folds in the soul, but are enacted in certain secluded or valorized spaces, through sensualized equipment of beds, drapes and silks, routines of dressing and undressing, aestheticized devices for providing music and light, regimes of partitioning of time and so forth (Ranum, 1989).

We might thus counterpose a *spatialization* of being to the narrativiz-ation of being undertaken by sociologists and philosophers of modernity and postmodernity. That is to say, we need to render being intelligible in terms of the localization of routines, habits and techniques within specific domains of action and value: libraries and studies; bedrooms and bathhouses; courtrooms and schoolrooms, consulting rooms and museum galleries; markets and department stores. The five volumes of *The History of Private Life* compiled under the general editorship of Philippe Ariès and George Duby provide a wealth of examples of the way in which novel human capacities such as styles of writing or sexuality depend upon and give rise to particular forms of spatial organization of the human habitat (Veyne, 1987; Duby, 1988; Chartier, 1989; Perrot, 1990; Prost and Vincent 1991). However, there is nothing privileged about what has come to be termed 'private life' for the emplacement of regimes of subjectification – it is in the factory as much as the kitchen, in the military as much as the study, in the office as much as the bedroom, that the modern subject has been required to identify his or her subjectivity. To the apparent linearity, unidirectionality and irreversibility of time, we can counterpose the multiplicity of places, planes and practices. And in each of these spaces, repertoires of conduct are activated that are not bounded by the enclosure formed by the human skin or carried in a stable form in the interior of an individual: they are rather webs of tension across a space that accord human beings capacities and powers to the extent that they catch them up in hybrid assemblages of knowledges, instruments, vocabularies, systems of judgement and technical artefacts.

To this extent a genealogy of subjectification needs to think human being as a kind of machination, a hybrid of flesh, knowledge, passion and technique (Haraway, 1991). One of the characteristics of our current regime of the self is a way of reflecting upon and acting upon all these diverse domains, practices and assemblages in terms of a unified 'personality' to be revealed, discovered or worked on in each: a machination of the self that today forms the horizon of the thinkable. But this machination needs to be recognized as a specific regime of subjectification of recent origin – and the aim of a genealogy of subjectification is to unsettle it sufficiently to reveal the fragility of the lines that have made it up and hold it in place.

Subjectification today: a new configuration?

Those who stress the 'postmodern' features of our present suggest that subjectivity, today, has characteristic and novel features such as uncertainty, reflexivity, self-scrutiny, fragmentation and diversity. From the perspective I have outlined in this chapter, the questions about ourselves and our present should be posed rather differently. Are we witnessing a transformation in the ontology through which we think ourselves, a mutation in the techniques through which we conduct ourselves, a reconfiguration of the relations of authority by means of which we divide ourselves and identify ourselves as certain kinds of person, exercise certain kinds of concern in relation to ourselves, are governed and govern ourselves as human beings of a particular sort? Does the diversity of authorities of the self in our present, the pluralization of moral codes, the apparent attenuation of the links between political government and the regulation of conduct, the heterogeneity of forms of life, the valorization of choices and freedom in the shaping of a style of life, the simultaneous celebration of individuality and proliferation of techniques of group identification and segmentation – does all this signify that new modes of subjectification have appeared today?

My aim in this chapter has been to suggest that investigations of such questions should concern themselves with the intersection of practices for the government of others and practices for the government of the self.

This is not the place to undertake a detailed exploration of them; however, let me make a few points in conclusion.

Autonomy, freedom, choice, authenticity, enterprise, lifestyle – this new ethical vocabulary should neither be derided with an aristocratic disdain, nor interpreted as the sign of cultural malaise or the death of God, but be understood in terms of new rationalities of government and new technologies of the conduct of conduct (Rose, 1992b; cf. Rieff, 1966, 1987). In a whole variety of different locales – not just in sexuality, diet or the promotion of goods and services for consumption, but also in labour and in the construction of political subjects – the person is presumed to be an active agent, wishing to exercise informed, autonomous and secular responsibility in relation to his or her own destiny. The language of autonomy, identity, self-realization and the search for fulfilment forms a grid of regulatory ideals, not making up an amorphous cultural space, but traversing the doctor's consulting room, the factory floor and the personnel manager's office, and organizing such diverse programmes as those for the training of unemployed youth and those for the electoral competition of political parties.

A critical analysis of these new ethical vocabularies and their govern-mental inscription might examine the ways in which they establish new 'dividing practices' within and between subjects. Thus the language of responsible self-advancement is linked to a new perception of those outside civility – the excluded or marginalized who through wilfulness, incapacity or ignorance cannot or will not exercise such responsibility. On the one hand, pathologies are re-individualized, removed from a 'social' determination into a moral order, thus providing the basis for new and harsher strategies of surveillance and control of those who, after all, bear the responsibility for their fate within their own hands – exemplary is the way in which, in the UK, the unemployed person has become a 'job seeker' and the homeless person a 'rough sleeper'. On the other hand, these new sectors of the population are opened up to new forms of intervention by experts, which would re-educate or 'empower' them, equipping them with the techniques of life planning and personal conduct to cope as autonomous subjects, deploying psychological techniques from social skills training to group relations.

Further, it is important to draw attention to the emergence of new modalities for folding authority into the soul associated in particular with the psy forms of expertise. The diverse techniques of the psycho-sciences – those of assessment, classification and discipline, those which produce a knowledge of social dispositions, those which deal with motivations, attitudes and desires – generate a multiplicity of techniques of reforma-tory intervention upon persons and groups. As I have already argued, the psy disciplines provide an array of techniques for the practical govern-ment of conduct in local sites, providing professionals of human conduct with a way of exercising their authority in keeping with, and not in opposition to, the valorization of autonomous subjectivity. In suggesting ways in which *those who have authority* can exercise it in relation to a knowledge of the inner nature of *those subject to authority*, psy accords authority a novel ethical justification as a kind of therapeutic activity.

Further, a whole new array of authorities of subjectivity have taken shape, in the form of broadcast images of dilemmas for the self, self-conduct and self-formation no longer in the realm of romance or adventure but in quotidian narratives of 'everyday life'. This public habitat of images and stories presupposes certain repertoires of person-hood as the *a priori* of the forms of life they display. It is amplified by a relation with the technologies of marketing and the shaping of consump-tion. These consumption technologies, themselves informed by the theories and techniques of the psy sciences, propagate images of conduct, in terms of new relations between the purchase of goods and services and the shaping of the self. New modes, techniques and images of self-formation and self-problematization are disseminated, spatialized in new ways according to market segments and lifestyle choices, and operating according to the objectives of profit or pleasure, rather than national well-being. They presuppose a certain kind of freedom in those whose subjectivity they engage, freedom here as the desire by each individual to conduct his or her existence as a project for the maximization of quality of life. And, in a kind of reverse move, the technologies of subjectification through advertising and marketing become the basis of a whole new regime for the government of conduct in relation to health, education and security: these too will be enjoined, by both public bodies such as health promotion agencies, and private organizations such as those selling health insurance, not as a matter of morality or public duty, but in the service of the prudent running of the enterprise of one's life and the maximization of its quality.

Finally, one can point to the consonance of the changes that I have noted with the revised problematizations of political rule that can be termed 'advanced liberal'. Advanced liberal programmes of rule seek to dismantle the apparatus of welfare and install novel governmental technologies: extending the rationalities of contracts, consumers and competition to domains where social logics previously reigned; breaking up bureaucracies and governing professionals 'at a distance' through budgets, audits, codes, market demands; making individuals themselves 'interested' in their own government (Rose, 1994). Advanced liberal programmes of rule presuppose the activity of subjects, and seek to act upon that activity to establish a consonance between the self-promoting endeavours of those who are to be the subjects of rule, and the objectives of those who are to exercise rule. Such transformations have been much criticized, especially from the Left. However, perhaps the ascendancy of these new technologies of rule, and the ways in which they have been taken up in so many different national political contexts by political forces of many different complexions, indicates that they have a versatility and a potency not recognized by their critics. This potency lies, in part at least, in their relentless inventiveness, their ability to find formulas for rule that will allow subjects to come to recognize themselves in the practices that govern them. If we are to gain a critical purchase upon these contemporary strategies for the conduct of conduct, it will be, in part, through historical investigations which can unsettle and de-valorize the regime of subjectification to which they are inextricably linked.

Notes

1 Versions of this chapter have been given at the following places: Department of Sociology, Open University; School of African and Asian Studies, University of London; Conference on 'De-Traditionalization', University of Lancaster; Department of Political Science, Australian National University. It has greatly benefited from all the comments I have received. A rather different version of some of this argument is published in S. Lash, P. Heelas and P. Morris (eds), *De-Traditionalization: Critical Reflections on Authority and Identity*, Basil Blackwell, Oxford, 1996. This version was written while I was a Visiting Fellow in the Political Science Programme of the Research School of Social Sciences at the Australian National University, Canberra, and I would like to thank this institution and all its staff for their generous hospitality and intellectual support.

2 To avoid any confusion, can I point out that subjectification is not used here to imply domination by others, or subordination to an alien system of powers: it functions here not as term of 'critique' but as a device for critical thought – simply to designate processes of being 'made up' as a subject of a certain type. As will be evident, my argument throughout this chapter is dependent upon Michel Foucault's analyses of subjectification.

3 It is important to understand this in the *reflexive*, rather than the substantive mode. In what follows, the phrase always designates this relation, and implies no substantive 'self' as the object of that relation.

4 Of course, this is to overstate the case. One needs to look, on the one hand, at the ways in which philosophical reflections have themselves been organized around problems of pathology – think of the functioning of the image of the statue deprived of all sensory inputs in sensationalist philosophers such as Condillac – and also of the ways in which philosophy is animated by and articulated with, problems of the government of conduct (on Condillac, see Rose, 1985; on Locke see Tully, 1993; on Kant see Hunter, 1994).

5 Similar arguments about the necessity for analysing 'the self' as technological have been made in a number of quarters recently. See especially the discussion in Elspeth Probyn's recent book (Probyn, 1993). Precisely what is meant by 'technological' in this context is, however, less clear. As I suggest later, an analysis of the technological forms of subjectification needs to develop in terms of the relation between technologies for the government of conduct and the intellectual, corporeal and ethical devices that structure being's relation to itself at different moments and sites. I develop this argument further in Rose (1996).

6 This is not, of course, to suggest that knowledge and expertise do not play a crucial role in non-liberal regimes for the government of conduct – one only has to think of the role of doctors and administrators in the organization of the mass extermination programmes in Nazi Germany, or of the role of party workers in the pastoral relations of East European states prior to their 'democratization', or the role of planning expertise in centralized planning regimes such as GOSPLAN in the USSR. However, the relations between forms of knowledge and practice designated political and those claiming a non-political grasp of their objects were different in each case.

7 This is not the place to argue this point, so let me just assert that only rationalists, or believers in God, imagine that 'reality' exists in the discursive forms available to thought. This is not a question to be addressed by reviving the old debates on the distinction between

knowledge of the 'natural' and 'social' worlds – it is merely to accept that this must be the case unless one believes in some transcendental power that has so shaped human thought that it is homologous with that which it thinks of. Nor is it to rehearse the old problem of epistemology, which poses an ineffable divide between thought and its object and then perplexes itself as to how one can 'represent' the other. Rather, perhaps one might say that thought makes up the real, but not as a 'realization' of thought.

References

Bauman, Z. (1991) *Modernity and Ambivalence*, Cambridge: Polity Press.

Beck, U. (1992) *Risk Society: towards a New Modernity*, London: Sage.

Bourdieu, P. (1977) *Outline of a Theory of Practice*, trans. R. Nice, New York: Cambridge University Press.

Brown, P. (1989) *The Body and Society*, London: Faber & Faber.

Burchell, G., Gordon, C. and Miller, P. (1991) *The Foucault Effect: Studies in Governmentality*, Hemel Hempstead: Harvester Wheatsheaf.

Burckhardt, J. (1990) *The Civilization of the Renaissance in Italy*, (1860) trans. S.G.C. Middlemore, London: Penguin.

Butler, J. (1990) *Gender Trouble: Feminism and the Subversion of Identity*, London: Routledge.

Butler, J. (1993) *Bodies that Matter: on the Discursive Limits of 'Sex'*, London: Routledge.

Chartier, R. (ed.) (1989) *A History of Private Life, Vol. 3: Passions of the Renaissance*, trans. Arthur Goldhammer, Cambridge, MA: Belknap Press of Harvard University Press.

Cline-Cohen, P. (1982) *A Calculating People: the Spread of Numeracy in Early America*, Chicago: University of Chicago Press.

Collini, S. (1979) *Liberalism and Sociology: L.T. Hobhouse and Political Argument in England 1880–1914*, Cambridge: Cambridge University Press.

Collini, S. (1991) *Public Moralists: Political Thought and Intellectual Life in Britain 1850–1930*, Oxford: Oxford University Press.

Dean, M. (1994) '"A social structure of many souls": moral regulation, government and self-formation', *Canadian Journal of Sociology*, 19: 145–68.

Deleuze, G. (1988) *Foucault*, trans. S. Hand, Minneapolis: University of Minnesota Press.

Deleuze, G. (1990) *Pourparlers*, Paris: Editions de Minuit.

Deleuze, G. (1992) *The Fold: Leibniz and the Baroque*, Minneapolis: University of Minnesota Press.

Duby, G. (ed.) (1988) *A History of Private Life: Vol. 2: Revelations of the Medieval World*, trans. Arthur Goldhammer, Cambridge, MA: Belknap Press of Harvard University Press.

Du Gay, P. (1994) 'Making up managers: bureaucracy, enterprise and the liberal art of separation', *British Journal of Sociology*, 45(4): 655–74.

Eisenstein, E.L. (1979) *The Printing Press as an Agent of Change*, Cambridge: Cambridge University Press.

Elias, N. (1978) *The Civilizing Process, Vol. 1: The History of Manners*, trans. Edmund Jephcott, Oxford: Basil Blackwell.

Elias, N. (1983) *The Court Society*, trans. E. Jephcott, Oxford: Basil Blackwell.

Foucault, M. (1967) *Madness and Civilization: a History of Insanity in the Age of Reason*, London: Tavistock.

Foucault, M. (1977) *Discipline and Punish: the Birth of the Prison*, London: Allen Lane.

Foucault, M. (1979) *The History of Sexuality, Vol. 1: The Will to Truth*, London: Allen Lane.

Foucault, M. (1986a) *The Care of the Self: the History of Sexuality Vol. 3*, trans. R. Hurley, New York: Pantheon.

Foucault, M. (1986b) On the genealogy of ethics: an overview of work in progress', in P. Rabinow (ed.), *The Foucault Reader*, Harmondsworth: Penguin (340–72).

Foucault, M. (1988) 'Technologies of the self', in L.H. Martin, H. Gutman and P.H. Hutton (eds), *Technologies of the Self*, London: Tavistock (16–49).

Foucault, M. (1991) 'Governmentality', in G. Burchell, C. Gordon and P. Miller (eds), *The*

Foucault Effect: Studies in Governmentality, Hemel Hempstead: Harvester Wheatsheaf (87–104).

Fraser, N. (1989) 'Foucault on modern power: empirical insights and normative confusions', in *Unruly Practices*, Minneapolis: University of Minnesota Press.

Giddens, A. (1991) *Modernity and Self-Identity: Self and Society in the Late Modern Age*, Cambridge: Polity Press.

Goody, J. and Watt, I. (1963) 'The consequences of literacy', *Comparative Studies in Society and History*, 5. Reprinted in J. Goody, (ed.) (1975) *Literacy in Traditional Societies*, Cambridge: Cambridge University Press (27–84).

Gordon, C. (1991) 'Introduction', in G. Burchell, C. Gordon and P. Miller (eds), *The Foucault Effect: Studies in Governmentality*, Hemel Hempstead: Harvester Wheatsheaf (1–51).

Hadot, P. (1992) 'Reflections on the notion of "the cultivation of the self" ', in T.J. Armstrong (ed.), *Michel Foucault, Philosopher*, Hemel Hempstead: Harvester Wheatsheaf (225–32).

Haraway, D. (1991) *Simians, Cyborgs and Women: the Re-Invention of Nature*, New York: Routledge.

Hunter, I. (1993a) 'The pastoral bureaucracy: towards a less principled understanding of state schooling', in D. Meredyth and D. Tyler (eds), *Child and Citizen: Genealogies of Schooling and Subjectivity*, Queensland: Griffith University, Institute of Cultural Policy Studies (237–87).

Hunter, I. (1993b) 'Subjectivity and government', *Economy and Society*, 22(1): 123–34.

Hunter, I. (1993c) 'Culture, bureaucracy and the history of popular education', in D. Meredyth and D. Tyler (eds), *Child and Citizen: Genealogies of Schooling and Subjectivity*, Queensland: Griffith University, Institute of Cultural Policy Studies (11–34).

Hunter, I. (1994) *Rethinking the School: Subjectivity, Bureaucracy, Criticism*, St Leonards, Australia: Allen & Unwin.

Jambet, C. (1992) 'The constitution of the subject and spiritual practice', in T.J. Armstrong (ed.), *Michel Foucault, Philosopher*, Hemel Hempstead: Harvester Wheatsheaf (233–47).

Joyce, P. (1994) *Democratic Subjects: the Self and the Social in Nineteenth Century England*, Cambridge: Cambridge University Press.

Lash, S. and Friedman, J. (eds) (1992) *Modernity and Identity*, Oxford: Basil Blackwell.

Lash, S., Heelas, P. and Morris, P. (eds) (1996) *De-Traditionalization: Critical Reflections on Authority and Identity*, Oxford: Basil Blackwell.

MacIntyre, A. (1981) *After Virtue: a Study in Moral Theory*, London: Duckworth.

Markus, T.A. (1993) *Buildings and Power: Freedom and Control in the Origin of Modern Building Types*, London: Routledge.

Mauss, M. (1979) 'Body techniques', in *Psychology and Sociology: Essays*, London: Routledge & Kegan Paul.

Minson, J.P. (1993) *Questions of Conduct*, London: Macmillan.

Nietzsche, F. (1956) *The Genealogy of Morals*, trans. Francis Golffing, New York: Doubleday.

Oestreich, G. (1982) *Neo-Stoicism and the Early Modern State*, Cambridge: Cambridge University Press.

Osborne, T. (1994) 'Bureaucracy as a vocation: liberalism, ethics and administrative expertise in the nineteenth century', *Journal of the Historical Society*, 7(3): 289–300.

Osborne, T. (1996) 'Constructionism, authority and the ethical life', in I. Velody and R. Williams (eds), *Social Constructionism*, London: Sage.

Pasquino, P. (1991) 'Criminology: the birth of a special knowledge', in G. Burchell, C. Gordon and P. Miller (eds), *The Foucault Effect: Studies in Governmentality*, Hemel Hempstead: Harvester (235–50).

Patton, P. (1994) 'Foucault's subject of power', *Political Theory Newsletter*, 6(1): 60–71.

Perrot, M. (ed.) (1990) *A History of Private Life, Vol. 4: From the Fires of Revolution to the Great War*, trans. Arthur Goldhammer, Cambridge, MA: Belknap Press of Harvard University Press.

Probyn, E. (1993) *Sexing the Self: Gendered Positions in Cultural Studies*, London: Routledge.

Prost, A. and Vincent, G. (eds) (1991) *A History of Private Life, Vol. 5: Riddles of Identity in Modern Times*, trans. Arthur Goldhammer, Cambridge, MA: Belknap Press of Harvard University Press.

Ranum, O. (1989) 'The refuges of intimacy', in R. Chartier (ed.), *A History of Private Life,*

Vol. 3: Passions of the Renaissance, trans. Arthur Goldhammer, Cambridge, MA: Belknap Press of Harvard University Press (207–63).

Rieff, P. (1966) *The Triumph of the Therapeutic: Uses of Faith after Freud*, Chicago: University of Chicago Press.

Rieff, P. (1987) *The Triumph of the Therapeutic: Uses of Faith after Freud, with a new Preface by Philip Rieff*, Chicago: University of Chicago Press.

Rose, N. (1985) *The Psychological Complex: Psychology, Politics and Society in England 1869–1939*, London: Routledge & Kegan Paul.

Rose, N. (1989) *Governing the Soul: the Shaping of the Private Self*, London: Routledge.

Rose, N. (1992b) 'Engineering the human soul: analyzing psychological expertise', *Science in Context*, 5(2): 351–70.

Rose, N. (1994) 'Government, authority and expertise under advanced liberalism', *Economy and Society*, 22(3): 273–99.

Rose, N. (1996) *Inventing Our Selves: Psychology, Power and Personhood*, New York: Cambridge University Press.

Smith, R. (1992) *Inhibition: History and Meaning in the Sciences of Mind and Brain*, Berkeley: University of California Press.

Sprawson, C. (1992) *Haunts of the Black Masseur: the Swimmer as Hero*, London: Jonathan Cape.

Taylor, C. (1989) *Sources of the Self: the Making of Modern Identity*, Cambridge: Cambridge University Press.

Tully, J. (1993) 'Governing conduct', in *An Approach to Political Philosophy: Locke in Contexts*, Cambridge: Cambridge University Press.

Valverde, M. (1996) 'Despotism and ethical self-government', *Economy and Society*, 25(3), November.

Veyne, P. (ed.) (1987) *A History of Private Life, Vol. 1: From Pagan Rome to Byzantium*, trans. Arthur Goldhammer, Cambridge, MA: Belknap Press of Harvard University Press.

Weber, M. (1978) *Economy and Society: An Outline of Interpretive Sociology*, Guenther Roth and Clauss Wittich (eds), Berkeley: University of California Press.

9

Organizing Identity: Entrepreneurial Governance and Public Management

Paul du Gay

These days it seems increasingly difficult to get away from 'culture'. Within the academy, for example, the theme of 'culture' has come to dominate debates in the social and human sciences. At the same time the substantive concerns of other spheres of existence have come to be represented in 'cultural' terms. In the domain of formal politics in the UK during the 1980s the ruling Conservative Party's radical programme of reform was represented in large part as a 'cultural' crusade, concerned with the attitudes, values and forms of self-understanding embedded in both individual and institutional activities. In other words, the government's political project of reconstruction was defined as one of cultural reconstruction – as an attempt to transform Britain into an 'Enterprise Culture'.

To my mind, one of the most interesting – indeed remarkable – instances of the contemporary turn to culture has occurred within the field of prescriptive organizational discourse. In recent years, people working in large organizations are very likely to have found themselves exposed to 'culture change' programmes as part of attempts to make enterprises more efficient, effective and profitable. Even in the most ostensibly 'material' of domains – that of business and organization – programmes of reform have come to be defined in cultural terms.

A cursory inspection of any number of recent management texts reveals the primacy accorded to 'culture' in governing contemporary organizational life. In this literature 'culture' is accorded a privileged position because it is seen to structure the way people think, feel and act in organizations. The problem is one of changing 'norms', 'attitudes' and 'values' so that people are enabled to make the right and necessary contribution to the success of the organization for which they work. To this end, managers are encouraged to view the most effective or 'excellent' organizations as those with the appropriate 'culture' – that ensemble of norms and techniques of conduct that enables the self-actualizing capacities of individuals to become aligned with the goals and objectives of the organization for which they work.

This focus on 'culture' as a means of producing a particular relationship to self amongst members of an enterprise suggests that its deployment as a governmental technique is intimately bound up with questions of identity. As Renato Rosaldo (1993: xi) has suggested, it is a pronounced feature of the present that 'questions of culture . . . quite quickly become . . . questions of identity' and developments in the organizational context seem to bear this out.

According to the popular management guru Tom Peters (1992: 227), contemporary attempts to govern the 'culture' of an organization have major implications for the sorts of identities that can flourish within an enterprise. He argues that 'emerging organizational forms' will turn every employee into a 'businessperson' or 'entrepreneur'. That is, contemporary organizational reform accords ontological priority to a particular category of person – the 'businessperson' or 'entrepreneur' – providing this *menschlichen Typus* with, in the words of Max Weber (quoted in Hennis, 1988: 59), 'the optimal chances of becoming the dominant type'.

In this chapter, I focus upon the new norms and techniques of conduct – or 'culture' – being instituted within organizations and the priority they accord to the 'entrepreneur' as a category of person. More specifically, I enquire into the political and ethical effects of re-imagining public sector bureaucrats as 'entrepreneurs', paying particular attention as to whether such a move is sufficiently pluralist (presupposing as it does a single ethical hierarchy with the entrepreneur at its apex).

Exploring the ethos of enterprise

In January, 1994 the Public Accounts Committee (PAC) of the House of Commons in the UK issued an unprecedented report entitled *The Proper Conduct of Public Business*. The report was published in the wake of a number of well publicized failures in 'administrative and financial systems and controls' within government departments and other public bodies which had led to 'money being wasted or otherwise improperly spent' (1994: v). According to the committee, these failings represented a significant departure from the standards of public conduct expected in liberal democratic societies in general and the UK in particular.

Along with many sections of the British press (*Financial Times*, 28 January: 17; *Guardian*, 28 January: 1 & 6; 29 January: 20; *Independent*, 28 January: 1) the Public Accounts Committee indicated that these failings had occurred at the same time as the introduction of more market-oriented and entrepreneurial systems of organization within the public sector. They also agreed that the two developments were related in some way. However, unlike some sections of the press, the Public Accounts Committee allotted no credence to the possibility that the 'cultural revolution' taking place within the public sector actively encouraged conduct amongst public servants that might be interpreted as 'improper'. Indeed, those who queried the politico-ethical propriety of the current reforms received short shrift. They were castigated for not wanting 'to accept the challenge of securing beneficial change' (1994: v).

This language of 'change' – invariably the sort that challenges – is a constitutive element of contemporary managerial discourse. It forms part of a discursive chain of equivalences that includes *inter alia* 'enterprise', 'empowerment' and 'customer'. This discourse is, of course, relational in character – its constitutive elements only get to mean what they do in relation to that which they are not. For example, the norms and values of conduct inscribed within contemporary managerial discourse are articulated in explicit opposition to those constituting the identity of 'bureaucratic' organization. Whereas the bureaucratic ethos encourages the development of particular capacities and predispositions amongst its subjects – strict adherence to procedure, the abnegation of personal moral enthusiasm and so forth – contemporary managerial discourse stresses the importance of individuals acquiring and exhibiting more 'proactive' and 'entrepreneurial' traits and virtues.

That the Public Accounts Committee report speaks from within the universe of contemporary managerialism can be in little doubt. In the report the managerial ethos with its 'greater delegation of responsibilities, streamlining, and . . . more entrepreneurial approach' is favourably compared to the traditional bureaucratic 'ethos of office' – the latter being uniformly associated with waste, inertia and unnecessary regulation (1994: v–vi).

As I have indicated, however, while expressing a belief in the public benefits of contemporary organizational change the report bemoans the diminution of 'principles and standards' of conduct expected of public officials in liberal democracies (1994: v). That these 'principles and standards' have arisen and have been fostered largely within a bureaucratic context does not seem to be relevant. Instead, the committee appears to assume that organizational reforms designed to make public organizations less bureaucratic and more entrepreneurial are uniformly positive; that they will increase economic efficiency – providing improved services at reduced cost – without affecting 'traditional public sector values'[1]. This can easily be interpreted as something of a leap of faith, however, if not an out and out *non sequitur*.

For one thing, assuming that the identity of a domain remains the same throughout all the changes it undergoes is extremely problematic. As I have already argued, given that any identity is basically relational in terms of its conditions of existence, any change in the latter is bound to affect the former. If, for example, the (bureaucratic) conduct of public administration is re-imagined in terms of entrepreneurial principles, then rather than having the same identity – (bureaucratic) public administration – in a new situation, a new identity is established.

Moreover, the production of this new identity will inevitably involve trade-offs. Rather than assuming, as the PAC report seems to do, that entrepreneurial public management is incontrovertibly a 'good thing' – that it is inherently positive – it might be more productive to examine its conditions of emergence, to analyse what its establishment must inevitably exclude and to assess what the politico-ethical effects of this exclusion might be.

Entrepreneurial governance and the critique of bureaucratic culture

The case against bureaucracy and for the sorts of 'flexible', 'entrepreneurial' forms and practices envisioned in contemporary discourses of organizational reform begins with changes in what is termed 'the external environment'. The conditions of existence of this discursive formation rest upon a number of developments, often gathered together under the heading of 'globalization'. While different texts highlight differing combinations of phenomena – the dislocatory effects consequent upon the increasing deployment of 'information technology'; those associated with the competitive pressures resulting from global systems of trade, finance and production, etc. – they all agree that the intensification of patterns of global interconnectedness has serious repercussions for the conduct of organizational life, in both the public and private sectors.

If 'globalization' constitutes the key 'predicament', then 'bureaucracy' is positioned as the crucial impediment to the successful management of its effects. Globalization, it is argued, creates an environment characterized by massive uncertainty. In such an environment only those organizations that can rapidly change their conduct and learn to become ever more enterprising will survive and prosper. Because 'bureaucracy' is held to be a 'mechanistic' form of organization best suited to conditions of relative stability and predictability, it becomes the first casualty of such an uncertain environment[2].

> In this environment, bureaucratic institutions . . . – public and private – increasingly fail us. Today's environment demands institutions that are extremely flexible and adaptable. It demands institutions that deliver high-quality goods and services, squeezing ever more bang out of every buck [*sic*]. It demands institutions that are responsive to their customers, offering choices of non-standardized services; that lead by persuasion and incentives rather than commands; that give their employees a sense of meaning and control, even ownership. It demands institutions that empower citizens rather than simply serving them. (Osborne and Gaebler, 1992: 15).

The dislocatory effects generated by the intensification of patterns of global interconnectedness require constant 'creativity' and the continuous construction of collective operational spaces that rest less upon mechanistic objective forms and their related practices – 'bureaucracy' –

and increasingly upon the development of more entrepreneurial organizational forms and modes of conduct.

The notion of 'enterprise' occupies an absolutely crucial position in contemporary discourses of organizational reform. It provides a critique of 'bureaucratic culture' and offers itself as a solution to the problems posed by 'globalization' through delineating the principles of a new method of governing organizational and personal conduct.

Quite obviously one key feature of 'enterprise' as a principle of government is the central role it allocates to the 'commercial enterprise' as the preferred model for any form of institutional organization of goods and services. However, of equal importance is the way in which the term refers to the habits of action that display or express 'enterprising qualities on the part of those concerned', whether they be individuals or collectivities. Here, 'enterprise' refers to a plethora of characteristics such as initiative, risk-taking, self-reliance, and the ability to accept responsibility for oneself and one's actions (Keat, 1990:3).

Thus, as Burchell (1993: 275) has noted, the defining characteristic of entrepreneurial governance is the 'generalization of an "enterprise form" to *all* forms of conduct – to the conduct of organizations hitherto seen as being non-economic, to the conduct of government, and to the conduct of individuals themselves'. While the concrete ways in which this governmental rationality has been operationalized have varied quite considerably, the forms of action they make possible for different institutions and persons – schools, general practitioners, housing estates, prisons and so forth – do share a general consistency and style.

As Burchell (1993: 276, following Donzelot) has argued, a characteristic feature of this style of government is the fundamental role it accords to 'contract' in redefining social relations. The changes affecting schools, hospitals, government departments and so forth often involve the reconstituting of institutional roles in terms of *contracts strictly defined*, and even more frequently involve a *contract-like way* of representing relationships between institutions and between individuals and institutions (Freedland, 1994: 88). An example of the former, for instance, occurs when fund-holding medical practices contract with hospital trusts for the provision of health care to particular patients where previously that provision was made directly by the National Health Service. Examples of the latter include the relationships between central government departments and the new executive or Next Steps agencies – where no technical contract as such exists but where the relationship between the two is governed by a contract-like 'Framework Document' which defines the functions and goals of the agency, and the procedures whereby the department will set and monitor the performance targets for the agency.

Thus, 'contractualization' typically consists of assigning the performance of a function or an activity to a distinct unit of management – individual or collective – which is regarded as being accountable for the efficient performance of that function or conduct of that activity. By assuming active responsibility for these activities and functions – both for carrying them out and for their outcomes – these units of management are in effect affirming a certain kind of identity or personality. This is essentially entrepreneurial in character. Contractualization requires these units of management to adopt a certain entrepreneurial form of relationship to themselves 'as a condition of their effectiveness and of the effectiveness of this form of government' (Burchell, 1993: 276). Or, to put it in the language of Tom Peters (1992: 273), contractualization 'businesses' individuals and collectivities.

As Colin Gordon (1991: 42–5) has argued, entrepreneurial forms of governance such as contractualization involve the re-imagination of the social as a form of the economic. 'This operation works,' he argues, ' by the progressive enlargement of the territory of economic theory by a series of redefinitions of its object.'

> Economics thus becomes an 'approach' capable in principle of addressing the totality of human behaviour, and, consequently, of envisaging a coherent purely economic method of programming the totality of governmental action. (Gordon, 1991:43)

The levelling function that this process performs ensures that formerly diverse institutions, practices, goods and so forth become subject to judgement and calculation exclusively in terms of economic criteria – giving rise to the increasing dominance of what Lyotard (1984:46) terms 'the performativity principle'. However, it would be misguided to view this development as simply the latest and purest manifestation of the irresistible rise of *homo economicus*.

As Gordon (1991: 43) has indicated, the subject of 'enterprise' is both a 'reactivation and a radical inversion' of traditional 'economic man'. The reactivation consists 'in positing a fundamental human faculty of *choice*, a principle which empowers economic calculation effectively to sweep aside the anthropological categories and frameworks of the human and social sciences'. The great innovation occurs, however, in the conceptualization of the economic agent as an inherently manipulable creation. Whereas, *homo economicus* was originally conceived of as a subject the wellsprings of whose activity were ultimately 'untouchable by government', the subject of enterprise is imagined as an agent 'who is perpetually responsive to modifications in its environment'. As Gordon points out, 'economic government here joins hands with behaviourism' (ibid.). The resultant subject is in a novel sense not just an 'enterprise' but 'the entrepreneur of himself or herself' . In other words, entrepreneurial government 'makes up' the individual as a particular sort of person – as an 'entrepreneur of the self' (Gordon, 1987: 300).

This idea of an individual human life as 'an enterprise of the self' suggests that no matter what hand circumstance may have dealt a person, he or she remains always continuously engaged (even if technically 'unemployed') in that one enterprise, and that it is 'part of the continuous business of living to make adequate provision for the preservation, reproduction and reconstruction of one's own human capital' (Gordon, 1991:44).

Because a human being is considered to be continuously engaged in a project to shape his or her life as an autonomous, choosing individual driven by the desire to optimize the worth of its own existence, life for that person is represented as a single, basically undifferentiated arena for the pursuit of that endeavour. Because previously distinct forms of life are now classified primarily if not exclusively as 'enterprise forms', the conceptions and practices of personhood they give rise to are remarkably consistent. As schools, prisons, government departments and so forth are re-imagined as 'enterprises' they all accord an increased priority to the 'entrepreneur' as a category of person. In this sense, the character of the entrepreneur can no longer be represented as just one amongst a plurality of ethical personalities but must be seen as assuming an ontological priority.

This conception of the individual as an 'entrepreneur of the self' is firmly established at the heart of contemporary programmes of organizational reform. In keeping with the entrepreneurial imbrication of economics and behaviourism, contemporary programmes of organizational reform characterize employment not as a painful obligation imposed upon individuals, nor as an activity undertaken to meet purely instrumental needs, but rather as a means to self-development. Organizational success is therefore premised upon an engagement by the organization of the self-optimizing impulses of all its members, no matter what their formal role. This ambition is to be made practicable in the workplace through a variety of techniques such as 'delayering' and performance-related pay. The latter, whose deployment throughout the public sector has grown dramatically in the last decade, often involves the development of an ongoing 'contract' between an individual employee and their line manager whereby an employee's pay is made more dependent upon whether s/he has met or exceeded certain performance objectives (Millward et al, 1992: 268, 361; Marsden and Richardson, 1994).

Thus, performance management and related techniques entail a characteristically 'contractual' relationship between individual employees and the organization for which they work. This means 'offering' individuals involvement in activities – such as managing budgets, training staff, delivering services – previously held to be the responsibility of other agents such as supervisors or personnel departments. However, the price of this involvement is that individuals themselves must assume responsibility for carrying out these activities and for their outcomes. In keeping with the constitutive principles of enterprise as a rationality of government performance, management and related techniques function as forms of 'responsibilization' which are held to be both economically desirable and personally 'empowering'.

Entrepreneurial organizational governance therefore entails the reconstruction of a wide range of institutions and activities along the lines of the commercial firm. At the same time, guaranteeing that the optimum benefits accrue from the restructuring of organizations along market lines necessitates the production of particular forms of conduct by all members of an organization. In this sense, governing organizational life in an enterprising manner involves 'making up' new ways for people to be; it refers to the importance of individuals acquiring and exhibiting specific 'enterprising' capacities and dispositions.

Refracted through the gaze of enterprise, 'bureaucratic culture' appears inimical to the development of these 'virtues' and hence to the production of enterprising persons. The bureaucratic commitment to norms of impersonality, strict adherence to procedure and the acceptance of hierarchical sub- and super-ordination is seen as antithetical to the cultivation of those entrepreneurial skills and sensibilities which alone can guarantee a 'manageable' and hence sustainable future.

While proponents of entrepreneurial governance are not averse to admitting that bureaucratic norms and techniques have proved efficient and effective in certain circumstances they clearly believe that such circumstances are no longer to be found, nor are they likely to recur in the foreseeable future. The implication is that organizational survival and flourishing in the dislocated environments of the present requires the cultivation of an appropriate entrepreneurial competence and style through which at one and the same time organizations conduct their business and persons conduct themselves within those organizations.

As I argued earlier, because the discourse of enterprise presupposes that no organizational context is immune to the effects of 'globalization', it assumes that ostensibly different organizations – hospitals, charities, banks, government departments – will have to develop similar norms and techniques of conduct, for without so doing they will lack the capacity to pursue their preferred projects. The urgency with which such claims are deployed gives the very definite impression that 'There Is No Alternative'. As Kanter (1990: 356) forcefully declares, organizations 'must either move away from bureaucratic guarantees to post-entrepreneurial flexibility or . . . stagnate – thereby cancelling by default any commitments they have made'.

While such insistent singularity has obvious attractions – for one thing it offers the sort of easily graspable and communicable *Weltanschauung* that can act as a catalyst for change – it neglects the fact that the generalization of an enterprise form to all forms of conduct may of itself serve to incapacitate an organization's ability to pursue its preferred projects by redefining its identity and hence what the nature of its project actually is.

In the public sector, which is part of government and which should therefore be subject to the rule of law, organizations are concerned with such things as equity and treating like cases in a like manner. These are not values primarily served by commercial enterprises and there is no *prima facie* reason why they should be. However, they are central to government and the rule of law in liberal democratic regimes. There is a clear danger here that the introduction of entrepreneurial principles into public sector organizations might undermine these basic principles of public provision and this serves to highlight the fact that in liberal democratic societies there is a good reason for assuming that markets have political and moral limits and that 'plotting some of the boundaries of markets will also involve putting enterprise in its legitimate place' (Plant, 1992: 86).

The entrepreneurialist may reply that without 'enterprising up' public sector organizations the liberties and equalities that citizens take for granted might become unaffordable, but this argument once again assumes that the generalization of an enterprise form to the conduct of public administration, for example, will not affect the identity and integrity of public administration but will simply make it 'work better'. Yet, in relation to the report of the Public Accounts Committee, it is extremely problematic to assume that the identity of a domain of activity can remain the same when its basic organizing principles are fundamentally altered.

Instead of simply accepting the case that the contemporary 'enterprising up' of the public sector is a uniformly positive as well as inherently necessary development I seek to advance the unfashionable view that there are a number of important political and ethical reasons for representing bureaucracy as the most efficient and effective form of public sector organization. In putting forward arguments to support this position I begin by specifying what the bureaucratic ethos consists of, indicating what sort of conceptions and practices of personhood the bureau gives rise to and delineating the relationship between these and what Michael Walzer (1984) terms 'the liberal art of separation'.

Office as a vocation

The idea that public sector organizations need reform has achieved a somewhat axiomatic status. To what extent and in what directions remains a matter of considerable debate. In recent years one particular approach has become pre-eminent and it is this approach that underpins many of the public sector reforms now taking place across the 'advanced' economies.

This new *modus operandi* is often termed the 'New Public Management', and more recently 'entrepreneurial governance'. According to two of its most fashionable proponents – Osborne and Gaebler (1992: 19–20) – 'entrepreneurial governance' consists of ten 'essential principles' which link together to 'reinvent' the public sector:

> entrepreneurial governments promote *competition* between service providers. They *empower* citizens by pushing control out of the bureaucracy, into the community. They measure the performance of their agencies, focusing not on

inputs but on *outcomes*. They are driven by their goals – their *missions* – not by their rules and regulations. They redefine their clients as *customers* and offer them choices – between schools, between training programs, between housing options. They *prevent* problems before they emerge, rather than simply offering services afterward. They put their energies into *earning* money, not simply spending it. They *decentralize* authority, embracing participatory management. They prefer *market* mechanisms to bureaucratic mechanisms. And they focus not simply on providing public services but on *catalyzing* all sectors – public, private and voluntary – into action to solve their community's problems.

The chief target of 'entrepreneurial governance' – that which it defines itself in opposition to – is the public sector bureaucracy. This is represented as the enemy of 'good governance' for many of the reasons outlined earlier. For example, the 'bureaucratic model' is seen as unsuited to the dynamics of the 'global marketplace', the 'information age' and the 'knowledge based-economy', being too 'slow, inefficient and impersonal' to meet their imperatives (1992: 14–15).

Although advocates of entrepreneurial governance such as Osborne and Gaebler are critical of all forms of bureaucratic conduct, it is the perceived failure of bureaucracy in opening up people's personal involvement and ideals – 'empowering' them – which comes in for some of the most severe criticism .

According to Osborne and Gaebler (1992:38) many employees in bureaucratic organizations 'feel trapped':

> Tied down by rules and regulations, numbed by monotonous tasks they know could be accomplished in half the time if they were allowed to use their minds, they live lives of quiet desperation. When they have the opportunity to work for an organization with a clear mission and minimal red tape . . . they are often re-born. When they are moved into the private sector, they often experience the same sense of liberation.

One can recognize a certain truth in their starting point – that bureaucratic organization can and often does create problems of 'motivation' for individuals, particularly those at lower levels of the hierarchy – but they seem to neglect the fact that certain forms of organization have 'defects' as a result of delivering politically sanctioned 'virtues'. The rules and regulations against which Osborne and Gaebler rail were not invented with the sole purpose of inhibiting individual entrepreneurial activity but to prevent corruption and to ensure fairness, probity and reliability in the treatment of cases. Jettisoning rules and regulations in the pursuit of entrepreneurial innovation will not eradicate problems but simply change them. Rather than offering a 'permanent win/win' situation in opposition to a bureaucratic 'no win situation', entrepreneurial forms of conduct exhibit both 'virtues' and 'defects'. The question is whether on balance the 'defects' associated with ordered, cautious, reliable administration are more widely acceptable than those associated with a more creative, risky, entrepreneurial style (Jordan, 1994; du Gay, 1994).

One thing is for certain: advocates of entrepreneurial government cannot even conceive of such a question. They seem unable to represent 'bureaucracy' in anything other than negative terms . Inciting readers to develop a 'public and passionate hatred of bureaucracy' (Peters, 1987:459) leaves little room for any positive evaluation of bureaucratic conduct. Indeed, texts such as those by Osborne and Gaebler (1992) and Peters (1987, 1992) tell their readers very little about the technical, ethical or social organization of the bureau, full stop. Instead their main role appears to be to frame the difference between the vocational ethics of the bureaucrat and those of the entrepreneur from the perspective of entrepreneurial principles. Rather than describing the ethos of office the entrepreneurial critique seeks to assess bureaucracy in terms of its failure to realize objectives which enterprise alone has set for it.

Delineating the bureaucratic ethos

According to the advocates of entrepreneurial government, bureaucracy is both economically and morally bankrupt. They argue that bureaucratic organization is always likely to mean significant human, and hence financial, cost because the privilege it accords to 'instrumental rationality' involves the simultaneous repression and marginalization of its Other – the personal, the emotional and so forth.

> In the traditional bureaucratic corporation, roles were so circumscribed that most relationships tended to be rather formal and impersonal. Narrowly defined jobs constricted by rules and procedures also tended to stifle initiative and creativity, and the atmosphere was emotionally repressive. (Kanter, 1990: 280)

In this reading, bureaucratic organization is based upon a series of 'foundational' exclusions whose 'absent presence' erupts onto the organizational surface in the form of cumulatively disabling 'dysfunctions'. To back up this claim, advocates of entrepreneurial government continually point to, amongst other things, a perceived lack of commitment, motivation and identification amongst the bureaucratic workforce which they attribute directly to 'rationalist' systems 'that seem calculated to tear down their workers' self-image' (Peters and Waterman, 1982: 57).

Inefficiency, waste and inertia are directly related to the fact that bureaucratic organization does not function as an instrument of 'self-optimization' for its members. Instead its very 'essence' is seen to be based upon a separation of 'reason and emotion' and 'pleasure and duty', which is disastrous for the productive health of the nation, the organization and the moral and emotional character of the individual employee.

Although the entrepreneurial critique utilizes (highly) selective elements of the work of the premier theorist of bureaucratic culture, Max Weber, in making its case – particularly those passages where bureaucratization is seen as equivalent to a general process of disenchantment and

dehumanization: the infamous 'iron cage of bureaucracy' – their con-
clusions concerning the ethical defects of bureaucracy are in fact quite the
opposite to those expressed by Weber.

In his classic account of bureaucratic culture Weber (1968) refuses to
treat the impersonal, expert, procedural and hierarchical character of
bureaucratic reason and action as inefficient and morally bankrupt.
Instead, he makes it quite clear that the bureau consists in a particular
ethos or what he terms *Lebensführung* – not only an ensemble of purposes
and ideals within a given code of conduct but also ways and means of
conducting oneself within a given 'life-order'. He insists that the bureau
must be assessed in its own right as a particular moral institution and that
the ethical attributes of the bureaucrat must be viewed as the contingent
and often fragile achievements of that socially organized sphere of moral
existence.

According to Weber, the bureau comprises the social conditions of a
distinctive and independent organization of the person. Among the most
important of these conditions are, that access to office is dependent upon
lengthy training in a technical expertise, usually certified by public
examination; and that the office itself constitutes a 'vocation', a focus of
ethical commitment and duty, autonomous of and superior to the
bureaucrat's extra-official ties to class, kin or conscience. In Weber's
discussion of bureaucracy these conditions delineate the bureau as a
particular department of life, and they provide the bureaucrat with a
distinctive ethical bearing and mode of conduct.

The ethical attributes of the good bureaucrat – strict adherence to
procedure, acceptance of sub-and superordination, commitment to the
purposes of the office – do not represent an incompetent subtraction from
a 'complete' entrepreneurial conception of personhood. Rather, they
should be viewed as a positive moral achievement in their own right.
They represent the product of particular ethical techniques and practices
through which individuals develop the disposition and ability to conduct
themselves according to the ethos of bureaucratic office (Hunter, 1991;
Minson, 1993).

Instead of lending support to the entrepreneurial stereotype of
bureaucracy as inimical to self-realization, Weber points to the historical
specificity of the 'rational' character of bureaucracy. Rather than representing the denial of personal involvement in, or the possibility of
deriving personal pleasure from, the conduct of office, Weber's (1968:359)
stress on the 'impersonal', 'functional' and 'objective' nature of bureaucratic norms and techniques refers simply to the setting aside of
pre-bureaucratic forms of patronage. What is to be excluded as 'irrational'
by this form of conduct is not personal feelings *per se* but a series of
'private' group prerogatives and interests which 'governed as they were
by a completely different ethos, it was at other times deemed quite
legitimate and "reasonable" to pursue' (Minson, 1991: 15). The normative
scope of bureaucratic rationality is quite particular. As Weber (1968: 973)

remarks: 'this freely creative administration would not constitute a realm of free arbitrary action and discretion, of personally motivated favour and valuation as we find among the pre-bureaucratic forms'.

Weber proceeds to indicate that bureaucratic rationality does not operate to exclude all sentiment from organizational existence. Such an accusation – levelled by the advocates of enterprise amongst many others – completely misses the point that bureaucratic culture engenders no antipathy towards emotional or personal relations within the domain of the office as long as these do not open the possibility of corruption through, for example, the improper use of patronage, indulging incompetence or through the betrayal of confidentiality. As Minson (1993: 135) argues, 'the supposition of an essential antipathy between bureaucracy and informal relations such as friendship hinges on a romantic identification of such relations with freedom from normative compulsion, spontaneous attraction, intimacy, and free choice'. When Weber describes bureaucratic conduct as precluding 'personally motivated' actions it is therefore important not to follow the advocates of enterprise and extend his intended reference from the exercise of personal patronage to the universal exclusion of the personal and /or 'private' realms[3].

In a similar move, Weber also indicates that far from being morally and emotionally vacuous 'formally rational' modes of conduct do have an ethical basis. As Charles Larmore, (1987: xiii–xiv) has argued, Weber's concept of 'formal rationality' has been consistently misappropriated and made to serve a function he never intended. It differs from its twin concept of 'substantive rationality' not by being narrowly 'instrumental' and dependent upon arbitrarily given ends – as the advocates of enterprise suggest – but by taking account of the heterogeneity of morality. In other words, while the ethos associated with formal rationality is certainly premised upon the cultivation of indifference to certain moral ends, that very indifference is predicated upon an awareness of the *irreducible plurality of and frequent incommensurability between passionately held moral beliefs* and thus on the possible moral costs of pursuing any one of them. Viewed within this frame, formal rationality is not associated with the development of an amoral instrumentalism but with the cultivation of a *liberal pluralist 'ethics of responsibility'* which does take account of the consequences of attempting to realize essentially contestable values that frequently come into conflict with other values.

In this sense, the bureau represents an important ethical and political resource in liberal democratic regimes because it serves to divorce the administration of public life from private moral absolutisms. It has become, as Larmore (1987: 41–2) indicates, 'a condition of freedom' because it permits 'a significant and liberating separation of the public and the private'. Without the emergence of the ethical sphere and persona of the bureau and the bureaucrat, the construction of a buffer between civic virtues and personal principles – one of the constitutive principles of modern liberal democracy – would never have become possible. As Michael Walzer (1984:320) argues, the 'liberal art of separation' that bureaucracy effects is a source of pluralism, equality and freedom:

> Under the aegis of the art of separation, liberty and equality go together. Indeed, they invite a single definition: we can say that a (modern, complex, differentiated) society enjoys both freedom and equality when success in one institutional setting isn't convertible into success in another, that is, when the separations hold.

Businessing bureaucracy: enterprise and public management

The ethos of office, with its chief point of honour, the capacity to set aside one's private political, moral, regional and other commitments, should not be regarded as obsolete.[4] The question then remains: what effect is a shift to entrepreneurial forms of government likely to have upon this ethos?

The very identity of entrepreneurial government is constituted in opposition to bureaucratic culture. Advocates of enterprise tend to represent 'bureaucracy' in language which leaves no room for positive evaluation. However, it is only possible to begin to answer the question posed above by indicating the ways in which the norms and techniques of entrepreneurial governance might pose a threat to the bureaucratic 'art of separation'.

According to the philosopher Amélie Rorty (1988:7) the liberal art of separation is most often undermined when the concerns of one particular context of life-order are imposed on other different departments of existence. The discourse of enterprise is involved in just such a 'take-over bid' by seeking to render a variety of discrete ethical domains amenable to one method of government.

The defining feature of entrepreneurial government is the generalization of an enterprise form to all forms of conduct – public, private, voluntary, etc. In this way, a certain conception of the person as an entrepreneur, which derives from and properly belongs to a particular sphere of existence (the life-order of the market) is imposed upon other departments of life (each of which has given rise to its own conceptions and practices of personhood). This blurs the boundaries between distinct spheres of existence and, I would suggest, the liberties and equalities predicated upon the 'art of separation' are put into question.

As Weber (1968: 1404) argued, the ethos governing the conduct of the 'bureaucrat', the 'entrepreneur' and the 'politician' are not identical. In addressing the different kinds of responsibility that these 'persons' have for their actions, Weber insisted upon the irreducibility of different spheres of ethical life and on the consequent necessity of applying different ethical protocols to them:

An official who receives a directive he considers wrong can and is supposed to object to it. If his superior insists on its execution, it is his duty and even his honor to carry it out as if it corresponded to his innermost conviction and to demonstrate in this fashion that his sense of duty stands above his personal preference. . . . This is the ethos of office. A political leader acting in this way would deserve contempt. He will often be compelled to make compromises, that means, to sacrifice the less to the more important . . . 'To be above Parties' – in truth, to remain outside the struggle for power – is the official's role, while this struggle for personal power, and the resulting political responsibility, is the lifeblood of the politician as well as the *entrepreneur*. (my emphasis)

By demanding – in the name of the 'market', the 'customer' or whatever – that the ethical conduct of the public administrator be judged according to the ethos of the entrepreneur the discourse of enterprise requires public sector bureaucrats to assume the role of businesspersons. As Larmore (1987: 99) argues, such 'confusion of realms' can have disastrous consequences. In seeking to instil a strong sense of personal 'ownership' for particular policies amongst public administrators, for example, proponents of 'enterprise' (Osborne and Gaebler, 1992) seem to have completely lost sight of the bureau's crucial civic and ethical role in *separating public administration from personal moral enthusiasms.*[5]

Such 'forgetfulness' is inscribed within all too many of the public sector reforms currently taking place across liberal democratic societies. In Britain, for example, the introduction of 'entrepreneurial' norms and techniques into the civil service as a result of the Next Steps initiative seems destined to undermine the bureaucratic ethos. Top civil servants, it would appear, are increasingly being encouraged to adopt a 'can do' style of conduct characterized by 'decisiveness and an ability to get things done, rather than the more traditional approach which lays greater emphasis on analysis of options and recommendations for action based upon that analysis' (RIPA, 1987). The obvious danger here is that public servants are now required to develop 'personal' enthusiasms for specific policies and projects and as a consequence the bureaucratic (liberal pluralist) 'ethos of responsibility' is being eroded. As Richard Chapman (1991b: 3) has argued with regard to these reforms, 'the emphasis on enterprise, initiative, and a more business-like style of management . . . seems oddly at variance with the expectations of officials working in a bureaucracy'.

The central mechanism of Next Steps – the replacement of a 'unified' civil service by a host of 'autonomous' agencies – is explicitly represented as a means of enterprising up the public sector. The 'new' agencies, it is argued, are structured to enable civil servants to 'obtain a sense of ownership and personal identification with the product' (Goldsworthy, 1991:6). Rather than seeking to moderate the perfectly understandable enthusiasms of public officials for particular projects and policies the agency system seems designed to incite them.

Staff, we are told, now often think of themselves as belonging to a particular department or agency, not to a wider civil service. They work in units that, far from displaying a team spirit with a common ethos, compete with each other. . . . [E]fforts are now made to stimulate feelings of enterprise and initiative in them and there can be no doubt that these have resulted in a fundamental change from an ethos . . . which contributed to the identity of the civil service. (Chapman, 1991b: 3).

The advocates of these reforms seem unable to imagine that business management and public administration are not identical in every respect. While there is a sense in which the state and the business concern are both rational 'enterprises' – deliberately and explicitly directed towards advancing goals and objectives in an efficient and effective manner – public administration differs from business management primarily because of the constraints imposed by the *political* environment within which the management processes are conducted. As Neville Johnson (1983: 193–4) amongst others has argued:

Undoubtedly, the official in public service is . . . engaged extensively in the use and deployment of resources taken away from the people he or she serves and returned to them as benefits and entitlements legitimated by the system of government. It is clear that in these circumstances he or she bears a responsibility for the efficient use of resources and to this end must be ready and able to use such methods of management as will offer the best prospect of optimal performance. But the function of officials cannot be exhaustively defined in terms of achieving results efficiently. There is also a duty to observe the varied limits imposed on action by public bodies and to satisfy the political imperatives of public service – loyalty to those who are politically responsible, responsiveness to parliamentary and public opinion, sensitivity to the complexity of the public interest, honesty in the formulation of advice, and so on. It is out of these commitments that a professional ethic was fashioned in the public services. Even if this has weakened in recent years we cannot afford to dispense with it. This is because a system of representative government does require officials to act as the custodians of the procedural values it embodies. The contemporary concern with efficient management, with performance, and with securing results, should not be allowed to obscure this fact. The pursuit of better management in government, important though it is, has to recognize the political limits to which it is subject.

Simply representing public bureaucracy in economic terms as an inefficient form of organization fails to take account of the crucial ethical and political role of the bureau in liberal democratic societies. If bureaucracy is to be reduced or abandoned and an entrepreneurial style of management adopted then it must be recognized that while 'economic efficiency' might be improved in the short term, the longer term costs associated with this apparent 'improvement' may well include fairness, probity, complex equality and other crucial 'qualitative' features of liberal democratic government. As Chapman (1991a: 17) argues:

When attention is focused on public sector management as distinct from management in other contexts, a distinctively bureaucratic type of organiz-ation, with accountability both hierarchically and to elected representatives, may mean that far from being inefficient it is in fact the most suitable type of organization. . . . Consequently, regarding bureaucracy as an inefficient type of organization may reflect a superficial understanding of bureaucracy and, perhaps, a blinkered appreciation of public sector management. Bureaucracy may be more expensive than other types of organization, but that is not surprising when democracy is not necessarily the cheapest form of government.

We are in no danger of forgetting the disasters and dangers to which bureaucracies are prone if we remind ourselves every now and again of the threats – including those posed by an unbridled entrepreneurialism – against which they offer protection.

Concluding remarks

There may well be a compelling case for making certain bureaucracies more responsive to the publics they serve. It is also possible that particular 'entrepreneurial' approaches to such a project are not without merit – certain services currently supplied by state bureaucracies might be better run by civic organizations, enhancing rather than endangering the liberal democratic art of separation. However, these decisions should be made on a case by case basis. Admitting the sagacity of such a move in one case does not mean that all services can or should be removed from public bureaucracies and handed over to civic organizations. To harbour the desire that they should is to lose sight of the bureau's crucial political and ethical role in separating public administration from moral absolutism.

The public bureaucracy is a key institution of liberal democratic societies. Reforms of this institution – such as reductions in its size and cost – may be welcomed as long as they do not undermine its ethical and political role as outlined above.

Similarly, arguing that there are distinct limits to the efficacy of deploying entrepreneurial norms and techniques within the public sector does not amount to saying that such forms of governance are uniformly bad. It simply means that such norms and techniques and the conceptions of personhood they give rise to should not be unilaterally imposed upon other spheres of existence.

Suitably regionalized, both bureaucratic and entrepreneurial forms and styles of conduct can be reconciled, if never definitively. Not definitively because the liberal democratic 'art of separation' never manages to achieve anything like total regionalization. Since the lines of demarcation are ambiguous they are always liable to be drawn here and there, experimentally and often wrongly. This is the unavoidable risk of liberal democracy. As Lefort (1988:19) has argued, the emergence of liberal democratic regimes means 'the dissolution of the markers of certainty'.

However, even when the separations do hold they must always be in tension, for the distinctive habits of action of the different constitutive 'spheres' will tend to undercut each other. It is doubtful whether the lines can ever be stabilized, and the changing character of states and markets requires, in any case, their continual revision, 'so the arguing and fighting over the location of the lines has no foreseeable end' (Walzer, 1984: 328–3).

Notes

1 William Waldegrave, the Minister responsible for public services, admitted being 'greatly cheered by the ringing endorsement in the report of the belief of the Public Accounts Committee that there is absolutely no contradiction between the new efficiency structures we have brought in and the maintenance of proper standards' (reported in the *Guardian*, 28 January 1994, p. 1).

2 It is interesting to note that bureaucracy is always represented as an entirely passive form. There is never any acknowledgement of the productive capacities of bureaucratic organization; that 'bureaucracy' actively constructs a predictable environment rather than simply being 'suited to' some already existing stable space.

3 In this regard it needs to be remembered that at the time of its emergence – in the period of the European religious wars fought in the name of moral absolutes – it was precisely the bureaucracy's capacity to divorce public administration from private moral enthusiasms that helped establish it as the privileged instrument of pragmatic statecraft. The bureaucratic capacity to provide a buffer between personal principles and civic virtues is a political achievement that it is always easy to underestimate (I would like to thank Ian Hunter for drawing my attention to this and the following point).

4 Think of those modern political arenas in which public conduct and personal ideals are not divorced – including the former Yugoslavia and Lebanon. It is all too easy, especially for social and human science 'radicals', to forget that the capacity of bureaucracy to divorce politics from absolute principles is a historically contingent and fragile achievement that those of us who live in pacified societies should not take for granted.

5 There are a number of famous examples of the disasters that can befall when public officials act in manner befitting the conduct of an entrepreneur or a politician. With regard to British public administration, see, for example, Richard Chapman's (1988: 302–3) discussion of the Crichel Down case.

References

Burchell, G. (1993) 'Liberal government and techniques of the self', *Economy & Society*, 22(3): 266–82.

Chapman, R.A. (1988) *Ethics in the British Civil Service*, London: Routledge.

Chapman, R.A. (1991a) 'Concepts and issues in public sector reform: the experience of the United Kingdom in the 1980s', *Public Policy and Administration*, 6(2): 1–19.

Chapman, R.A. (1991b) 'The end of the civil service?', *Teaching Public Administration*, 12(2): 1–5.

Du Gay, P. (1994) 'Colossal immodesties and hopeful monsters: pluralism and organizational conduct', *Organization*, 1(1): 125–48.

Freedland, M. (1994) 'Government by contract and public law', *Public Law*, Spring: 86–104.

Goldsworthy, D. (1991) *Setting Up Next Steps: a Short Account of the Origins, Launch and Implementation of the Next Steps Project in the British Civil Service*, London: HMSO.

Gordon, C. (1987) 'The soul of the citizen: Max Weber and Michel Foucault on rationality and government', in S. Whimster and S. Lask (eds.), *Max Weber: Rationality and Modernity*, London: Allen & Unwin.

Gordon, C. (1991) 'Governmental rationality: an introduction', in G. Burchell, C. Gordon and P. Miller (eds.), *The Foucault Effect*, Hemel Hempstead: Harvester Wheatsheaf.

Hennis, W. (1988) *Max Weber: Essays in Reconstruction*, London: Allen & Unwin.

Hunter, I. (1991) 'Personality as a vocation: the political rationality of the humanities', *Economy & Society*, 19(4): 391–430.

Johnson, N. (1983) 'Management in government', in M.J. Earl (ed.), *Perspectives on Management*, Oxford: Oxford University Press.

Jordan, G. (1994) 'Reinventing government': but will it work?', *Public Administration*, 72: 1271–9.

Kanter, R. (1990) *When Giants Learn to Dance*, London: Unwin Hyman.

Keat, R. (1990) 'Introduction', in R. Keat and N. Abercrombie (eds.), *Enterprise Culture*, London: Routledge.

Larmore, C. (1987) *Patterns of Moral Complexity*, Cambridge: Cambridge University Press.

Lefort, C. (1988) *Democracy and Political Theory*, Cambridge: Polity Press.

Lyotard, J-F. (1984) *The Postmodern Condition*, trans. G. Bennington and G. Massumi, Minneapolis: University of Minnesota Press.

Marsden, D. and Richardson, R. (1994) 'Performing for pay? The effects of "merit pay" on motivation in a public service', *British Journal of Industrial Relations*, 32(2): 243–61.

Millward, N., Stevens, M., Smart, D. and Hawes, W.R. (1992) *Workplace Industrial Relations in Transition*, Aldershot: Dartmouth.

Minson, J. (1991) *Bureaucratic Culture and the Management of Sexual Harassment*, Institute for Cultural Policy Studies Occasional Paper no. 12, Griffith University, Brisbane.

Minson, J. (1993) *Questions of Conduct*, Basingstoke: Macmillan.

Osborne, D. and Gaebler, T. (1992) *Re-Inventing Government*, Reading, MA: Addison Wesley.

Peters, T. (1987) *Thriving on Chaos*, Basingstoke: Macmillan.

Peters, T. (1992) *Liberation Management*, Basingstoke: Macmillan

Peters, T. and Waterman, R. (1982) *In Search of Excellence*, New York: Harper & Row.

Plant, R. (1992) 'Enterprise in its place: the moral limits of markets', in P. Heelas and P. Morris (eds), *The Values of the Enterprise Culture: the Moral Debate*, London: Routledge.

Public Accounts Committee (1994) *The Proper Conduct of Public Business*, London: HMSO.

RIPA [Royal Institute of Public Administration] (1987) *Top Jobs in Whitehall: Appointments and Promotions in the Senior Civil Service*, (working group report), London: RIPA.

Rorty, A. (1988) *Mind in Action*, Boston: Beacon Press.

Rosaldo, R. (1993) *Culture and Truth*, London: Routledge.

Walzer, M. (1983) *Spheres of Justice*, Oxford: Basil Blackwell.

Weber, M. (1968) *Economy and Society* (3 vols), New York: Bedminster.

10

The Citizen and the Man About Town

James Donald

Who is the man about town?

O. Henry was an American writer of meretricious but, in their turn-of-the-century day, hugely popular short stories. In the late 1950s or early 1960s, a television series was based on them. One episode has always stuck in my mind. It was called 'Man About Town'. Intrigued by the persistence of this screen memory, and wondering how I might have creatively misremembered it, I decided to check the original story.[1] To my surprise, it matched my recollection almost exactly.

The narrative tells of O. Henry's wish to find out what a Man About Town is. He asks a number of people around New York: a reporter, a barman, a 'Salvation lassie', and a critic. They offer him a variety of more or less helpful, more or less inconsequential suggestions. Inspired by these, he determines to meet a Man About Town face to face. 'I am going to find my Man About Town this night if I have to rake New York from the Battery to the Little Coney Island.'

> I left the hotel and walked down Broadway. The pursuit of my type gave a pleasant savour of life and interest to the air I breathed. I was glad to be in a city so great, so complex and diversified. Leisurely and with something of an air I strolled along with my heart expanding at the thought that I was a citizen of great Gotham, a sharer in its magnificence and pleasures, a partaker in its glory and prestige.

So absorbed is the narrator in his search that he steps absentmindedly into the road, and is run over. When he wakes up in hospital, a young doctor shows him a newspaper report of the accident.

> I read the article. Its headlines began where I heard the buzzing leave off the night before. It closed with these lines: '. . . Bellevue Hospital, where it was said that his injuries were not serious. He appeared to be a typical Man About Town'.

From the mass of tacky television tales that I absorbed in childhood, why should this one stay with me? If I could not measure my investment in the story by what I had added to it or altered in it, what could be the fascination?

One explanation is obvious enough. I too would like to find out that I am the Man About Town. In my fantasy world, His Majesty My Ego can often be seen roaming the metropolis 'with something of an air'. Much of my life has been happily wasted in reading about tough detectives braving the cliché of those mean streets, and in watching movies about doomed, Promethean gangsters or flawed heroes ensnared by fatal *femmes*. In my academic work, too, I am repeatedly drawn to the asphalt jungle as the locus of modernity. My concern is only partly with the rationalized urban environment of planners and reformers. What fascinates me above all is the enigma of modernity represented by the city: the possibilities of public life and worldly self-creation, yet also the ineradicable dangers of the metropolitan labyrinth. The reassuringly familiar location of New York, tonight, with its cast of stock characters is no doubt part of the appeal of O. Henry's story. But that cannot be a sufficient explanation. There must also be something about its narrative structure to which I respond.

I certainly feel an affinity with the dissonance between image and self-image at the heart of the story. It plays on our non-transparency to ourselves, the tantalizing impossibility of seeing ourselves as others see us, and our frustrating sense of a self which is not me, but a reflection of the world's perception of me. It is on the specularity and alterity of male subjectivity that the story's twist turns.[2] The narrator conducts himself as a Man About Town, he exhibits all the habits and characteristics of the Man About Town, and yet he cannot recognize himself as the person he is obsessively searching for. Inside, he simply does not feel like the image he projects.

Not only does the story appeal to a pattern of imaginary identification in me, then, to the fantasy of being seen as a Man About Town. It may also plug into a symbolic identification with an assumed position from which I could be identified and judged. There again you can see the attraction of the symbolic space of the city as a topic of study. *The city* provides an imagery for the way we represent ourselves as actors in the theatre of the world, and for what it feels like to present ourselves in that way. This stage for the drama of the self is not only to be found in detective novels and *films noirs*. It is the backdrop and theme for many of the great novels from *Wilhelm Meister* at the end of the eighteenth century to *Ulysses* in the 1920s. It also provides the mystery that is to be unravelled (and to some extent celebrated) in the cultural history of the city initiated by Simmel and Benjamin.

Is there any way in which such representations of the city might shed light on the political imaginary shaping current debates about citizenship?

Who is the citizen?

If I ask, 'Who is the citizen?' I may end up like O. Henry's narrator. After scurrying around quizzing those who ought to know where I might track down such a creature, I could just be told to look in the mirror. I have my passport, and no doubt soon I shall have my identity card. I have done jury service. I am sent my voting card at election time, and my tax demand once a year. These rights and obligations confirm my status as a member of the state. What more do I want to know? What's the problem?

The problem, of course, is that this legal status as citizen does not feel as though it has anything much to do with my sense of self. It tells me what I am, not who I am.

Let me illustrate what is at stake in that distinction by examining the central flaw in Habermas's contribution to the citizenship debate: his eminently sensible argument that a nation of state-citizens whose affective loyalties were expressed in a *constitutional patriotism* would be the best hope for a mature and sustainable democracy.[3] Here the problem takes this form: could any set of institutional arrangements, however rational and just, really plug into structures of the self with the same peremptory authority as the claims of *nation* and *people*? Could they command our loyalty or solicit our desire?

If the answer is no, does that mean we are doomed forever to slide back from the political aspiration to a civilized democracy into the pre-political loyalties of nationalism and ethnic exclusivism? It is easy to sympathize with Habermas's desperate concern, writing in Germany during the throes of reunification, to challenge traditional versions of identity. He makes a powerful case for a post-traditional identity which exists 'only in the method of the public, discursive battle around the interpretation of a constitutional patriotism made concrete under particular historical circumstances'.[4] Here Habermas shows his determination to pre-empt the re-emergence of any idea of Germany as a community of fate. Membership of a cultural or ethnic community should never be the grounds for having or not having rights. No one should be disbarred from having rights. Constitutional patriotism, as expressed in the discursive battle to defend and proliferate rights, would be the measure of citizens' commitment to that principle.

The trouble with Habermas's formulation here is that his horror of traditional identity leads him to conflate different questions about citizenship which are better kept apart. One is the question of who, in particular historical circumstances, does and does not bear the rights entailed by full membership of the state. That is, *who are* citizens (and, by the same token, who are not?). A second question concerns individuals' self-understanding as belonging to a collectivity. This comes closest to my question, *who is* the citizen? Habermas narrows it down, though. What he wants to know is, what would it be like to be a post-traditional citizen of a reunified German state? And a third question concerns the *practice* of citizenship understood as the formation of opinion and the self-definition of a community within civil society. In other worlds, *what are* citizens? What do people *do* when they are being citizens?

Almost as if recognizing that the notion of constitutional patriotism is incoherent, Habermas insists in principle on the need to distinguish between *demos*, the political sovereignty of the people, and *ethnos*, filiation to an imagined cultural community. The conundrum is whether *civic* identity, the membership of this or that state, can ever be extricated from *national* identity, self-recognition as a member of a *nation* state. In his book on *Citizenship and Nationhood in France and Germany*, Rogers Brubaker suggests that history gives a thumbs down. 'The politics of citizenship today,' Brubaker concludes, 'is first and foremost a politics of nation-hood. As such, it is *a politics of identity*, not *a politics of interest* (in the restricted, materialist sense)'.[5] He contrasts the French and German traditions of citizenship and nationhood. In the former, since even before the Revolution, the nation has been understood politically, in relation to the institutional and territorial frame of the state. Even so, this political and secular conception has still had cultural implications. The cost of universal citizenship is always and inevitably cultural assimilation. A unitary state cannot tolerate alternative centres of value legitimation and loyalty.[6]

In Germany, on the other hand, the nation emerged out of a cultural nationalist aspiration to define and embody the specificity and destiny of a *Volk*.

> Since national feeling developed before the nation-state, the German idea of the nation was not originally political, nor was it linked to the abstract idea of citizenship. This prepolitical German nation, this nation in search of a state, was conceived not as the bearer of universal political values, but as an organic cultural, linguistic, or racial community – as an irreducibly particular *Volksgemeinschaft*. On this understanding, nationhood is an ethnocultural, not a political fact.[7]

Habermas is, of course, entirely aware of these histories, and his argu-ment is only partly that the Germans need to be a bit more like the French. More fundamentally, he tries to cut through Brubaker's citizenship-ethnicity knot by arguing for a sense of identity that should forever be up for grabs in the 'daily plebiscite' of democracy. This evanescence, this re-flexivity and this instability are what, for him, makes an identity post-traditional. It is not handed down from the past, but constantly scruti-nized, challenged and remade here and now.

Although that sense of democracy as a noisy, fractious and routine negotiation seems right, why am I still unconvinced? The answer probably lies in my O. Henryish nosiness. Habermas tackles the question, what bonds will be both democratic and effective in tying the legitimate members of the state to its constitution? His answer provokes in me a different question: where might I find a post-traditional democratic state-citizen and how would I recognize her? Habermas is still trying to give the legal *status* of citizenship a cultural *identity*, even though this post-traditional identity will supposedly have had all traces of ethnicity bleached out of it.

Although Habermas tries to break the equation of state-membership with ethnic identity, he does not ask the prior question: must bearing the rights and obligations of state-membership necessarily entail a cultural identity, whether traditional *or non-traditional*? Does it not make more sense to argue that, on the contrary, the very principle of universality inherent in the idea of citizenship means that this status cannot be colonized by any claim to define it in cultural terms? The premise would then be that 'the citizen' can have no substantial identity. Intuitively, that matches my own experience of the status as citizen making little impact on any sense of identity. More importantly, it suggests a stronger political and theoretical argument: that the position of the citizen *must not* have a substance. Any claim to identify citizenship in terms of cultural identity – even, I would say, the identity of post-traditional constitutional patriotism – undermines democratic popular sovereignty and the rights of citizenship by drawing a line separating those who are members of this political community from those who are not.

My argument is therefore that 'the citizen' should be understood in the first instance not as a type of person (whether German nationalist or constitutional patriot) but as a position in the set of formal relations defined by democratic sovereignty. Just as 'I' denotes a position in a set of linguistic relations, an empty position which makes my unique utterances possible but which can equally be occupied by anyone, so 'the citizen' too denotes an empty place. It too can be occupied by anyone – occupied in the sense of being spoken from, not in the sense of being given a substantial identity.

To say that (for example) only white male property owners can be citizens is therefore like saying that (for example) only people six foot two in height with green eyes and a red beard can speak from the position 'I'. That is why Slavoj Zizek equates 'the subject of democracy' with 'the Cartesian subject in all its abstraction, the empty punctuality we reach after subtracting all its particular contents'.

> . . . there is a structural homology between the Cartesian procedure of radical doubt that produces the *cogito*, an empty point or reflective self-reference as a remainder, and the preamble of every democratic proclamation 'all people *without regard to* (race, sex, religion, wealth, social status)'. We should not fail to notice the violent act of abstraction at work in this 'without regard to'; it is an abstraction of all positive features, a dissolution of all substantial, innate links, which produces an entity strictly correlative to the Cartesian *cogito* as a point of pure, nonsubstantial subjectivity.[8]

Rather than fill the position of citizenship (or the subject of democracy) with a post-traditional content, as Habermas does, I would follow Zizek and insist on the substancelessness of citizenship. The logic is, in part, that the universality of rights should be instituted as a regulative ideal in the daily plebiscite of democracy, even if that ideal cannot be realized in practice. This move has, of course, often been criticized by Marxists and feminists. They dismiss the idea of a desirable but unachievable universality as an excuse for ignoring, or even colluding in, actual inequalities and domination. Their scepticism is neither surprising nor ill-founded. Hypothetical green eyes and red beards are not at stake, but the oppression and exploitation suffered by real people in the real world. It seems indecent, almost perverse, to worry about democracy always being a formal link between abstract subjects, instead of righting such wrongs.[9] So why is it important nonetheless?

My case is that it is only the *symbolic* relationship between subjects instituted by the category of rights that makes it possible to mediate the social relations between people through the third term of Law. Only this allows their needs to be articulated as demands or claims, and their wrongs to be assessed as injustices. Social disputes can then be arbitrated in the language of law and not just through the assertion of power. It is only the principle of universality inherent in citizenship (and so its *identitylessness*) that makes it possible to articulate the fact of a denial of rights or an exclusion from state membership as an injustice that demands redress. It creates the perspective from which (for example) the injuries of patriarchal domination can be discerned and called to account.

Having established that democratic relations have their basis in a symbolic order, I can now rephrase my doubts about Habermas. Even though he wants to displace ethnic identity in favour of loyalty to a constitution, Habermas's new verison of rational patriotism and provisional identity still envisages an *imaginary* identification. To experience yourself as a constitutional patriot would be to recognize yourself in a constitutional patriotic interpellation. 'Yes, that state-citizen is me!' The underlying question in Habermas's daily plebiscite would still be, 'Who are we?' I agree with Claude Lefort. It is the wrong question. What matters is less the imaginary identity of the citizen, than the *symbolic* order of citizenship rights. Democracy is founded on *'the legitimacy of a debate as to what is legitimate and what is illegitimate – a debate which is necessarily without any guarantor and without any end'.*[10]

The citizen as empty space or as pure Cartesian *cogito* may seem a pretty anaemic answer to the question, 'Who is the citizen?' But it drives home one point: that the status of citizenship is contingent on an operative symbolic order that needs to be distinguished from any claims to a cultural identity for the citizen. To *become* a citizen is therefore to become a subject within this symbolic order, to be subjected to it, just as we are forced to take up the empty space of 'I' when we become speaking subjects.[11] This citizen-subject has no identity other than that produced by the Law. That is not to say that subjectivity is merely a facsimile of the Law. On the contrary, assigned identities are transformed and recreated as individuals negotiate the Law's play of power. But it is the lack of any primordial identity that produces the *need for identification*: 'the subject attempts to fill out its constitutive lack by means of identification, by identifying itself with some master-signifier guaranteeing its place in the symbolic network'.[12]

This fantasy structure of identification shows why citizenship inevitably becomes enmeshed with questions of national belonging and communal self-definition. Without question, Brubaker is right to see one history of citizenship as the history of parties, sects and movements attempting to occupy the empty place of popular sovereignty, to give community a fixed and exclusive identity, to speak for and through the citizen. On the other hand, teasing out the logic of the connection between the symbolic and the imaginary as I have explains how the desire for identification is produced, but without reducing either the symbolic order of citizenship or the habits and rhetorics it generates to the absolutism of identity politics.

From a mask to a person . . .

An obvious question follows from this. If the subject of democratic citizenship is the substanceless *cogito*, how can citizens actually make an appearance about town, in the forum of public life? Descartes himself gives us a clue. In his earliest extant jotting, he wrote:

> Actors, taught not to let any embarrassment show on their faces, put on a mask. I will do the same. So far, I have been a spectator in this theatre which is the world, but I am now about to mount the stage, and I come forward masked.[13]

He, presumably, was referring to the need to take up a position within discourse in order to participate in philosophical debate. Nevertheless, it is striking how frequently Descartes's metaphors of drama and masquerade recur in attempts to capture the nature both of citizenship and of metropolitan life.

In his famous Huxley Memorial Lecture of 1938, the anthropologist Marcel Mauss sketched a history of 'the notion of person' and 'the notion of "self"' as 'a category of the human mind'. The central argument is that the structure of personality we experience as the most fundamental and the most pyschologically implacable fact of life is not a biological given. It is contingent. It has a history. Mauss therefore looks beyond cultural identities to their subjective conditions of existence. In a profoundly radical turn, he tells a story of how the various elements in our specific organization of 'being a person' were set in place.

He starts in ancient Rome, with the original meaning of *persona*. It was, literally, a mask. Mauss sees 'the person' as the bearer of status and responsibilities beginning to emerge as the word's meaning expanded to incorporate the roles legitimately allowed to the wearer of a given mask and the bearer of a given name. In doing so, he claims, the category of the person became 'a fundamental fact of law'.[14] This turns on its head a common-sense assumption, as well as a Rawlsian fiction. These picture an original or pre-social state consisting of people, or persons, who would

naturally seek to satisfy their various needs and desires. Only secondarily, as a calculated strategy to mitigate the dangers of this state
descending into a war of all against all, would Law have emerged as a
means of mediation and arbitration, as a codification of individual rights
and mutual obligations. Mauss does not believe this scenario of persons
first and Law second. Roman law not only defined but *produced* the
category of the person. The person emerges as an effective entity when
individuals were ascribed an identity in terms of membership of a family
or clan, and then, on that basis, were granted the right to a say in the
forum of politics. It was through this move that the *personal* character of
the law was instituted. Equally, however, in this moment of its inception,
the symbolic institution of personhood was engendered by, and has
always remained contingent on, the existence of a particular legal and
political order.

Being a person was not yet perceived to be a universal attribute of
humanity, let alone experienced as a psychological reality. It was a status
defined by law, ascribed to some and not to others in a ritual of naming,
and enacted through a public dramaturgy of citizenship. (To underline
the non-essential nature of the category, people who were slaves could
not be persons, whereas, before the law, corporations and religious
institutions could be.) The name and status that betokened personhood
were of their nature exterior. This mask did not hide the true identity of its
wearers. It declared who and what they were, and so made public
discourse possible. It provided a role and bestowed the right to speak.
Whether the performance entailed any characteristic sense of an inner
life, it is impossible to know. We need not assume that it did, and it would
certainly be wrong to suppose that it would have been experienced as an
innate personality or an ethical substance moulded or repressed by the
demands of citizenship.

That modern sense of self, for Mauss, only began to appear with the
rise of Christianity. First, a moral sense of personhood was added to the
legal and political definition, 'a sense of conscious, independent,
autonomous, free responsible being'.[15] To act as a person meant less
putting on your mask of identity and performing a public role than
searching your private conscience. Second, in the transition from the idea
of man invested with a status to the notion of Man as a being with an
ulterior inner nature, Christianity ascribed to personhood a new universality, a universal structure of individuation defined by the relationship between each person and a personal God.[16]

Read in this context, what is the significance of Descartes's image of a
detached, observing, interior self emerging, masked and doubting, on to
the stage of an exterior, discursive, public world? It suggests the final
twist in Mauss's history: the emergence of the modern *category of the self*.
In a slow but dramatic evolution, personhood no longer consists in the
mask. It now exists as that abstracted position of ethical apperception
which *lies behind* the public mask. Or rather, it appears to lie behind. It is in

fact created retrospectively by the masquerade, yet as if it were not only topologically behind but temporally prior to the mask. Mauss ends by linking this modernization of the self to Kant and Fichte. For Kant, individual consciousness was the sacred basis of Practical Reason. For Fichte, the 'ego' was the precondition of consciousness and science, of Pure Reason. Then, in an intriguing, almost throwaway conclusion, Mauss again picks up the intricate links between the psychological interiority of modern personhood and the socio-symbolic structures of citizenship. 'Since that time,' Mauss observes, 'the revolution in our mentalities has been achieved, we each have our own "self" or ego, *an echo of the Declarations of Rights which preceded Kant and Fichte.*'[17]

The subject of the Enlightenment

That echo rumbles on. In a recent article, Etienne Balibar, like Mauss, sees 1789 and the *Declaration of the Rights of Man* as marking the ruptural emergence of a radically new category of subjectivity – a category which only makes sense in terms of the revolutionary citizen. Athough the *Declaration* proclaims the rights *of man*, Balibar sees them as being really the rights of *man as citizen*. The objective of the *Declaration* is the constitution of citizenship, but now a citizenship that demands not absolute loyalty and obedience to the monarch (subjection) but a new capacity for self-determined agency (subjectification) and so new forms of intersubjective *and* intrasubjective relationships. Democratic sovereignty requires a symbolic equality of all citizens, because all citizens are the nominal source of its authority, as well as being subject to that authority. The *sovereign equality* of democratic authority thus institutes citizenship as a certain kind of freedom, and anchors this liberty not in a relationship to God but in the nature of Man. The privileged civic freedoms and equality of antiquity, embodied in rights and roles granted by law, give way to an understanding of equality and freedom as natural and universal. When Rousseau proclaims that 'Man was born free, and everywhere he is in chains', he is asserting that freedom and equality are innate attributes whose denial is not only an injustice, but an affront to nature. The symbolic order of rights and the modern sense of a self embodied in an inner voice of nature are each a condition of the other's existence.

So the question ceases to be, as it would have been in ancient Rome, and continues to be in the formulation of nationality laws and immigration policies, 'Who is a citizen?' (or: 'Who are citizens?'). For Balibar, concerned with the production of subjectivity, the question now is, *Who is the citizen?*

> The answer is: The citizen is a man in enjoyment of all his 'natural' rights, completely realizing his individual humanity, a free man simply because he is equal to every other man. This answer (or this new question in the form of an answer) will also be stated, after the fact: *The citizen is the subject*, the citizen is

always a *supposed subject* (legal subject, psychological subject, transcendental subject).[18]

By a different, more historical route, Balibar reaches the same conclusion as Zizek. The citizen is the *cogito*; the citizen is the subject. But Balibar's gloss on this pure, non-substantial subjectivity emphasizes less its emptiness than its perennial deferral. The citizen is always *becoming-a-subject* (*devenir-sujet*). The possibility of action is now mediated through a new sense of a primordial but incomplete self, the sense of a self in need of completion that is manifested in a psychic life of need, desire and guilt. To be a person now entails the remorseless aspiration to self-knowledge, self-expression, and self-fulfilment. The status, the rights and the responsibilities of citizenship come to be experienced as somehow constitutive of a sense of self, as subjective.

But (to repeat) they are not experienced or recognized as an identity. On the contrary, it is the traumatic lack of fit between the impulses of a supposed inner nature and the demands of an external reality – their necessary non-identity – that produces the characteristically modern sense of the self as divided and incomplete. Schiller's *On the Aesthetic Education of Man* (1791), for example, articulates the Romantic conception of this split as an opposition between natural feeling and 'all-dividing Intellect':

> It was civilization itself which imposed this wound upon modern man. Once the increase of empirical knowledge, and more exact modes of thought, made sharper divisions between the sciences inevitable, and once the increasingly complex machinery of State necessitated a more rigorous separation of ranks and occupations, then the inner unity of human nature was severed too, and a disastrous conflict set its harmonious powers at variance.[19]

At first sight this may sit oddly with Balibar's definition of the citizen subject as a person 'completely realizing his individual humanity'. Remember, though, that Balibar sees this not as an achieved state of wholeness, but as the process of unendingly *becoming* a subject. That superficially paradoxical notion of the subject becoming a subject is vital. Taking up a position within the symbolic, because it is to occupy a necessarily empty position which makes it possible to articulate need as desire, always entails a sense of loss. It produces the sense of subjectivity as *lack* that motivates the compulsion to heal the wound of modern culture, the drive to recreate a harmony or fullness that feel as though they must once have existed.

If you want to hear that foundational myth of modern selfhood voiced with unrivalled vivacity and paranoid conviction, then you need only listen to Jean-Jacques Rousseau. Rousseau above all proclaimed the self to be the locus of primordial nature, one subjugated to society but guided by a conscience which still 'speaks to us in the language of nature'.[20] That voice, he believed, can all too easily be drowned out by the noise of society, and especially by the babble and chatter of the city. The least worst city would therefore be the one which allows the nearest alignment

of its codified principles of justice (Law) to the demands of nature
(Conscience). It would allow a degree of authenticity in interpersonal
relations, without disavowing the necessary deformation of the natural
self entailed by the subject's entry into society. The artifice and
theatricality of the city were to be deplored because they were incompat-
ible with this striving for subjective authenticity. Not only did they lead to
the corruption of morals and culture (*moeurs*), they were against nature.
The question for politics was not just how to arbitrate between the public
good and selfish hedonism, but, given the intractable conflict between
nature and society, how to create good citizens.

In making the link between the public codes and conducts of cities and
the subjective repertoire of action and self-understanding available to
citizens, Rousseau was one of the most perceptive early theorists of
modern urbanism as well as modern politics.[21] Yet he despised the
cosmopolitanism of Paris, and the way that here people disguised their
true natures as a matter of course. He could not stand the impossibility of
knowing for sure who is a citizen and who is a man about town.

> The men to whom one speaks are not at all those with whom one communi-
> cates. Their sentiments do not come from their hearts, their insight is not in
> their character, their speech does not represent their thoughts. Of them only
> their appearance is perceived. . . . Until now I have seen a great many masks;
> when shall I see the faces of men?[22]

His moral repugnance at the masquerade of the big city was no mere
metaphor. Rousseau's most sustained assault on cosmopolitanism and
his most passionate defence of a strict civic republicanism were provoked
by the encyclopaedist d'Alembert's suggestion that Geneva would
benefit from having a theatre.

D'Alembert's argument was that civilized behaviour could be learned
from the pedagogic example of theatrical performances. To Rousseau,
this was absurd and disgusting. The artifice evident in the performances
of men (and especially women) about town – let alone the morals of actors
and actresses! – implied not refinement but corruption. The presentation
of self in the cosmopolitan world of Paris did not allow an interior nature
to express itself. It was an obstacle to open intersubjective relationships.
In this drama, honesty and authenticity were sacrificed for the tawdry
prize of reputation.

> In a big city, full of scheming, idle people without religion or principle, whose
> imagination, depraved by sloth, inactivity, the love of pleasure, and great
> needs, engenders only monsters and inspires only crimes; in a big city, . . .
> *moeurs* and honour are nothing because each, easily hiding his conduct from the
> public eye, shows himself only by his reputation.[23]

To dispel this opacity and illegibility of others, Rousseau wanted to
render social relations transparent. He would have liked all office holders
to wear badges or emblems denoting their rank or position, so that at least
there could be no doubt about *what* they were.[24] In the big city, he fretted,

how can you know *who* strangers really are if you cannot take their courtesies, or even intimacies, at face value?

> People meet me full of friendship; they show me a thousand civilities; they render me services of all sorts. But that is precisely what I am complaining of. How can you become immediately the friend of a man whom you have never seen before? The true human interest, the plain and noble effusion of an honest soul – these speak a language far different from the insincere demonstrations of politeness (and the false appearances) which the customs of the great world demand.[25]

It was to counteract the city's masquerade of false appearances that Rousseau was willing to endorse the imposition of a quite tyrannical transparency. Every citizen should forever be subject to the surveillance of government, to the gossip of women's circles, and to the inner voice of conscience. In an exemplary republican small town like Geneva, 'the authorities have everyone under their eye'. Paradoxically, because 'individuals are always in the public eye, critics of one another from birth', they are freed from the pressure of 'public opinion' and so are better able to develop and grow.[26] Stripped of their masks of fashion, artifice and anonymity, people are forced back on their natural inner resources, and this provides a more fertile soil for the cultivation of good citizens.

This, then, was the Rousseauian dream of a transparency of the self to the self and to others that revolutionized European politics.

> It was the dream of a transparent society, visible and legible in each of its parts, the dream of there no longer existing any zones of darkness, zones established by the privileges of royal power or the prerogatives of some corporation, zones of disorder. It was the dream that each individual, whatever position he occupied, might be able to see the whole of society, that men's hearts should communicate, their vision be unobstructed by obstacles, and that opinion of all reign over each.[27]

Foucault is no doubt right in this assessment of how Rousseau's will to transparency is related to the new phenomenon of 'governmentality'. Techniques of surveillance, a pastoral concern with the capacities of a population, and the force of public opinion all helped to shape the social and political terrain of the nineteenth-century city.

Any yet, despite the tendency to totalitarianism in the fantasy of absolute transparency, it would be wrong to see only the infancy of Big Brother in Rousseau's response to the city. For, contradictorily, and no doubt despite himself, Rousseau was also a man about town. However vehemently he denounces Paris and lauds Geneva, the story he tells in the *Confessions* is of a callow youth who leaves an emotionally and intellectually stifling provincial town, acquires his sentimental education through a series of adventures, and eventually makes his name in the capital city. Isn't this the blueprint for the *Bildungsroman* narrative of the nineteenth century? And doesn't it therefore entail a different image of the metropolis? Artificial and illegible it may be, but for many a young fictional hero, as for Rousseau, the big city offered a field of liberating possibilities. Here were the urbane pleasures of squares and cafés, the chance encounters with strangers, the *frisson* of amorous adventure and political intrigue, the opportunity to make your reputation in the community of letters or the world of theatre. Its anonymity could be cruel, its dark zones could harbour hidden dangers, but the city at least allowed the space for self-formation and self-creation, for experimentation and change.

Reading the *Confessions* is like riding a rollercoaster, as Rousseau recounts his triumphs, his real or imagined slights, and his farcical and often self-inflicted humiliations. Could it be that these extraordinary vicissitudes are symptomatic of the way that Rousseau acted out, in all its ambivalence, the uneasy relationship between the citizen and the man about town? Each is a characteristically modern type, and each is by definition an urban type. But each seeks to heal or salve the wound of civilization in a different way. The citizen, not without pain and sacrifice, embraces the ascetic comforts of civic virtue as a means to psychologically authentic personal relations. The man about town pursues a different, though not necessarily less demanding, ethic: the increasingly aesthetic cultivation – and perhaps creation – of the self. Rousseau unquestionably committed himself, morally and intellectually, to the former. By the end of the nineteenth century, however, his idea of a primordial inner nature had to a significant degree been superseded by a new sense of interiority: not now a nature deformed by society, but the only defensible space of an authenticity threatened with obliteration.

Modern man

An apparently trivial example can illustrate this shift. It is the question of how a man should dress about town. By his own admission, Rousseau was a slob, but typically he defended his slobbishness in ethical terms. Excessive ornament and non-functional adornment – or 'garishness of dress' – he found not only offensive but inconvenient. It cramped his style. 'In order to retain all possible liberty, when I am among other men, I would want to be dressed in such a way that in every rank, I appeared to be in my place, and that I did not stand out in any,' he declared. 'In this way I would be more the master of my conduct, and I would put the pleasures of all stations always within my reach'.[28] Although this deliberate opaqueness in his own case is inconsistent with the transparency he would impose on others, it points forward to a later, modernist presentation of the masculine self. By 1908, for the Viennese architect Alfred Loos, Rousseau's eccentricity had become a norm.

> The person who runs around in a velvet suit is no artist but a buffoon or merely a decorator. We have become more refined, more subtle. Primitive men had to differentiate themselves by the use of various colours, modern man needs his

clothes as a mask. . . . His individuality is so strong that he cannot express it any longer by his clothing. The lack of ornament is a sign of intellectual power. Modern man . . . concentrates his own power of invention on other things.[29]

These 'other things' concern less the display of rank or reputation than the defensive cultivation of an inner authenticity. Here we are in the mental landscape of the metropolis analysed by Georg Simmel. For modern man, in contrast to Rousseauian man, the battle is to 'preserve the autonomy and individuality of his existence in the face of overwhelming social forces', to resist 'being levelled down and worn out by a social-technological mechanism'.[30]

The result of this conflict, suggests Simmel, was a hyper-inflation of individualism. Modern man dedicates his power of invention to hiding his sense of an interior, intimate self from the world. The Roman mask of identity and distinction has long disappeared. Now a mask of anonymity conceals difference and so guards a sense of identity.[31] For Simmel and Loos and other modernist men about town, a commonplace exterior is an aesthetic tactic which turns all the imposed technologies and narratives of the self back on themselves.

> The commonplace is good form in society. . . . It is bad taste to make oneself conspicuous through some individual, singular expression. . . . Obedience to the standards of the general public in all externals [is] the conscious and desired means of reserving their personal feelings and their taste.[32]

'How should one dress?' asked Loos. 'Modern,' he answers. And that means creating an unreadable surface. 'One is modernly dressed when one stands out the least.' Loos takes Nietzsche's view that it is the 'remarkable antithesis between an interior which fails to correspond to any exterior and an exterior which fails to correspond to any interior' which makes a modern man modern. The masks of public life are no longer either mimetic or indexical. 'No one dares to appear as he is, but masks himself as a cultivated man, as a scholar, as a politician. . . . Individuality has withdrawn within: from without it has become invisible.'[33]

Loos followed this logic of interiority through to his architecture. Houses should be like men about town. Their outsides should present an inconspicuous face to the world, as standardized as dinner jackets. 'The house does not have to tell anything to the exterior,' he insisted; 'instead, all its richness must be manifest in the interior.'[34] Inside, all the lines of sight were directed into the house, not out on to the city. His windows were often opaque or curtained. Sofas stood with their backs resolutely to windows.

This turning away from the world, or turning inward to the domestic interior, Simmel again explained in terms of the essential defensiveness of style. Surrounding yourself with the fashionable accessories of the *Jugendstil*, because it was at once personal and shared with a wider taste community, provided 'a counterbalance and a cloak' for 'the exaggerated subjectivism of the times'. The obsessive stylization of the domestic interior was less a means of self-expression than a symptom of self-protection.

> What impels people so strongly toward style is the unburdening and masking of the personality that is the essence of style. Subjectivism and individuality have accelerated almost to breaking point and in the stylised creations of form . . . there lies a tempering and toning down of this extreme individuality into something general and more universal.[35]

Modern man exercises his power of invention less in a dandyism than in the cultivation of an interior world. This is not just a *private* world, but one that carries a newly charged sense of *intimacy*. It is evident not only in the style of your room, but above all in the world of the psyche.

In his essay on 'Fashion', Simmel uses an image that echoes Loos's dictum that 'all the richness must be manifest in the interior'. 'Over an old Flemish house,' he remarks, 'there stands the mystical inscription: There is more within me'.[36] The implication is that behind the mask of masculine anonymity, just as behind the façade of the house, there lies complexity, depth and plenitude. The mask, like the obsession with domestic style, represents a phobic reaction to the hyperactivity and overstimulation of the modern metropolis. Take it off and you will find the real man. But, of course, this is where we came in – with O. Henry's joke that there's no there there behind the image. Ego is always and only imaginary, formed in the play of display and reflection in public life.

A cynic might therefore see modern man's clothes as a not-so-subtle piece of advertising. Even if gorgeous excess has given way to the surrealist insouciance of Magritte's suit and bowler hat or the demotic semiotics of Gap, that ordinary sartorial exterior is now presented as the promise of extraordinary richness within. In that sense, men's clothing remains a display of authority. This is the double bluff of modern masculinity: the assertion of authority through its manifest disavowal. We need no badges of office or pompous uniforms, we protest disdain-fully. The only authority we claim is the authenticity of who we really are. But that authority, however ironic, however austere, is an imposture nonetheless. The phallus is still a fraud. 'If the penis was the phallus, men would have no need of feathers or ties or medals,' comments the Lacanian analyst Eugénie Lemoine-Luccioni. She may be wrong about the style, but her inference is valid. 'Display [*parade*], just like the [feminine] masquerade, thus betrays a flaw: no one has the phallus.'[37]

Is the argument that the modern man about town gets his new clothes from the same tailor as the Emperor? Not quite, because that would again suggest that when you strip away the clothes you find the real man, however puny he may be. I agree with Lacan. The ego is nothing but 'the superimposition of various coats borrowed from the bric-à-brac of its props department'.[38] Beneath the man about town's clothes – behind the mask – is *nothing*. Even so, this masculinity is not quite a confidence trick. This nothing is once again the necessary nothing we keep coming up against, the abstraction that is the subject, the empty place that makes appearance, conduct and consciousness possible. Being a citizen, being a man about town, being a person – these are not identities, they are performances.

Now, of course, such performances are fundamentally implicated in logics of sexual differentiation. That is why the metaphor of masquerade has been used primarily in recent years to theorize the experience of being a woman in a man's town. Recent writers from Lacan onwards have taken up Joan Riviere's assertion in the late 1920s that womanliness and the masquerade 'whether radical or superficial. . . . are the same thing' in order to explain the excessive or fetishistic or parodic nature of feminine self-presentation. Masquerade, they suggest, embraces the dislocation between subjectivity and role, and the performativity of the gendered ego.[39] The comparative latitude of ego as performance, and so the possibilities of cross-dressing and other subversive tactics, have been seized on as ways to undermine the tendency to essentialism in the notion of identity. Women have always found ways to get out on the town.

Citizens and difference

What might be the implications of these arguments for an understanding of citizenship and personhood? Some initial questions and possibilities present themselves.

For a start, it is not hard to see that Rousseau's image of the natural self being deformed as it is forced to choose to acquiesce to the General Will of society, Schiller's image of the wound imposed by civilization, and Freud's image of symbolic castration are all variations on a single theme. They share a model of the self being formed as alienated because subject to the authority of the Other – the Law Giver for Rousseau, Culture for Schiller, the Name-of-the-Father for Freud. It is this model that explains the recognition of oneself as not whole, and so the desire for identification articulated in terms of a master-signifier.

Given this modern (post-Enlightenment) structure of subjectivity, we might ask what sort of masquerade citizenship is. How does the empty, lacking subject of democracy mount the stage of this theatre which is civil society? With an intense imaginary commitment to political participation and a passionate belief in the life-and-death importance of the role, is often the answer. Here is a random example of that attitude, expressed in this case by David Marquand:

> the central message of civic republicanism is that the Self can develop its full potential and learn how to discharge its obligations to other selves only through action in the public realm of a free city – that politics is both a civilised and a civilising activity; that it is, indeed, the most civilised and civilising activity in which human beings can take part.[40]

Implicit in this romantic-republican ethic,[41] and sustaining its masquerade, is a fantasy scenario in which the fulfilment of the self is linked to the longed-for development of society as a rational and non-conflictual community. To recognize this scenario as a fantasy (which is not to trivialize it) should make it possible to examine how different ways of performing politics have been authorized for men and women, in the same way that the symbolic space of the city allows or prohibits different modes of appearing in public.

Renata Salecl takes a more radical step, however. She sees in the sexually differentiated masquerade of citizenship further evidence that citizenship denotes an empty place. Men cannot *be* this symbolic place any more than women can. Rather, masculine and feminine enactments of citizenship embody different ways of experiencing the impossibility of identity.

> 'Masculine' and 'feminine' are . . . the two modes of the subject's *failure* to achieve the full identity of Man. 'Man' and 'Woman' together do not form a whole, since *each of them is already in itself a failed whole*.[42]

Salecl then goes on to distinguish two logics of citizenship. The first, 'male' logic is a logic of universality. That is: 'all people have rights, with the exception of those who are excluded from this universality (for example, women, children, foreigners, etc.)'. In contrast, in a 'feminine' logic, 'there is no one who does not have rights; i.e. everybody taken individually possesses rights, but precisely because of this we cannot say that people as such have rights'. This underlies the importance of not confusing the position of the subject with the identity of the citizen. The claim that no one should remain without rights 'means that no one can universally possess them'.[43]

That makes me wonder whether a politics of identity, understood as a claim to recognition (and support) for a self-defined group by the state, would fall within her male or feminine logic. In so far as the assertion of collective identity as the warrant for citizenship rights is still premised on the Rousseauian logic of politics as the bridge back to this primordial identity, then I suspect the logic is male.

So how would it then be possible to imagine an emancipatory politics outside the logic of lucid self-knowledge and authentic identity? What would it mean to live without the comforting myth of self as ultimate truth?

For a start, it would mean saying yes to the inevitably fictional nature of identity and the otherness of the self. Strip away all the masks of social performance, and what will you find? Nothing unique, nothing natural, suggests Lévi-Strauss in his introduction to Mauss's work, but nonetheless a potential for action.

> Going down into the givens of the unconscious, the extension of our understanding, if I may put it thus, is not a movement towards ourselves; we reach a level which seems strange to us, not because it harbours our most secret self, but (much more normally) because, without requiring us to move outside ourselves, it enables us to coincide with forms of activity which are both at once *ours* and *other* . . .[44]

In this light, emancipation would not be the recovery or liberation of the true self, but an uncanny sense of the self as contingent. This is the experience of freedom which Gianni Vattimo aptly defines as 'a continual oscillation between belonging and disorientation'. It embraces the historicity and finiteness of subjectivity. And yet it is, genuinely, freedom. Vattimo quotes Nietzsche. It is the freedom of 'continuing to dream knowing one is dreaming'.[45]

The citizen and the monster

What is the relationship between the citizen and the man about town? Distant kinsmen linked by a bond of affection, it might appear, if the opening of Robert Louis Stevenson's *Strange Case of Dr Jekyll and Mr Hyde* (1886) is anything to go by.[46] Every Sunday, that exemplary citizen, 'Mr Utterson the lawyer', and 'Mr Richard Enfield, his distant kinsman, the well-known man about town', take a stroll around London together. For both men, these largely silent walks are 'the chief jewel of each week'.

It is Enfield who gives Utterson the first account of Hyde, having witnessed him trampling over a little girl at three o'clock one morning. The memory is prompted when they notice a sinister door. Through this Enfield had seen Hyde disappear, although he fails to recognize it as the rear entrance to the home of Dr Jekyll. He knows that Hyde has some claim on Jekyll, but he cannot imagine what it is.

The man about town sees the terrible things that can happen in the city at night. But eventually it is the man of law who discovers their significance. To Utterson are entrusted the documents which allow the story to be told, and it is eventually he who breaks down the door to Jekyll's laboratory to confirm the dreadful truth. That secret is, of course, Jekyll's non-identity.

This doubling of the self suggests a less sanguine perspective on the relationship between the citizen and the man about town. The split is not between the good Jekyll and an evil Hyde. Hyde is wholly evil, it is true, but for Jekyll he embodies the wish to act the man about town more than a respectable doctor can allow himself to do. The worst of Jekyll's youthful faults had been 'a certain impatient gaiety of disposition, such as has made the happiness of many, but such as I found it hard to reconcile with my imperious desire to carry my head high, and wear a more than commonly grave countenance before the public'. Hence repression, or at least masquerade: 'I concealed my pleasures'. And hence the split already latent in Jekyll, his 'profound duplicity of life'.

Normally, such anxieties might have been displaced or projected on to the Other, on to Woman.[47] In this *Strange Case*, however, there are no significant women characters. The founding anxiety of masculine sexuality is turned back on itself, and produces Hyde as the embodiment of perversion, as abjection, as the ruin of 'the very fortress of identity'. The tension between the citizen and the man about town is revealed as constitutive of modern male sexuality. Its magnetic poles are the demands of civic virtue and the hedonism of the city at night.

Twenty years or so after *Jekyll and Hyde*, in the same year that Loos commented on the defensive masquerade of modern man's clothes and Simmel wrote his essay on fashion, Freud published ' "Civilised" sexual morality and modern nervous illness' (1908):

> Experience teaches us that for most people there is a limit beyond which their constitution cannot comply with the demands of civilisation. All who wish to be more noble-minded than their constitution allows fall victims to neurosis; they would have been more healthy if it could have been possible for them to be less good.[48]

This is a reminder, if one were needed, that for all their historicity and contingency, structures of personality have real psychological and somatic effects. Their history is also the history of erotic compulsion and emotional disorder.

Yet it would miss the point to reduce Jekyll and Hyde to a case of 'mental illness'. Hyde *is* monstrous, and he is a thoroughly modern monster. To suggest where the Enlightenment project went wrong, Slavoj Zizek uses the analogy of the baby and the bathwater. Philosophers like Rousseau wanted to get rid of all the gunk of corrupt civilization in order to recover the healthy, unspoiled and natural infant of the ego. Not only did they manage to throw out that baby in the process. In its place, they found themselves left with a monstrous residue: all those monsters from Frankenstein's creation to George Romero's shopping mall zombies which register the 'specific dimension of the uncanny that emerges with modernity'.[49] The pure 'subject of the Enlightenment', concludes Zizek, 'is a monster which gives body to the surplus that escapes the vicious circle of the mirror relationship'.[50]

Here lies the danger of trying to fill in the empty place of subjectivity, rather than learning to live with an ego whose fugitive identities are conjured up in the inescapable play of images and reflections. The search for lucid self-knowledge or absolute self-fulfilment may unleash Hyde, that which should have remained hidden. The monsters of the Enlightenment remind us why, by the same token, we should learn to respect the opacity of others. Communitarians tell us that every nook and cranny of the social body should be 'cracked open to politics' (Roberto Unger) or that the opacity of participants in social life should be dissolved (Michael Sandel).[51] Would that produce the mutual harmony and clear-sighted rationality of a Rousseauian utopia? Or are such injunctions no more than the elevation of narcissism to a political principle? The fantasy of transparency may produce monsters as much as the sleep of reason. The good citizens and zealous republicans should leave us flawed men and women about town some space.

Notes

1 See David Rosenberg (ed.), *The Movie that Changed my Life*, Viking, New York, 1991.

2 Specularity and alterity come from Kaja Silverman, *Male Subjectivity at the Margins*, Routledge, London, 1992.

3 Jürgen Habermas, 'Yet again: German identity – a unified nation of angry DM-burghers?', *New German Critique*, 1992.

4 Ibid., p. 98.

5 Rogers Brubaker, *Citizenship and Nationhood in France and Germany*, Harvard University Press, New Haven, 1992, p. 182.

6 Ibid., p. 1.

7 Ibid.

8 Slavoj Zizek, *Looking Awry*, MIT Press, Cambridge MA, 1991, p. 163.

9 Renata Salecl, *The Spoils of Freedom: Psychoanalysis and Feminism after the Fall of Socialism*, Routledge, London, 1994, p. 119.

10 Quoted ibid., p. 121.

11 Ibid., p. 126.

12 Zizek, *Looking Awry*, p. 163.

13 René Descartes, *The Philosophical Writings of Descartes*, trans. John Cottingham, Robert Stoothoff and Dugald Murdoch, Cambridge University Press, Cambridge, 1985, p. 2.

14 Marcel Mauss, 'A category of the human mind, the notion of person; the notion of self', in *Sociology and Psychology: Essays*, trans. Ben Brewster, Routledge & Kegan Paul, London, 1979, p. 78.

15 Ibid., p. 84.

16 Ibid., pp. 85–6. See also Nikolas Rose's discussion in *Governing the Soul: The Shaping of the Private Self*, Routledge, London, 1990, pp. 217–19.

17 Mauss, 'A category', p. 89 (emphasis added).

18 Etienne Balibar, 'Citizen subject', in Eduardo Cadava, Peter Connor and Jean-Luc Nancy (eds), *Who Comes after the Subject?*, Routledge, London, 1991, p. 45.

19 Friedrich Schiller, *On the Aesthetic Education of Man* (1791), Clarendon Press, Oxford, 1967, p. 33. See the discussions in Ian Hunter, 'Setting limits to culture', *New Formations*, 4, Spring 1988, and Jeffrey Minson, *Questions of Conduct: Sexual Harassment, Citizenship, Government*, Macmillan, London, 1993.

20 Jean-Jacques Rousseau, *Émile*, trans. Barbara Foxley, J.M. Dent, London, 1974, p. 254.

21 Richard Sennett, *The Fall of Public Man*, Cambridge University Press, Cambridge, 1974, p. 115.

22 Jean-Jacques Rousseau, *La Nouvelle Héloïse*, quoted in Charles E. Ellison, 'Rousseau and the modern city: the politics of speech and dress', *Political Theory*, 13, 4, 1985, p. 507.

23 Rousseau, *Letter to d'Alembert*, quoted in Sennett, *Fall of Public Man*, p. 118.

24 See Ellison, 'Rousseau and the modern city', p. 526.

25 Rousseau, *Julie*, quoted in Sennett, *Fall of Public Man*, p. 119.

26 *Letter to d'Alembert*, in John Hope Mason, *The Indispensable Rousseau*, Quartet, London, 1979, p. 129.

27 Michel Foucault, *Power/Knowledge*, ed. Colin Gordon, Harvester Press, Brighton, 1980, p. 152.

28 *Émile*, quoted in Ellison, 'Rousseau and the modern city', p. 518.

29 Alfred Loos, 'Ornament and crime', quoted in Beatriz Colomina, *Privacy and Publicity: Modern Architecture as Mass Media*, MIT Press, Cambridge, MA, 1994, p. 35.

30 Georg Simmel, 'The metropolis and mental life', in *The Sociology of Georg Simmel*, ed. K.H. Wolff, Free Press, New York, p. 409.

31 See Colomina, *Privacy and Publicity*, p. 37.

32 Simmel, 'Fashion' (1904), quoted ibid., p. 273.

33 Nietzsche, 'On the uses and disadvantages of history for life,' quoted ibid., pp. 32, 8.

34 Loos, 'Architecture' (1910), quoted ibid., p. 274.

35 Simmel, 'The problem of style' (1910), quoted and discussed in David Frisby, *Fragments of Modernity*, Polity Press, Cambridge, 1985, p. 101.

36 Quoted in Colomina, *Privacy and Publicity*, p. 35.

37 Quoted in Stephen Heath, 'Joan Riviere and the masquerade', in Victor Burgin, James Donald and Cora Kaplan (eds), *Formations of Fantasy*, Methuen, London, 1986, p. 56.

38 Quoted in Silverman, *Male Subjectivity*, pp. 6–7.

39 See Riviere and Heath in Burgin et al., *Formations of Fantasy*. Also the essays on masquerade by Mary Ann Doane, *Femmes Fatales: Feminism, Film Theory, Psychoanalysis*, Routledge, London, 1991.

40 David Marquand, 'Civic republicans and liberal individualists: the case of Britain', *Archive of European Sociology*, 32, 1991, p. 343.

41 The phrase is Minson's.

42 Salecl, *Spoils of Freedom*, p. 116.

43 Ibid., p. 133.

44 Claude Lévi-Strauss, *Introduction to the Works of Marcel Mauss* (1950), Routledge & Kegan Paul, London, 1987, p. 35.

45 Gianni Vattiomo, *The Transparent Society*, Polity Press, Cambridge, 1992, p. 8.

46 I am grateful to Chris Blake for reminding me of this passage and its relevance.

47 Here I follow Stephen Heath's analysis of the story: 'Psychopathia sexualis: Stevenson's *Strange Case*', *Critical Quarterly*, 28, 11/12, 1986.

48 Quoted ibid., p. 97.

49 Mladen Dolar, 'I shall be with you on your wedding-night', *October*, 58, 1991, p. 7.

50 Slavoj Zizek, *Enjoy Your Symptom!* Routledge, London, 1992, p. 136.

51 R. Unger in Minson, *Questions of Conduct*, p. 193; N. Sandel, *Liberalism and the Limits of Justice*, Cambridge University Press, Cambridge, 1982, p. 183. See the discussion in Iris Marion Young, *Justice and the Politics of Difference*, Princeton University Press, Princeton, 1990, p. 230.

Index